C000075961

Literacy in Context
for AQA A

Literacy in Context
for AQA A

John O'Connor

with **John Nield**

General editor **Joan Ward**

CAMBRIDGE
UNIVERSITY PRESS

PUBLISHED BY THE PRESS SYNDICATE OF THE UNIVERSITY OF CAMBRIDGE
The Pitt Building, Trumpington Street, Cambridge, United Kingdom

CAMBRIDGE UNIVERSITY PRESS
The Edinburgh Building, Cambridge CB2 2RU, UK
40 West 20th Street, New York, NY 10011-4211, USA
477 Williamstown Road, Port Melbourne, VIC 3207, Australia
Ruiz de Alarcón 13, 28014 Madrid, Spain
Dock House, The Waterfront, Cape Town 8001, South Africa

http://www.cambridge.org

© Cambridge University Press 2003

This book is in copyright. Subject to statutory exception and to the provisions of
relevant collective licensing agreements, no reproduction of any part may take place
without the written permission of Cambridge University Press.

First published 2003

Printed in the United Kingdom at the University Press, Cambridge

Typefaces Bebop, Stone Sans   *System* QuarkXPress®

A catalogue record for this book is available from the British Library

ISBN 0 521 53528 X paperback

Prepared for publication by Pentacor Book Design plc

ACKNOWLEDGEMENTS

Cover images: Burglar at door, © L. Clarke/CORBIS; dancing mice, Lowe; Claire Danes and Leonardo DiCaprio as Romeo and Juliet, The Kobal Collection/
20th Century Fox/Morton, Merrick.

Thanks are due to the following for permission to reproduce copyright textual material:

pp. 21–3, Department of Health; p. 27, SOS Children's Villages UK; pp. 40–1, pp. 102–3, pp. 111–13, *Daily Mail*; pp. 42–3, *Channel 4 News*/ITN; p. 47, pp. 100–1,
© the *Guardian*; pp. 50–1, Warwick Castle; p. 51, Tower Bridge Experience; p. 52, Bletchley Park Trust; p. 53, Cabinet War Rooms; p. 57, American Air Museum, Duxford;
pp. 62–3, William Jefferson Clinton; p. 70, The Living Rainforest; p. 71, Rainforest Concern, Tel: 0207 2292093, Fax: 0207 2214094, 27 Lansdowne Crescent, London
W11 2NS, www.rainforestconcern.org; pp. 72–3, GAP Activity Projects (GAP UK Ltd), a not-for-profit organisation, is the UK's leading year out provider for the 18–19
age range, sending up to 2000 school leavers annually on fixed-term overseas voluntary work experience placements in 34 countries worldwide. Programmes range from
heritage and conservation to community management; p. 77, Natural History Museum; pp. 80–3 Thames Valley Police – CP Keith Raw and Crime Services Agency –
CSO Roy Townsend; pp. 90–1, Lee Krystek/The Museum of Unnatural History; pp. 92–3, p. 97, Paul Stonehill; pp. 120–3, The Amber Spyglass, by Philip Pullman, 2002,
the third book in the *His Dark Materials* trilogy, published by Scholastic Children's Books, reproduced by permission of Scholastic Limited; pp. 130–1, Reprinted by
permission of Harper Collins Publishers Limited © Pamela Stephenson 2002; pp. 132–3, Sally Morgan, Time Warner Books UK; p. 141, by Lawrence Ferlinghetti, from
THESE ARE MY RIVERS, copyright © 1979 by Lawrence Ferlinghetti. Reprinted by permission of New Directions Publishing Corp.; p. 142 *l*, *By kind permission of*
JOHN AGARD c/o Caroline Sheldon Literary Agency *from* GET BACK PIMPLE *published by* Puffin 1996; p. 142 *r*, Curtis Brown Publishers; p. 150, p. 151 *l*, *r*, Seamus
Heaney, published by Faber and Faber Ltd; p. 152 *l*, *r*, p. 153 *l*, by Gillian Clarke, published by Carcanet Press Ltd; p. 160, from *The World's Wife* by Carol Ann Duffy,
published by Pan Macmillan Ltd; p. 161 *l*, 'Stealing' is taken from *Selling Manhattan* by Carol Ann Duffy published by Anvil Press Poetry in 1987; p. 161 *r*, 'Education for
Leisure' is taken from *Standing Female Nude* by Carol Ann Duffy published by Anvil Press Poetry in 1985; pp. 170–3, p. 177, © Barry Hines, 1968; pp. 180–3, Reproduced
from *An Inspector Calls* by JB Priestley (Copyright © JB Priestley 1947) by permission of PFD on behalf of the Estate of JB Priestley.

Thanks are due to the following for permission to reproduce photographs:

p. 10, p. 193 *r*, Kobal Collection; p. 13, p. 17, The Kobal Collection/20th Century Fox/Morton, Merrick; p. 14, The Kobal Collection/Paramount; pp. 30–3, Lowe;
pp. 40–1, © Wolfgang Kaehler/CORBIS; p. 42, p. 43 *b*, British Antarctic Survey; p. 43 *tl*, *tc*, *tr*, MODIS images courtesy of NASA's Terra satellite, supplied by Ted Scambos,
National Snow and Ice Data Center, University of Colorado, Boulder; p. 60, © Alan Schlein Photography/CORBIS; p. 61, © Lester Lefkowitz/CORBIS; p. 62
© Wally McNamee/CORBIS; p. 63 *l*, © Chris Collins Studio/CORBIS; p. 63 *r*, © Liba Taylor/ CORBIS; p. 67, © CORBIS; p. 80 *l*, p. 81 *r*, Getty Images; p. 80 *r*, p. 81 *l*,
© L. Clarke/CORBIS; p. 83, © Bill Stormont/ CORBIS; p. 90, p. 91 *r*, Fortean Picture Library; p. 101, © South Tyrol Museum of Archaeology, Italy, www.iceman.it,
Photo: Augustin Ochsenreiter; p. 112 *l*, © Hulton-Deutsch Collection/CORBIS; p. 112 *r*, p. 117 *t*, *rc*, *lc*, © Bettmann/CORBIS; p. 113 *t*, © Don Mason Photography/
CORBIS; p. 113 *b*, © Randy Faris/CORBIS; p. 117 *b*, Paul Chauncey/CORBIS; p. 130, © Mike Laye/CORBIS; p. 131 *l*, © Hulton-Deutsch Collection/CORBIS;
p. 131 *r*, © Dan Maclellan/CORBIS; p. 137 *l*, © David Turnley/ CORBIS; p. 137 *r*, PA Photos; p. 150, © O. Alamany & E.Vicens/CORBIS; p. 151, © Patrick Johns/
CORBIS; p. 152, © Michael Rose; Frank Lane Picture Agency/CORBIS; p. 153, © Dean Conger/CORBIS; p. 161, © Brian Bailey/CORBIS; p. 170, p. 171, The Kobal
Collection/Woodfall/ Kestrel/Barnett, Michael; p. 172, Rex Features; p. 182, p. 193 *l*, p. 194 *l*, Donald Cooper/Photostage; p. 191, p. 193 *c*, Copyright BBC Photo Library;
p. 194 *r*, Joe Cocks Studio Collection, The Shakespeare Centre Library, Stratford-upon-Avon.

Every effort has been made to reach copyright holders. The publishers would be glad to hear from anyone whose rights they have unknowingly infringed.

The publishers have tried to ensure that the URLs for external websites referred to in this book are correct and active at the time of going to press.
However, the publishers have no responsibility for the websites and can make no guarantee that a site will remain live or that the content will remain appropriate.

Literacy in Context for AQA A is a collection of texts and activities that will prepare you for your English and English Literature GCSEs.

● Each unit gives you a **text** – an example of writing in a particular genre, such as a news article, a TV advert or a poem. These texts cover a wide variety of subjects, from conservation to tourist attractions, Billy Connolly to 'Bigfoot'.

  In many units you will be given the opportunity to **compare** two or more texts. This will help you to understand the way texts work much more clearly.

● Each unit then focuses on three or four key **language features** typical of that genre – such as paragraphing or the use of quotes. You will read a clear explanation of each of these features, and then work through a range of **activities** which will help you to understand them.

● Finally you have a choice of **tasks** which are closely modelled on the kind of questions you will be given in your GCSE exams. Tasks are provided in each unit at both **Foundation tier** and **Higher tier**. Your teacher will advise you on which are the most useful tasks for you to attempt.

● Every unit includes either '**The examiner's view**' or '**The moderator's view**'. This is designed to help you review what you have learned and apply it to an exam-style writing task. Written by a senior examiner, it aims to give you an insight into what the examiner is looking for and help you to improve your grades.

I hope you enjoy using *Literacy in Context for AQA A* and understanding more about the fascinating range of texts that we come across in our daily lives.

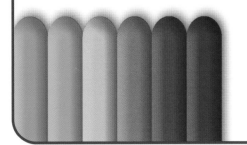

John O'Connor

Contents

UNIT	TEXTS	TEXT TYPE	PURPOSE

Comparing media texts

UNIT	TEXTS	TEXT TYPE	PURPOSE
Writing to analyse, review and comment on media texts Star-cross'd lovers 10–19	*Romeo and Juliet*, William Shakespeare	film sequence	examine film techniques and compare film openings
Analysing print-media advertisements People are... 20–9	*People are proud* *People are terrifying* *People are mystifying*	narrative-text advert	examine the combination of image and text
Analysing moving-image advertisements No-one wants jigging mouses! 30–9	Storyboard for a television advert for the Aero chocolate bar	television advert	examine the techniques of moving-image advertising
Comparing news reports Ice titan 40–9	*The ice monster*, Tim Utton *Breaking the ice*, Andrew Veitch	newspaper article web-page	compare two treatments of the same news item
Comparing print-media advertisements Two thousand years of history... 50–9	Warwick Castle leaflet Tower Bridge Experience leaflet Station X leaflet Cabinet War Rooms leaflet	tourist leaflet	examine and compare the design and language of tourist leaflets

Reading and writing non-fiction and literary non-fiction

UNIT	TEXTS	TEXT TYPE	PURPOSE
Writing to argue A message from the president 60–9	*The Gettysburg Address*, Abraham Lincoln *The struggle for the soul of the 21st century*, Bill Clinton	political speech	examine the language of argument and compare two speeches
Writing to persuade Save the rainforest! 70–9	*The Living Rainforest* *Rainforest Concern* *Gap: Go Global!*	tourist leaflet charity advert project advert	examine the language of persuasion and compare how it is used in three texts
Writing to advise Crimestoppers 80–9	*Crimestoppers*, Thames Valley Police	crime prevention booklet	examine the language of advice texts
Writing to inform Snow monster 90–9	*Bigfoot of North America*, Lee Krystek *Bigfoot, Sasquatch, Yeti...*, Paul Stonehill	information article	examine the language of information texts
Writing to explain Mysteries of the dead 100–9	*Oetzi the Iceman*, Rory Carroll *The Man Who Never Was*, Bill Mouland	explanatory newspaper article	examine the language of journalism
Writing to describe The finger of fate 110–19	*The finger of fate*, Michael Hanlon	descriptive article	examine the language of description and report

KEY LANGUAGE FEATURES	TASKS	SPECIFICATION REF
• setting • film techniques • themes	• *F* summarise the story • *F* summarise the background to the story • *F&H* compare two film versions of the opening speech • *H* compare the openings of two films	8.3 English 12.5 English
• use of narrative • typography • graphic novel techniques	• *F* write a report, summarising a narrative • *F* write a letter to your MP • *F&H* compare three advertisements • *H* compare campaign advertisements	8.3 English 12.5 English
• moving-image techniques • awareness of target groups • message and slogan	• *F* summarise the advertisement • *F* create a storyboard for a television advertisement • *F&H* compare television advertisements • *H* compare moving-image techniques	12.5 English 8.3 English
• the language of writing to inform • adjectives • quotes	• *F* summarise the news reports • *F* write a speech • *F&H* compare the reports • *H* compare scientific news articles	8.4 English
• imperatives • vocabulary • combination of text and image	• *F* summarise a leaflet • *F* write a letter to a friend • *F&H* compare the leaflets • *H* compare war museum leaflets	8.3 English 12.5 English
• structure • the language of speeches • the language of argument	• *F* summarise the main points of a speech • *F* explain how speakers use language to argue a point • *F&H* compose a speech • *H* compare the speeches	8.3 English
• the language of persuasive texts • purpose • presentational devices	• *F* summarise the information • *F* write a letter to a newspaper • *F&H* create a leaflet • *H* examine the language of persuasion	8.3 English
• imperatives and directives • adverbials • conditional sentences	• *F* summarise the booklet • *F* explain how writers use language to advise • *F&H* create an advice leaflet • *H* examine the language of the booklet	8.3 English
• chronological writing • parenthesis • active and passive	• *F* summarise the Bigfoot history • *F* rewrite an account as autobiography • *F&H* write a magazine article • *H* explain how writers use language to inform	8.4 English
• photograph, headline and intro • paragraphs • pyramid writing	• *F* write a tabloid newspaper article • *F* write a summary • *F&H* write a tabloid newspaper article • *H* compare two articles	8.4 English
• non-chronological writing • adverbials • adjectives	• *F* retell an account in chronological order • *F* write a newspaper crime report • *F&H* write a non-chronological newspaper report • *H* explain how the writer creates an informative article	8.4 English

UNIT	TEXTS	TEXT TYPE	PURPOSE
Approaches to original writing			
Writing to imagine The vulture woman 120–9	*The Amber Spyglass*, Philip Pullman	fantasy novel	learn about narrative craft and ways of telling stories
Writing biography and autobiography Outsiders 130–9	*Billy*, Pamela Stephenson *My Place*, Sally Morgan	biography autobiography	examine the language of biography and autobiography
Reading and comparing poetry			
Reading and responding to poems from different cultures and traditions 140–9	*Nothing's Changed*, Tatamkhulu Afrika *Two Scavengers in a Truck, Two Beautiful People in a Mercedes*, Lawrence Ferlinghetti *Half-Caste*, John Agard *Island Man*, Grace Nichols *Not my Business*, Niyi Osundare from *Unrelated Incidents*, Tom Leonard	poetry	consider the different contexts in which the poems are set examine the ways in which the poets achieve their effects
Compare and contrast poems by Seamus Heaney and Gillian Clarke 150–9	*Death of a Naturalist, Digging, Blackberry-Picking*, Seamus Heaney *A Difficult Birth, Easter 1998; Cold Knap Lake; The Field-Mouse*, Gillian Clarke *Inversnaid*, Gerard Manley Hopkins	poetry	compare the poets' treatment of a particular theme examine the ways in which the poets achieve their effects
Compare and contrast poems by Carol Ann Duffy and Simon Armitage 160–9	*Salome, Stealing, Education for Leisure*, Carol Ann Duffy *Hitcher, Those bastards in their mansions..., I've made out a will...*, Simon Armitage *The Man He Killed*, Thomas Hardy *Patrolling Barnegat*, Walt Whitman	poetry	compare the use of different poetic forms examine the ways in which the poets achieve their effects
Reading and responding to post-1914 prose			
A Kestrel for a Knave 170–9	*A Kestrel for a Knave*, Barry Hines	post-1914 novel	examine the techniques used in a modern novel
Language and techniques of 20th-century drama			
An Inspector Calls 180–9	*An Inspector Calls*, JB Priestley	post-1914 play	examine the context of the play and the dramatic conventions used
Reading and responding to Shakespeare			
Studying a character in performance Shylock and the pound of flesh 190–9	*The Merchant of Venice* (Act 1 Scene 3), William Shakespeare	Shakespeare play	examine the language of Shakespeare study a character and compare interpretations

KEY LANGUAGE FEATURES	TASKS	SPECIFICATION REF
• genre • comparisons • language that appeals to the senses	• *F* describe a scene from the extract • *F* write an extract from a fantasy story • *F&H* write an extract from a novel in a particular genre • *H* write about your impressions of the extract	12.6 English
• direct speech • juxtaposition • biographical and autobiographical writing	• *F* write about an episode from your own life • *F* write a biographical article • *F&H* write a section from a biography • *H* analyse the language of biography and autobiography	12.6 English
• context • meaning and language • first and third person	• *F* write about the people in the poems • *F* compare poems which point out contrasts • *F&H* examine and compare the contexts of two poems • *H* compare poems written in Standard English and in non-standard forms	8.4 English
• themes • comparisons • alliteration	• *F* recount an episode from one of the poems • *F* create a storyboard • *F&H* compare how the poets treat the theme of nature and people • *H* show how the poets use imagery and alliteration to convey ideas and develop themes	8.3 English Literature & 8.4 English Literature
• rhyme • rhythm • voice	• *F* describe what happens in a poem • *F* compare the description of people in two poems • *F&H* compare the different voices in four poems • *H* compare the poets' use of rhyme and rhythm	8.3 English Literature & 8.4 English Literature
• character description • dialogue • comic and serious writing	• *F* write a scene involving the characters from the novel • *F* write about how the author creates a character • *F&H* write about your impression of a character's life • *H* analyse the mixture of comic and serious writing	12.4 English 9.1 English Literature
• dialogue and stage directions • genre • historical and social context	• *F* write a scene in a play • *F* write about characters from the extract • *F&H* write about the use of stage directions in the extract • *H* analyse a scene from the play	13.4 English Literature
• Shakespeare's language • setting • interpretation	• *F* summarise the story of the scene • *F* create a storyboard • *F&H* compare interpretations of Shylock • *H* compare cut and uncut versions of the scene	12.3 English 8.5 English Literature

Star-cross'd lovers

In this unit you will:

- study the opening sequences of two films of Shakespeare's *Romeo and Juliet*
- examine some film techniques
- compare the two openings

Shakespeare's play *Romeo and Juliet* opens with a figure called the Chorus, who gives us the background to the story and some idea of what is going to happen. Then, in the opening scene, we meet two men of the house of Capulet boasting about their hatred of the rival house of Montague.

FRANCO ZEFFIRELLI'S 1968 *ROMEO AND JULIET*

This storyboard shows the opening sequence of a film version directed by Franco Zeffirelli.

SHOT	TIME	SOUND & MUSIC	DESCRIPTION OF SHOT	SHOT	DIALOGUE/ VOICE OVER
1a–c	00–34 secs	Music (romantic, orchestral).	(1a) Camera pans over long-shot of fifteenth-century Verona, (1b) with the director's name superimposed, (1c) to focus on a misty sun.		The Chorus is heard in voice-over (VO): *Two households, both alike in dignity, In fair Verona (where we lay our scene) From ancient grudge break to new mutiny, Where civil blood makes civil hands unclean.*
1d	35–41		The camera zooms in on the sun and the words *William Shakespeare's* appear below it.		*From forth the fatal loins of these…*
2a	42		Cut to a shot from inside the city walls.		*…two foes…*
2b	43–47		Title superimposed on the same shot.		*…A pair of star-cross'd lovers take their life…*

SHOT	TIME	SOUND & MUSIC	DESCRIPTION OF SHOT	SHOT	DIALOGUE/ VOICE-OVER
2c	48 secs –1 min 03 secs	The music ends.	Citizens enter through the gate and the camera pans left.		*Whose misadventured piteous overthrows Doth with their death bury their parents' strife.*
3	1.04–1.08	Market sounds (which continue as background noise).	Shot looking down on a busy market.		
4	1.09–1.10		The yellow-and-red-clad legs of two men walking through the market.		(The men are laughing heartily.)
5	1.11–1.15	Someone shouts 'Villain!'	One of the legs kicks a dog.		(They laugh even more loudly.)
6	1.16–1.24		First shot of the two men's faces – they are Capulet servants (**C1** and **C2**).		**C1** *The quarrel is between our masters, and us, their men.* **C2** *Ah, 'tis all one.*
7	1.25–1.27		Capulet servants seen from behind a market stall.		**C1** *Here come the house of the Montagues!*
8	1.28–1.30		Cut to another stall where the Montague priest (**Mp**) is seen talking to the stall-holder (**S**).		**Mp** *Good morrow.* **S** *Good morrow to you, sir.*
9	1.31–1.33		Cut back to the Capulets.		**C2** *Quarrel. I will back thee.* **C1** *(hesitantly) Right… Fear me not.*

BAZ LUHRMANN'S 1996 *ROMEO + JULIET*

This storyboard shows the opening sequence of a film version directed by Baz Luhrmann.

SHOT	TIME	SOUND & MUSIC	DESCRIPTION OF SHOT	SHOT	DIALOGUE/ VOICE-OVER
1a–c	00–06 secs	Interference noise from the TV which fades as the credits appear.	A television appears in the centre of a black screen – no picture, only interference. Then credits appear: Twentieth Century Fox…		
1d	07–41		A newsreader (**N**) appears on the TV screen, behind her an image of a broken ring, with the caption STAR-CROSS'D LOVERS.		**N** *Two households, both alike in dignity, In fair Verona, where we lay our scene…*

…From ancient grudge break to new mutiny, Where civil blood makes civil hands unclean.
From forth the fatal loins of these two foes, A pair of star-cross'd lovers take their life,
Whose misadventured piteous overthrows Doth with their death bury their parents' strife.
The fearful passage of their death-marked love, And the continuance of their parents' rage,
Which, but their children's end, nought could remove, Is now the two hours' traffic of our stage.

SHOT	TIME	SOUND & MUSIC	DESCRIPTION OF SHOT	SHOT	DIALOGUE/ VOICE-OVER
1e–2	42–49	As she finishes speaking, dramatic music (which continues to the end of shot 6).	As she completes her report, the camera zooms in to a blurred image, which resolves itself into the street of a major city, seen from above.		

Shots 2 and 3 appear several times in the space of two seconds…

SHOT	TIME	SOUND & MUSIC	DESCRIPTION OF SHOT	SHOT	DIALOGUE/ VOICE-OVER
3			The caption: IN FAIR VERONA		
4	50–52		The enormous statue of Christ on top of a church.		
5	53		A city skyline showing, on each side of the statue, tower blocks bearing the names MONTAGUE and CAPULET.		

SHOT	TIME	SOUND & MUSIC	DESCRIPTION OF SHOT	SHOT	DIALOGUE/ VOICE-OVER
6–16	54 secs– 1 min 02 secs		*A sequence of split-second shots showing …a speeding car's wheels, a police car, the statue of Christ, the MONTAGUE building, the CAPULET building, a zooming shot over the city, a police helicopter, a street riot scene, the statue again, the helicopter again, and a final zoom in on the statue, cutting to…*		
17	1.03	Sombre music (to end of sequence)	A grainy photo of the statue, which, when the camera pulls back, is seen to be part of a newspaper spread showing the two families.	The Verona Beach Herald Montagues Capulets	**VO** *(In fact, the voice of the Priest – the Friar in Shakespeare's play)* Two households…
18–30	1.05–1.19		*Flames give way to the newspaper headline – 'Montague v Capulet', more flames lead to a repeat of shot 6 (IN FAIR VERONA), another aerial shot across the city featuring the police helicopter, further newspaper headlines proclaiming 'Ancient grudge', 'New mutiny' and 'Civil blood', shots of rioting and police response, Captain Prince (the police chief), magazine front covers featuring the riots, ending in…*		…both alike in dignity, In fair Verona where we lay our scene, From ancient grudge break to new mutiny, Where civil blood makes civil hands…
31	1.20		…a gunman.		…unclean.
32	1.23		The Montague parents looking out of a car window.		From forth the fatal loins…
33	1.27		The Capulet parents.		…of these two foes…
34–35	1.30–1.32		Two captions: first A PAIR OF STAR-CROSS'D LOVERS then TAKE THEIR LIFE	A PAIR OF STAR CROSS'D LOVERS	A pair of star-cross'd lovers take their life…

The power of language

Key features of the texts are:

1 choosing settings

2 using film techniques

3 introducing themes

1 **SETTING**

The setting of a film is the particular time and place in which the events of the story happen.

Choosing a time

Shakespeare wrote his play *Romeo and Juliet* in the 1590s, but he based the story on events which were said to have taken place perhaps a hundred years earlier. So some directors set the story in the 1590s, when Shakespeare wrote it (a **Shakespearean setting**); some in the fifteenth century, when it supposedly happened (a **historical setting**). Other directors ignore both of these options and set their story in the modern world, even though the characters still speak Shakespeare's language – a **modern setting**.

a) Zeffirelli chose a fifteenth-century setting for his film, Luhrmann a modern one.

Write down some examples of images at the beginning of each film which tell you when it is set. For example, think about:

- costumes
- buildings and surroundings
- transport
- props ('properties' – any object an actor uses: an apple, a newspaper, a gun...)
- any other features of daily life

Choosing a place

Shakespeare's Chorus tells us that the story opens in the Italian city of Verona, and this is where Zeffirelli has set his film version. Luhrmann, however, has set his story in an imagined Verona Beach, USA.

b) What impression do we form of Verona Beach in this opening sequence? Describe it in 100 words, picking out the key visual details which help to create this impression. For example, the camera picks out two particular tower blocks and a massive statue which dominate the skyline (shots 4 to 10). What do they tell us about the institutions which have power and influence in Verona Beach? What might it be like to live there (look at the sequence of shots 18 to 31, for example)?

c) In small groups, discuss what you think the advantages and disadvantages are of setting a film of *Romeo and Juliet* (a) in the fifteenth century, and (b) in the modern world. In your discussion consider the following questions:

- Is the fifteenth-century setting more appropriate because that is when the story is supposed to have happened? Or does it make the story too remote and less relevant for a modern audience?
- Does the modern setting help us to feel that the story is still 'alive' and relevant today? Or does it sound silly to have modern people speaking Shakespeare's dialogue?

2 FILM TECHNIQUES

A single uninterrupted run of the camera is called a **shot**. When the camera moves across a scene in a single shot, it **pans**. The camera takes shots from different **angles**.

a) Write a paragraph commenting on the content of the shots chosen by Baz Luhrmann. What information do they give us? What could we learn about the background to the story by looking at shots 2 to 35 without the voice of the Chorus?

A single individual picture is a **frame**. A photograph taken from a film frame is known as a **still**. The skill of placing people or objects in a particular place within the edges of the film frame is called **framing**.

Directors use framing to gain particular effects. For example, in our first view of the Capulets, Zeffirelli frames the boys' legs in their red and yellow house colours (shot 4); this makes us focus on them not as individuals but as representatives of the Capulet household.

b) Write a paragraph on Baz Luhrmann's use of framing:

- Describe the framing of Luhrmann's shot 5 of the Verona Beach skyline. What effect does he achieve by filling the frame with the two buildings and the statue?

- Study frame 32 of the Montague parents and explain what effect Luhrmann achieves by both the framing and the camera angle.

3 THEMES

Themes are the main subjects or ideas that run through a play, film or book, and are explored throughout it in different ways.

In films, themes are often introduced by visual images. For example, the image of blood being dripped onto a severed hand at the opening of Roman Polanski's *Macbeth* introduces the twin themes of violence and the supernatural.

a) Most people would agree that the main themes of *Romeo and Juliet* include: love and sex, conflict, fate, and religion. Write a paragraph to explain which of those four themes comes across most clearly in the opening of the Zeffirelli film, in your opinion, describing what happens in particular shots.

Changing from one shot to another is known as **cutting**. The skill of joining shots together in a sequence to convey a particular meaning is called **montage** (a French word, pronounced *mont-arje*).

For example, a simple montage of shots showing: 1) a woman standing alone at a bus stop, 2) a clock showing ten o'clock, 3) the woman now at the front of a queue and 4) the clock at eleven – would tell us that she has been waiting an hour for a bus.

b) Find the montage of fourteen shots in the Luhrmann film which tells the following story:

The city is dominated by religion and by the two powerful households; the feud between Capulets and Montagues causes endless civil disturbance; and the families (and possibly also the church) are responsible for the lovers' deaths.

(Some of these shots are referred to in the storyboard but not illustrated.)

Write a paragraph explaining how the particular shots in this montage succeed in telling this story without any words being necessary.

Writing to analyse, review and comment

FOUNDATION TIER TASKS

 1 SUMMARISING THE STORY

Look again at the opening of the Zeffirelli film (pages 10–11). Then describe in your own words the images which introduce the film, and what happens in this opening sequence.

Planning and drafting

The task is in two parts. Use these points in order to make preparatory notes.

Part 1: the images which introduce the film

Look at:

- the sequence represented by frames 1a to 2c

Part 2: what happens in this opening sequence

Look at:

- the market-place
- the Capulets
- how the Capulets behave and what they say
- the arrival of the Montagues
- what the Capulets plan to do

You could start:

In the opening shot we are given a view across the roofs and towers of the city of Verona. The camera pans across the rooftops until it picks out the sun beginning to shine through the early morning mist...

2 SUMMARISING THE BACKGROUND

Look back at the storyboard of the Baz Luhrmann version as far as shot 31. What do we learn in that opening sequence about the background to Romeo and Juliet's story? How is that information conveyed to us?

Planning and drafting

The task is in two parts:

Part 1: What do we learn about the background to Romeo and Juliet's story?

Part 2: How is that information conveyed to us?

Remember to refer both to:

- the Chorus's words, spoken by the newsreader and other voices
- the visual images

You might find this writing frame useful to start you off.

Shot	The Chorus's account	Images	You could start...
3	Two households...	TV presenter	*The TV news presenter gives us the background to the story. In the city of Verona...*
8		The skyline	*As the camera pans across the city, two tower blocks stand out...*
18		Newspaper headline	*For a long time there has been a feud between two powerful families...*
18–31	From ancient grudge...	Flames, newspaper headlines and photos, rioting, police activity	*Now the rioting has blown up again...*

FOUNDATION & HIGHER TIER TASK

 COMPARING THE TWO OPENINGS

Shakespeare's play opens with the following speech by the Chorus:

> Two households, both alike in dignity,
>   In fair Verona (where we lay our scene),
> From ancient grudge break to new mutiny,
>   Where civil blood makes civil hands unclean.
> From forth the fatal loins of these two foes
>   A pair of star-cross'd lovers take their life;
> Whose misadventured piteous overthrows
>   Doth with their death bury their parents' strife.
> The fearful passage of their death-marked love,
>   And the continuance of their parents' rage,
> Which, but their children's end, nought could remove,
>   Is now the two hours' traffic of our stage;
> The which if you with patient ears attend,
>   What here shall miss, our toil shall strive to mend.

Compare the openings of Baz Luhrmann's and Franco Zeffirelli's film versions of *Romeo and Juliet*. Which version is more successful in representing the Chorus's speech, in your opinion? (See pages 18–19 for 'the moderator's view' on how to tackle this question.)

HIGHER TIER TASK

 COMPARING THE TWO OPENINGS

Compare the openings of Baz Luhrmann's and Franco Zeffirelli's film versions of *Romeo and Juliet*, saying which version you prefer, and giving your reasons.

Planning and drafting

You could divide your answer into sections and ask yourself a number of questions:

INTRODUCING THE STORY

- How much introductory information does a film audience need for this story? Which version provides the appropriate amount in the first minute and a half?

INTRODUCING THE THEMES

- Is it a good idea to introduce the major themes from the outset? Which version introduces themes more effectively?

CHOOSING A SETTING

- Which setting seems to work better — fifteenth-century Verona, or modern-day Verona Beach? Why?

USING FILM TECHNIQUES

- Which director has made most effective use of film techniques?

CAPTURING OUR INTEREST

- Which opening encourages you to continue watching?

You could start:

Zeffirelli and Luhrmann are both dealing with the same material — the opening of Shakespeare's Romeo and Juliet. *But they make very different decisions about how they want to introduce the story and its major themes...*

The moderator's view

Compare the openings of Baz Luhrmann's and Franco Zeffirelli's film versions of *Romeo and Juliet*. Which version is more successful in representing the Chorus's speech, in your opinion?

STEP 1: READ THE TEXT

This kind of task, writing based on a response to a media text, could be set either as a piece of coursework (your media coursework) or in the reading section of Paper 1 in your English exam (Paper 1, Section A).

The task asks you to **compare** the openings to two versions of the same film. Prepare for this task by rereading the texts on pages 10–13, paying special attention to the similarities and differences in the use of the Chorus's speech.

STEP 2: COMPARING

Students studying at both Foundation and Higher tiers should use the following process when comparing and contrasting.

1. **Read** the question and **underline** what has to be compared.
2. **List** the ways in which the two items are **similar**.
3. **List** the ways in which the two items are **different**.
4. **Sequence** the two lists by numbering them and adding *compare* **words and phrases**.
5. **Write** your answer, using the *compare* **words and phrases** in every paragraph.
6. **Evaluate** by stating which of the two you think is better, and why.

STEP 3: THE USE OF LANGUAGE

You need to build up a bank of compare words and phrases which you can use whenever you compare.

- Brainstorm a list of words and phrases which show similarities.

- Brainstorm a list of words and phrases which show differences.

- Write down three phrases which could be used to introduce some evaluation.

STEP 4: PLANNING AND DRAFTING

1 Before you tackle the question, make some notes on what the Chorus actually says, to do with:

- where the story is set (lines 1–2)
- who the main characters are (lines 1–6)
- what has happened in the past (line 3)
- what has just happened (line 3)
- what will happen in the rest of the story (lines 5–12)
- the actors who are about to perform the story (lines 13–14)

2 Then ask yourself the following questions:

- How much of the Chorus's speech ought to be included at the beginning of a film?
- Which parts of the speech are essential and which parts could be cut?

3 Finally, compare the different ways in which the two versions deal with the material that you think is important. Which is more successful?

- How much of the speech does each version include?
- How is the speech delivered in each case? (Think about voice-over and captions.)
- How effectively does each director combine the Chorus's words with visual images? (Look back at question 2a, page 15, on shots.)
- Which film techniques does each director employ and how effective are they? (Look back at questions 2 and 3, page 15.)

STEP 5: WRITING TO ANALYSE, REVIEW AND COMMENT

Now answer the question – make sure that you:

- write with a clear purpose and for a particular audience
- structure your writing into clear and coherent paragraphs
- use an effective range of sentences and technical vocabulary
- present your answer accurately and attractively

(These are the assessment objectives used for marking media coursework.)

STEP 6: SAMPLE ANSWER

Read this opening from a sample answer.

> Any director making a film of Shakespeare's Romeo and Juliet has to decide what to do about the Chorus. In this essay, I am going to compare how each director deals with this opening section of the play and then evaluate how successful each has been.

By using the words *compare* and *evaluate* this student has already shown that they are attempting to show evidence of Higher tier reading skills.

Quick tip Compile a bank of compare words and phrases. These will be useful in many situations during your GCSE assessments.

People are ...

In this unit you will:

- study a series of three advertisements
- examine the combination of image and text
- compare the three advertisements

The three advertisements on these pages are all encouraging people to think about a career in social work.

People can be fascinating, mystifying, terrifying. Social work is work with people, it's that simple and that complicated. To find out more about training to be a qualified social worker call for a career booklet on **0845 604 6404** or visit www.socialworkcareers.co.uk (minicom: 0845 601 6121)

it's all about people.

GP   local doctor (general practitioner)

autism	autistic people have difficulty in relating to others and their language does not develop normally
congenital deficiency	a weakness in the genes inherited from your parents
cerebellum	the part of the brain which controls muscular movements, balance and co-ordination
traumas	harmful experiences
social isolation	being cut off from other people

The power of language

Key features of the advertisements are:

1. use of narrative
2. typography
3. graphic novel style

1 NARRATIVE

> A **narrative** is another term for a story or account. Biographies, autobiographies, novels and short stories are all examples of **narrative texts**.

Advertisements in print media (newspapers, magazines etc) mainly use two kinds of writing:

- writing to inform (giving you details about the product)
- writing to persuade (encouraging you to buy it)

But these three *People are...* advertisements are unusual because they are mainly narrative texts: they each tell a story.

a) In pairs, look back at the three advertisements and pick out examples of:

- writing to inform (giving you information about social work as a career)
- writing to persuade (encouraging you to train as a social worker)
- narrative writing (telling a story)

2 TYPOGRAPHY

> **Typography** is the name given to the way words are written, drawn or printed. It is a term used in **graphics** (the art of combining images and lettering for particular effects).

Graphic artists put as much thought into typography as writers do into choosing the right words.

a) Write a short paragraph on each of the following examples of typography from *People are terrifying*. For each example, describe the typography used and explain why you think it was chosen.

- the word *terrifying* in the title, and the text in the bottom left-hand corner (*Mother screams at you...*)
- the words *you get a message from a GP*
- the words *unlucky thirteen*
- the words *social work* in the bottom right-hand corner

EOF

3 GRAPHIC NOVEL STYLE

> A **graphic novel** is a story which is told through a combination of words and images. It closely resembles a cartoon-strip in its method of telling the story.

Graphic novels are similar in design to children's comics. But they are different in the following ways:

- they are much longer
- they deal with adult issues
- they contain a single, extended story
- they use a wide range of images – not just line drawings
- the drawing styles are adult
- the images are a very important part of the narrative – some frames contain no words at all

a) Look at the frames and images from the three advertisements listed in the right-hand column. In pairs, discuss how the illustration alone helps to tell the story in each case. For example, the text about Errol (*People are proud*) says: *as he tells you he's had a good life.*

The illustration gives much more information about him and also shows how fanatical he has always been about cricket.

People are proud

- frame 8: What does the road sign suggest about the location of, and the attitude of, Errol's family?
- frame 10: What does this image suggest? Look particularly at the way the word *home* has been reproduced.
- frame 11: How does the image of the umpire help to convey the idea that death itself was *a small thing to Errol*?
- frame 5 onwards: Which other images help to show Errol's obsession with cricket? How do they get it across?

People are terrifying

- frame 2: What evidence did the doctor have, apart from the sight of the bruising?
- frame 3: The girl on the horse doesn't look like the girl in the story – is it the same girl? Why has this picture been included?

People are mystifying

- What story is being told through the set of three frames near the bottom of the advert (starting with the text *the rewards*)? For example, why does the adult look exactly the same while the child has changed?
- What fact is being illustrated by the two frames of the cathedral at the bottom?

b) In pairs, talk about the way in which you first read the three advertisements. For example, did you find yourself looking at the images first, then the writing, or the other way round? What do you notice now that you look at them for the second or third time? What do you like about the graphic novel style of narrative? What can it do that traditional novel narrative cannot do?

c) After your discussion, write a paragraph headed *Graphic novel style*. Explain what it is and how a graphic novel text might be read differently from a traditional novel or short story.

Analysing print-media advertisements

FOUNDATION TIER TASKS

1 SUMMARISING THE NARRATIVE

Imagine you are a social worker whose job it is to help Errol (in *People are proud*). You visit him for the first time and have a long talk. Draft the brief report that you write up after your meeting.

> ### Planning and drafting
>
> Use the story told on page 21 as a basis for your report. First, review what you discussed for question 3a in the section on graphic novel style (page 25). That will remind you which parts of the narrative are told through the illustrations rather than the text.
>
> Write about:
>
> - your impressions of Errol when you first met him (get some ideas from the three frames on the top line)
> - what he told you about himself and his background:
>   - his age
>   - his family life
>   - his employment history (you could make up details about what jobs he had done)
> - his view of his past life (was he cheerful or sad, for example?)
> - his passion for cricket (mention the way he describes life in cricketing terms)
> - his current difficulties and needs
>
> Then write a section headed *Action*. State briefly what you plan to do to help Errol, including:
>
> - practical changes in his home
> - home-helps and visitors

> **You could start:**
>
> *I visited Errol Jones at his home on .... (date). As soon as he opened the door I got the impression of a man who...*

2 WRITING A LETTER

Write a letter to your local MP explaining why you think social workers are doing an excellent job. Use the three stories from the *People are...* advertisements as evidence.

> ### Planning and drafting
>
> You could write about:
>
> - the people social workers help
> - the practical support they offer
>
> Use the writing frame below as a guide.

Facts and ideas	Possible openers
Social workers can help...	
old people	*When old people live a long way from...*
young people	*If a young person is suffering...*
people suffering from autism	*Social workers can also help people who...*
Social workers know what practical help can be given...	
helping old people	*It can be hard for old people to manage at home...*
	Many old people need to make friends and...
helping people who have been abused	*Social workers can work alongside doctors...*
supporting families	*If a family has an autistic child...*

> **You could start:**
>
> *Dear................ (name of your MP),*
>
> *I am writing to you in support of the many social workers in our local community. I don't think many people appreciate...*

FOUNDATION & HIGHER TIER TASK

COMPARING THE THREE ADVERTISEMENTS

Write an analysis of the three *People are...* advertisements in which you compare their methods and decide which one is the most successful in persuading people to consider social work as a career.

(See pages 28–9 for 'the moderator's view' on how to tackle this question.)

HIGHER TIER TASK

COMPARING CAMPAIGN ADVERTISEMENTS

Compare the *People are...* advertisements with the following spread from a leaflet about SOS Children's Villages. What are the similarities and what are the differences?

> ### Planning and drafting
> Think about the features you are going to compare. Look, for example, at:
> - the use of images
> - the information provided
> - the stories which are told

"We wish we had a mummy to...

A mother's unconditional love. It's every child's right. The very least they can expect when they take their first steps into the world. Imagine, then, a child so starved of human contact they can hardly speak. A child that doesn't even know what a hug

or a kiss is, let alone how to ask for one. A child who already has the odds well and truly stacked against them. Sadly, this is the plight of children the world over. It's something that SOS Children's Villages is working tirelessly to defeat by giving over

50,000 orphaned and abandoned children a new mother, brothers and sisters, a home and a community.

This leaflet tells you the stories of just some of these brave children and the important role that you can play in their future.

Now Keemenao knows what a hug is

...give us a hug...

Most of us have a mother for life. Little Keemenao had one for just 18 short days. After she died he was left clinging to life in a hospital. No mother to sit by his bedside. No mother to hold him close when the tears started to fall. No mother to simply care whether this frail little baby made it through the night. Things didn't look hopeful when he

arrived at the SOS Children's Village in Tlokweng, Botswana. However, with our help he was eventually able to turn the corner. He received the medical treatment he urgently needed, the right food to build up his strength and gradually recovered his health. Best of all, with his new SOS mother, he was able to experience his very first hug.

...kiss us goodnight...

Children can arrive at an SOS Children's Village looking like startled wild animals, cowering away from any attempt at contact. Emotionally starved of a mother's love throughout their short lives. The first step for our SOS mothers is to simply hold these children. Then, gradually, over time,

the child learns to open their emotional defences and accept a mother's love. As one of our SOS mothers says, "At night, when they are asleep, I kiss each of my nine sons and daughters and it seems to me that they can tell I am there because they smile and stretch their hands out to me".

... hold our hands."

Achinea is growing up with brothers and sisters

The moderator's view

> Write an analysis of the three *People are...* advertisements in which you compare their methods and decide which one is the most successful in persuading people to consider social work as a career.

STEP 1: READ THE TEXTS

This kind of task could be set either for your media coursework (5% of your total mark for English) or in the reading section of Paper 1 in your English exam (15%).

Media coursework assignments test how well you can write to **analyse**, **review** and **comment**, in response to media texts – print-media advertisements in this case.

This task asks you to compare the three advertisements and decide which is the most successful. Reread the texts, paying special attention to:

- similarities
- differences

STEP 2: COMPARING PRINT-MEDIA TEXTS

Refer to the process for comparing and contrasting outlined on page 18.
Try to use this whenever you are asked to compare texts.

- **Analyse** the topics in each of the advertisements.
- **Review** the different ways in which image and language are linked.
- **Comment** on which advertisement is the most successful.

- C-grade answers will need to include some appropriate media terminology.
- A-grade answers will need to show a sophisticated and convincing use of technical terminology to describe media concepts.

STEP 3: READING PRINT-MEDIA ADVERTISEMENTS

- Choose one presentational device from each advertisement and explain how each helps to get the message of the advert across.

- Compare the ways meaning is conveyed in print and image in each of the advertisements.

STEP 4: PLANNING AND DRAFTING

When answering this question, include examples from all three advertisements and refer closely to both the text and graphics. Remember to organise your ideas carefully; use these notes to help you plan.

1   You could begin by stating what it is that links the three advertisements:

- the **purpose** (to persuade people to consider social work as a career)

- the **form** (graphic novel style)

- the **audience** (readers who might be considering which career to follow, or thinking about changing careers)

- the **topics** (vulnerable people in our society and the social workers who help them)

2   You could then explain that the methods used involve both language and images, and refer to:

- the different kinds of writing used: to inform, to persuade and to tell a story

- the choices made about typography and the effects achieved

- the graphic novel style and the part played by the illustrations in getting across details of the story which are not explained in the written narrative

3   Finally, decide which of the three is most successful in persuading people about the attractions and value of social work as a career.

STEP 5: WRITING TO ANALYSE, REVIEW AND COMMENT

In addition to the general assessment objectives given on page 19, your media coursework will be marked using the following assessment objectives:

- clear structure
- clear use of technical terminology (examples are highlighted in the sample answer below)

STEP 6: SAMPLE ANSWER

These three advertisements are linked by a common purpose, form, audience and topic...

> All three advertisements use the graphic novel style to help persuade the
> reader to their point of view. The images illustrate the text and tell a story in
> the same way that a comic book or cartoon tells a story. By using this unusual
> approach, the adverts appeal to the imagination of the target audience...

This student uses a variety of media terminology. Remember, you must not simply identify and name terms; you should explain how they are used.

! Quick tip   Plan to use effective words, or terminology, by preparing a list beforehand and ticking words off when you have used them.

No-one wants jigging mouses!

In this unit you will:

- study a television advertisement
- examine the techniques of moving-image advertising
- compare two moving-image advertisements

This is the storyboard for a thirty-second television advertisement for the Aero chocolate bar. It was shown in spring 2002.

SHOT NO.	TIME IN SECONDS	SOUND EFFECTS	DESCRIPTION OF SHOT	SHOT	DIALOGUE
1	00–02	Busy traffic	Delivery man (DM) walks from the back of his lorry up to the shop door. He carries two boxes.		
2	03–04	Faint traffic noise from outside	Inside the shop, the owner (O) is standing behind the counter, contentedly eating an Aero bar.		DM: *Hello, mate. It's your new Honeycomb Aero and a hundred promotional items.*
3	05–06		DM puts the boxes on the floor.		

SHOT NO.	TIME IN SECONDS	SOUND EFFECTS	DESCRIPTION OF SHOT	SHOT	DIALOGUE
4	07		O's face drops.		O: *Mouses? No-one wants jigging mouses!*
5	08		Close-up of shop counter, as O throws his Aero down angrily. DM's eyes peer over the top.		
6	09		O turns angrily to the cupboards in the wall behind him.		
7	10		O opens the doors one by one, to reveal dozens of mice, all dancing and playing with hula-hoops.		O: *All they want is bubbly…*
8	11–12		His voice fades away as he turns back to DM.		*…chocolate!*

SHOT NO.	TIME IN SECONDS	SOUND EFFECTS	DESCRIPTION OF SHOT	SHOT	DIALOGUE
9	13		His jaw drops in amazement as he watches DM…		
10	14–15		…who turns round and opens his hand to reveal…		DM (smugly): *These are from…*
11	16–17	Singing in Chinese from the mouse	…a dancing mouse standing up on his palm, which then sings in Chinese and dances.		…*Taiwan!*
12	18–19		A woman customer (C) walks behind O, just as the mouse is jumping onto his hand. Not noticing the mouse, she picks an Aero off the display…		C (looking at the Aero): *Oh, lovely!*
13	20		Hearing her enthusiastic comment, O turns round to her, smiling, while DM comments over his shoulder.		DM: *Off your hands before you can say…*

SHOT NO.	TIME IN SECONDS	SOUND EFFECTS	DESCRIPTION OF SHOT	SHOT	DIALOGUE
14	21–23		C starts to open the Aero, but a look of horror strikes her face as she sees the mouse. She screams.		C (screams)
15	24–27	Thud as she hits the floor.	Shot of DM and O from over C's shoulder. As she drops from view, their eyes follow her descent to the floor. DM says goodbye and leaves. O watches his departure in dismay.		DM: *Cheerio!*
16	28		Cut to the Aero display box on the counter with the mouse standing next to it.		Voice-over: *Honeycomb Aero* *All bubble…*
17	29–30		Closer shot of the Aero display box – cutting out the mouse.		*…No squeak!*

Promotional items are free gifts, given away with a product. These are often made, very cheaply, in Far East countries such as *Taiwan*.

33

Language in context

The power of language

Key features of the advertisement are:

 1 moving-image techniques

2 awareness of target groups

3 message and slogan

1 MOVING-IMAGE TECHNIQUES

Film, television, video, computer-generated moving images and similar technologies are known as **moving-image media**. Anybody creating a moving-image text has to think about **vision** (what the audience see), **sound** (what they hear, including sound effects and music) and **duration** (timing: how long the audience will watch each part of the text).

Vision

A single uninterrupted run of the camera is called a **shot**. A single individual picture is called a **frame** (and a photograph taken from a film frame is known as a **still**).

When you are filming a scene, you have a choice from a variety of different camera-shots, such as the close-up, the close-shot, the medium-shot and the long-shot. The Aero advertisement uses the following shots:

Extreme close-up	Close-up
Close-shot	Long-shot

a) In pairs, study the storyboard and discuss the following questions:

- What can you show the audience with a close-up which can't be achieved with other shots?
- What can you achieve with a long-shot?
- What kind of shot is useful for showing two or three people's expressions in a single frame?
- What kind of shot is used most frequently in the Aero advertisement? Why is it so useful in filming this scene?

The skill of placing people or objects in a particular place within the edges of the film frame is called **framing**.

Directors use framing to gain particular effects. For example, in this advertisement the mouse from Taiwan fills almost the whole of frame 11 so that we can see it in detail and be impressed by its amazing performance.

b) Write down how the framing helps to show:

- where the story is about to take place and what is happening (frame 1: note that the framing allows us to see the van with its doors open, the delivery man carrying boxes from it, and the shop entrance)
- the shop owner's reaction to the phrase 'promotional items' (frame 4)
- the actions of the customer (frame 12)
- the customer's reactions to seeing the mouse (frame 14)
- the shop owner's reaction when the customer faints and the delivery man makes a hasty departure (frame 15)
- the product (frame 17)

The camera can also take shots from different directions and different heights, such as looking up at an object, or viewing it from above. These views are called **camera angles**.

c) Write down what camera angle you could use if you wanted to:

- show people waiting on a platform as a train comes in
- make the villain in a film look menacing
- show the full effect of a massive traffic-jam in one shot

d) What effect does the camera angle have in frame 5 of the advertisement?

> Changing from one shot to another is called **cutting**.

For example, the director of this advertisement cuts from a shot of the cheerful shop owner (frame 2) to a shot of the delivery man depositing the boxes on the floor (frame 3).

e) In pairs discuss how the cutting helps to contrast the shop owner's feelings with the delivery man's (on two occasions: frames 2–5 and 9–10).

Duration

> A key difference between print-media texts (anything that appears on a printed page) and moving-image texts is **duration**: the fact that a moving-image text takes a set amount of time to be experienced by the audience.

f) In pairs:

- talk about the overall length of the Aero advertisement (How long is it? How does that length compare with the average television advertisement in your opinion?)
- think about the duration of the shots – pick two or three examples of one-second shots which illustrate the fact that a great deal can be conveyed in a very short piece of action
- find the shot which the director holds for the longest time and discuss why you think the camera stays with that shot as long as it does

Voice-over

> **Voice-over**, in moving-image media, is an effect in which we hear someone's voice but do not see the speaker.

2 TARGET GROUPS

> All advertisements are aimed at a particular audience. This is known as the **target group**.

For example, television advertisements for disposable nappies are aimed mainly at women in the 16–35 age group. When a new advertisement is being planned, the makers have to ask themselves at least two questions:

- Which **gender** are we aiming at: male, female, both?
- Which **age group** are we aiming at: up to 15, 16–24, 25–35, 36–55, over 55?

a) Look at the images and the humorous approach of the Aero advertisement – as well as the product itself – and decide which target groups (gender and age) it is aimed at. Write a paragraph to explain your decision.

3 MESSAGE AND SLOGAN

> The **message** of an advertisement is the main point that the advertisers are trying to get across. The message is often underlined in a **slogan** – a short, catchy phrase designed to stick in the memory.

a) Write a paragraph to explain what you think the message of the Aero advertisement might be and how the slogan (heard in voice-over at the end) helps to sum it up or put it into words.

Analysing moving-image advertisements

FOUNDATION TIER TASKS

 SUMMARISING THE ADVERTISEMENT

Imagine you were telling a friend about this advertisement. Summarise what happens.

Planning and drafting

- Use the seventeen storyboard frames, and the individual shot descriptions, as a guide.
- Write in the present tense (*he places the boxes on the floor... she looks up...*).
- Avoid repeating (*In the first shot... in the third shot...*).

Use the writing frame below as a guide.

Frame	Possible openers
1	*A delivery man is unloading...*
2	*Inside the shop, the owner...*
3	*The delivery man puts the boxes on the floor...*
4–8	*But when the owner realises...*
9–11	*He is amazed when...*
12–14	*Meanwhile, a woman customer has entered the shop...*
15	*The delivery man leaves...*
16–17	*In the final shots...*

You could start:

As the advertisement starts, a delivery man is seen unloading some boxes from his lorry which is parked in a busy street. He carries the boxes...

 CREATING A STORYBOARD

Draw six frames of a storyboard for a television advertisement. (Either choose an advertisement that you know well or make up your own.) Then, write a paragraph to explain how your six shots fit in to the advertisement as a whole.

Planning and drafting

You could choose to draw the opening or concluding six frames, or any six from the middle of the advertisement.

Drawing up the storyboard

Use the same storyboard framework as the one which represents the Aero advertisement on pages 30–3. Include:

- the shot number
- the duration of that particular shot (the length of time it takes)
- any sound effects or music
- a brief description of the shot
- a rough outline sketch of the shot (don't spend too much time on that)
- any dialogue

Writing an explanatory paragraph

Start by explaining what the overall message of the advertisement is. Then explain what part your six frames play in the advertisement as a whole. For example, do they introduce the situation and the characters, or round off the advertisement, underlining the message with a slogan?

Your explanatory paragraph could start:

I have chosen to represent the opening six shots of the television advertisement for Woolworths. These six shots introduce the main character – a woman shopper – and the Woolworths store itself. The message of the advertisement is...

FOUNDATION & HIGHER TIER TASK

 ## COMPARING TELEVISION ADVERTISEMENTS

Compare the Aero advertisement with any other television advertisement for a similar product. (Think about advertisements for chocolate bars such as Double Decker or Kinder Bueno.) Which one is more effective in getting its message across and encouraging us to buy the product, in your opinion?

(See pages 38–9 for 'the moderator's view' on how to tackle this question.)

HIGHER TIER TASK

 ## COMPARING MOVING-IMAGE TECHNIQUES

Compare the moving-image techniques used in the Aero advertisement with those used by either Franco Zeffirelli or Baz Luhrmann at the opening of their film versions of *Romeo and Juliet* (see pages 10–13).

Planning and drafting

1 Think about the techniques you are going to compare. Look, for example, at:

- varying the shots (long-shots, close-ups etc)
- framing
- different camera angles
- cutting and montage
- sound
- varying the duration of particular shots
- using sound effects, music and voice-over

2 List the similarities between the techniques used in the advertisement and those used in the film. Make sure that you write about the effects that these techniques have. How do they help to sell the product or tell the story?

3 List the differences between them.

4 Sequence the two lists by numbering them and adding *compare* words and phrases.

5 Write your answer, using the *compare* words and phrases in every paragraph.

You could start:

The television advertisement for the new Honeycomb Aero employs a number of moving-image techniques which are also seen in the opening of Baz Luhrmann's Romeo + Juliet...

The moderator's view

Compare the Aero advertisement with any other television advertisement for a similar product. (Think about advertisements for chocolate bars such as Double Decker or Kinder Bueno.) Which one is more effective in getting its message across and encouraging us to buy the product, in your opinion?

STEP 1: READ THE TEXT

This kind of task could be set either as media coursework or as the reading task in Paper 1 of your English exam. It assesses how well you can write to **analyse**, **review** and **comment**, based on the 'reading' of media: moving-image advertisements in this case.

You are asked to **compare** TV advertisements and decide which is more successful. To prepare for this task:

- brainstorm ideas about your chosen advert (include notes on shots, angles, cuts, sound effects, music etc)
- reread the storyboard on pages 30–3 and note down similarities and differences between this and your chosen advert

STEP 2: COMPARING MOVING-IMAGE MEDIA

Students studying at both Foundation and Higher tiers should use the process outlined on page 18 when comparing. In this kind of task you will also be expected to analyse, review and comment.

- Say what happens in each advert and explain how the 'story' is told (**analyse**).

- Give your opinion about what happens in each advert (**review**).

- Explain which of the two you believe to be the better (**comment**).

- **Compare** the purposes, audiences, methods and media techniques of the two adverts.

- **Evaluate** which of the two adverts is more successful in fulfilling its purpose for its particular audience.

STEP 3: THE USE OF LANGUAGE

- Write a list of words and phrases which show similarities and differences. For example *Similarly… On the other hand…*

- Try to begin some of your sentences with phrases that lead you into detailed **evaluation**, which means 'to judge or assess the worth of'. For example *I also think that … because… This also means that … However… In addition, I also think that … but… Another point is that … Nevertheless…*

STEP 4: PLANNING AND DRAFTING

Before you start writing, make some notes on another advertisement. It might help to draw up a rough storyboard. Then:

1 Think about the features of the two adverts that you are going to compare.
Look, for example, at how each one uses moving-image techniques such as:

- varied shots (long-shots, close-ups etc)
- framing
- varying the duration of particular shots
- different camera angles
- using sound effects, music and voice-over
- cutting and montage

You could also address the following questions:

- How successfully does each advert attract its target group?
- What is the message of each one and how effectively is it conveyed (through the storyline and the slogan)?

2 List the similarities between the two advertisements.

3 List the differences between them.

4 Sequence the two lists by numbering them and adding *compare* words and phrases.

5 Write your answer, using the *compare* words and phrases in every paragraph.

STEP 5: WRITING TO ANALYSE, REVIEW AND COMMENT

You are now going to use your notes and lists of *compare* and *evaluate* phrases to write your comparison of the two TV adverts. Aim to use all of the material at your disposal to make your work as interesting and detailed as possible.

STEP 6: SAMPLE ANSWER

Read this opening paragraph from a sample answer.

> The first advertisement I am going to write about aims to persuade people to buy the Honeycomb Aero chocolate bar. However, many other manufacturers use a variety of techniques to help sell their products. One such product is Cadbury's Creme Eggs. In the following piece of writing, I will analyse the purpose and target audience of the two adverts, review the media devices used by the advertisers and comment on which aspects of each advert are more effective, in my opinion.

Evaluation is a Higher tier reading skill and means to judge the worth of something. Real evaluation gives you the opportunity to give your opinion about different items/issues and usually begins with phrases like *It is my opinion that … because…* and *I believe … however…*

! Quick tip Using your first paragraph as a sort of contents page to your written work helps to make the purpose of your writing clear.

Ice titan

In this unit you will:

- read a newspaper article and a web-page covering the same item of news
- learn about the language and presentation of news items
- compare the different treatments of a news item

On 19 March 2002, reports started to come in that a huge Antarctic ice shelf, called Larsen B, had collapsed into the sea. This is how the story was reported in the *Daily Mail* and on the *Channel 4 News* website.

The ice monster

Fears as a 50 billion-ton Antarctic mass collapses

By **Tim Utton**
Science Reporter

AN Antarctic ice sheet the size of Cambridgeshire has collapsed into the sea in the latest terrifying sign of global warming.
5 It was described by one minister yesterday as 'a wake-up call to the whole world'.

Experts said the 50 billion-ton mass of ice had crumbled with
10 'staggering' speed, taking less than a month to break off and float away.

The collapse of the 650ft thick shelf, called Larsen B, is due to
15 an unprecedented temperature rise of 2.5C on the Antarctic Peninsula over the last 50 years – a rate five times faster than the rest of the Earth.
20 Dr David Vaughan, a glaciologist with the British Antarctic Survey, said: 'We have increased carbon dioxide and methane in the atmosphere to levels that
25 haven't been seen on Earth for at least half a million years, and probably longer.

'It would be surprising if we didn't see climate change as a
30 result.

'In 1998, the BAS predicted the demise of more ice shelves around the Antarctic Peninsula. Since then, warming on the

35 peninsula has continued and we watched as, piece by piece, Larsen B has retreated.

'We knew what was left would collapse eventually, but 40 the speed of it is staggering.

'It's hard to believe 50 billion tons of ice sheet have disintegrated in less than a month.

'Climate change has effective-45 ly been "taking the bricks out of the wall" one by one.'

Larsen B, which was twice the size 15 years ago, has now disintegrated into thousands of 50 icebergs.

In response to the collapse, Environment Minister Michael Meacher called for 'dramatic and fundamental' changes to 55 address global warming.

The ice sheet's rapid decline was 'the most significant evidence of continuing climate change'.

60 Speaking at the launch of a climate change exhibition at London's Science Museum, he added: 'It's an indication of global warming which is 65 extremely stark and the implications are that we have got to arrest climate change and adapt to it. But above all, we have got to reduce it.

70 'I think it's a wake-up call to the whole world that when an ice shelf of such enormous proportions can break up, that shows the effect we are having 75 on the planet.'

demise death (here: loss or destruction)

Forum I Contact us I Snowmail

CHANNEL 4 NEWS

Breaking the ice

Published: March 19, 2002

Reporter: Andrew Veitch

More stories

Security breached

Heathrow heist

Hunting vote

Performing miracles

Zimbabwe ban

Breaking the ice

Full show video

Snowmail

Forum

Get Real Player

An Antarctic ice shelf almost the size of Cambridgeshire has collapsed in less than a month, scientists reported today – and further south an iceberg the size of Cyprus has broken away from the continent.

Global warming – or a little local oddity? Our Science Correspondent Andrew Veitch has this:

Scientists had been watching the Larsen ice shelf melt as the Antarctic Peninsula grew warmer.

But the speed of the final collapse was astonishing.

VIDEO

View photos of Iceshelf collapse:

British Antarctic Survey

Links:

Kyoto Protocol – full text

Detr: Climate Change and Global Warming information and action

EPA Global Warming Site

National Environmental Trust

Sovereignty International

WWF Climate Change Campaign

The British Antarctic Survey ship *James Clark Ross* was there.

Dr Carol Pudsey, British Antarctic Survey, speaking from the *James Clark Ross*:

"That part of the ice shelf has been calving bergs for years. In early February eight miles broke off – it was the suddenness of the subsequent disintegration, 3,000 square kilometres almost overnight, that was a surprise. It looked like a mass of icebergs and fragments of ice covering the surface of the ocean as far as we could see."

The Antarctic Peninsula has warmed by a dramatic two and a half degrees centigrade over the last 50 years.

The top part of the Larsen ice shelf, Larsen A, has already gone.

Now, satellite images show the much bigger Larsen B disintegrating: 50 billion tonnes of ice, an area almost the size of Cambridgeshire, in less than a month.

Breaking the ice

Rapid Melting:

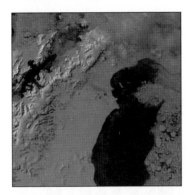

Three satellite photographs of the Larsen B ice shelf: 15 October 1995 (left), 31 January 2002 (centre) and 5 March 2002 (right). Visit <u>British Antarctic Survey</u> for larger images.

And in a separate event further south, an iceberg the size of Cyprus has broken from the Thwaites Glacier – one of the biggest bergs ever seen.

Dr David Vaughan, British Antarctic Survey:
"We can't tie it back concretely to global climate change. But we're getting more confident about that. Shelves have been there for 1,800 years and it must be more that a local natural fluctuation in climate."

Michael Meacher, Environment Minister:
"When an ice sheet which is 50 billion tonnes of ice breaks up that is a wake-up call for the entire planet. That has not happened before in human experience."

Scientists forecast that the first signs of global warming would appear at the poles because ice is sensitive to small changes in temperature.

Water forms lakes on the surface during the summer and seeps into cracks breaking the ice apart. And warmer seawater melts it from below.

It's been discovered that ice shelves melted during a global warm spell starting 8,000 years ago, and formed again as the planet cooled, 1,800 years ago.

The question is whether the loss of the sea ice will destabilise the glaciers on land: when they start melting, sea levels will rise substantially threatening coastal cities around the world.

<u>Forum</u> I <u>Contact us</u> I <u>Snowmail</u> I <u>Chat</u>

calving	producing (like a cow giving birth to calves)
subsequent	following
tie it back concretely	link it definitely
fluctuation	variation up and down

The power of language

Key features of the texts are:

1 the language of information texts

2 adjectives

3 quotes

---

1 WRITING TO INFORM

> Writing to **inform** focuses on conveying information and ideas clearly. To achieve this, writers of information texts need to have a very accurate understanding of who their **audience** is. This audience might have to be given **statistics** and access to **further information**.

In the articles on pages 40–3, statistics include the size of the ice shelf and changes in temperature. Further information might include other examples of global warming or a selection of comments by scientists.

Audience

Both writers know that their audience is very wide: it is the general public who read the *Daily Mail* or watch *Channel 4 News*.

a) Write a paragraph to explain what methods the two texts have used in order to get across the following scientific details to a wide audience:

- the size of the Larsen B ice shelf (look at the opening paragraph of the *Daily Mail* article, for example)

- the size of the iceberg that has broken from the Thwaites Glacier (on the *Channel 4 News* web-page)

- the way in which climate change has damaged the ice sheet (the *Daily Mail* article, lines 44–6)

Statistics

b) Reports of this kind can involve a great many statistics. Imagine you were creating a series of PLANET EARTH fact-cards. Read both texts and create a card on *Ice shelves and climate change*. You could use the following headings:

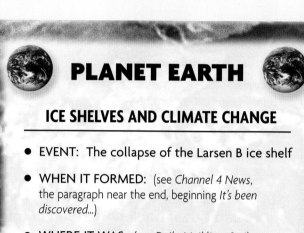

PLANET EARTH

ICE SHELVES AND CLIMATE CHANGE

- **EVENT:** The collapse of the Larsen B ice shelf

- **WHEN IT FORMED:** (see *Channel 4 News*, the paragraph near the end, beginning *It's been discovered...*)

- **WHERE IT WAS:** (see *Daily Mail* lines 1–4) Which continent was it part of?

- **ITS SIZE:** (see *Daily Mail*, 8–19; and *Channel 4 News*, Dr Pudsey's quote) How heavy was it? How thick? How many square kilometres?

- **WHAT CAUSED IT TO COLLAPSE:** (see *Daily Mail*, 13–27) How serious was the temperature rise?

- **HOW LONG IT TOOK TO COLLAPSE:** (see *Channel 4 News*, the paragraph beginning *Now, satellite...* and the photos on page 43)

2 ADJECTIVES

> An **adjective** is a word which gives us information about a noun or pronoun. A group of words which does this is called an **adjective phrase**.

Both texts use adjectives and adjective phrases to get across the magnitude and seriousness of the ice shelf's collapse.

a) Find the adjectives or adjective phrases which describe:

in the *Daily Mail* article

- the latest sign of global warming (lines 1–4)
- the speed at which the ice had crumbled (8–12)
- the temperature rise which caused the collapse (13–19)
- the changes needed to deal with global warming (51–5)
- the evidence of continuing climate change (56–9)
- the indication of global warming (60–9)
- the proportions of the ice shelf (70–5)

in the *Channel 4 News* text

- the speed of the final collapse (paragraph 4)
- the two-and-a-half-degree increase in temperature (the paragraph beginning *The Antarctic...*)
- Larsen B (the paragraph beginning '*Now, satellite...*)
- the iceberg that has broken from the Thwaites Glacier (the paragraph beginning *And in a...*)

b) Write two paragraphs to explain how the writers have used adjectives to get across how significant the collapse of Larsen B is.

3 QUOTES

> Journalists often use quotations (commonly called **quotes**): word-for-word comments from people closely involved with the story.

Quotes in an article can be used for a variety of purposes; for example:

- they help the reader to understand how urgent the subject is, if they are spoken by someone well known or important
- they add authority, especially if they are spoken by someone who has made a close scientific study of the subject

a) *Quotes to underline the urgency*

Look at the quotes in both texts from Michael Meacher. Write a paragraph to explain why they have quoted him at length. What is his position in government, for example? Why is it important for us to read his exact words, rather than the journalist's report of what he said? (Look at the powerful adjectives he uses, for example, and the warnings he gives.)

b) *Quotes to add authority*

Write a paragraph to explain the importance of the quotes from Dr David Vaughan (in both texts) and Dr Carol Pudsey (in the *Channel 4 News* text). Look, for example, at:

- the background information provided by Dr Vaughan
- Dr Pudsey's personal reaction to the ice shelf's collapse

Writing to analyse, review and comment

FOUNDATION TIER TASKS

 1 **SUMMARISING THE NEWS REPORTS**

Reread both texts and then summarise:

- what has happened to the Larsen B ice shelf
- why it has happened

Planning and drafting

The task is in two parts.

Part 1: what has happened to the Larsen B ice shelf

Part 2: why it has happened

Use the writing frame below for ideas.

	Where to look in the two reports	You could start...
Part 1	What has happened to the Larsen B ice shelf	
The collapse of the ice shelf	• *Daily Mail,* lines 1–12 and 47–50 • Channel 4 News, paragraph 1 and Dr Pudsey's quote	*In March 2002, news suddenly came of a dramatic event in Antarctica. The Larsen B...*
Part 2	Why it has happened	
Temperature rises in Antarctica	• *Daily Mail,* lines 13–19	*The collapse has been caused by...*
Global warming	• *Daily Mail,* lines 20–30 • *Channel 4 News,* and Dr Vaughan's quote	*Global warming has been a major problem...*

2 WRITING A SPEECH

Imagine that you are going to take part in a debate about the future of the planet. Your task in the debate is to argue that something urgently needs to be done about global warming and its effects. Write your speech.

Planning and drafting

You could first give an example of the effects of global warming: the collapse of the Larsen B ice shelf. Explain what happened and why it happened (use the points that you summarised in task 1).

You might then want to use Michael Meacher's quotes as a basis for some of your own arguments:

- the Larsen B collapse is an extremely important sign: *the most significant... It's an indication...*
- something has to be done about climate change: *...the implications are... But above all...*
- everyone around the world needs to take notice: *I think it's a...*

You could start:

Ladies and gentlemen, events in Antarctica in recent years have shown once and for all that we can no longer fail to take action against global warming. In March 2002, a huge ice shelf...

FOUNDATION & HIGHER TIER TASK

 COMPARING THE REPORTS

Write an analysis of these two news reports, comparing how effective they are in informing their audiences about the collapse of the Larsen B ice shelf and explaining how serious an event it is.

(See pages 48–9 for 'the moderator's view' on how to tackle this question.)

HIGHER TIER TASK

 COMPARING NEWS ARTICLES

Compare the *Daily Mail* report with this scientific article by Tim Radford.

Stumbling with dinosaurs...
at 20mph across ancient Oxfordshire

Tim Radford
in Boston

Millions of years after the event, scientists have reconstructed the case of the dinosaur that broke into a sprint at nearly 20mph across what is now Oxfordshire.

It was a Megalosaurus, a huge hunter-killer, a relative of Tyrannosaurus rex, and made its mark in history when it went for a walk along an intertidal zone in the Jurassic era.

It left a trail of neat clear three-toed footprints which dried in the lime-rich mud of the foreshore. Sand covered them. Some freak of time and geology preserved them. Sediments buried them. Continents shifted. The landscape sank beneath the waves, and then emerged again.

And 163m years later, quarrymen at Ardley, Oxfordshire, scraped away the rock and clay above and exposed one of the most extensive dinosaur track-ways in the world, with sets of footprints that could be followed for 180 metres.

Julia Day and colleagues from Cambridge and Oxford report in Nature today that they used global positioning satellite measurements and close observation to tell the story of at least one stalking beast on that forgotten foreshore.

The size of its footprints, and the distance and the angles between them, were all they had to go on. The length of the foot gave a clue to the creature's height at the hip. When it walked – at an estimated 4.25mph – it had a stride of 2.7 metres. When it accelerated, its stride stretched to 5.6 metres and its speed increased fourfold.

"It was about seven metres in length, and had a hip height of about two metres. It was a bipedal dinosaur, a relative of T rex," said Dr Day.

"It is walking and the footprints vary from the midline: it is walking pigeon-toed. Then it breaks into a run or a jog for a 35-metre section of the track-way, and in that section the feet are tucked underneath the body, the way a mammal would run. It is an erect gait with the feet in line, rather than a zig-zag arrangement."

She added: "We calculated its speed at about 18mph. It fits the higher end of people's previous estimates."

"Obviously if an animal that big falls over it is more likely to break a limb at that speed. We don't know if it could sustain its run, or whether it was doing short bursts."

Planning and drafting

1 Think about the features of the two news reports that you are going to compare. Look, for example, at:

- the writers' awareness of audience
- their method of helping the audience to understand scientific concepts and statistics
- their use of adjectives and adjective phrases
- their use of quotes

Then follow stages 2 to 5 outlined on page 18.

You could start:

Both of these articles are reporting on scientific news...

The moderator's view

 Write an analysis of these two news reports, comparing how effective they are in informing their audiences about the collapse of the Larsen B ice shelf and explaining how serious an event it is.

STEP 1: READ THE TEXT

This task assesses how well you can write to analyse, review and comment; it is based on the 'reading' of media, news media in this case. This kind of task could be set either for your media coursework or in the reading section of Paper 1 in your English exam.

You are being asked to **compare** how two different media have dealt with the same piece of news. Reread the two reports. Pay close attention to the way each has presented the information through:

- language
- layout/combination of text and image

What are the similarities in the reports' approach? What are the main differences?

STEP 2: USING QUOTATIONS

Using quotations effectively is a very important skill. Quotes can support points you make and help your writing sound more authoritative. You should try to use this three-stage process:

1 make a point
2 back it up with an example or quotation
3 explain how the quotation or example helps

- Write down one important quotation from each article.
- Explain why you think these quotations are important.

- Try to **embed** or **include** your quotations ⓗ within a sentence. For example:
  The journalist in the *Daily Mail* writes '................',
  which shows that '................' is important, because...

STEP 3: THE USE OF LANGUAGE

Sometimes, you will not want to use a quotation, but will want to write what the journalists are saying in your own words. Absorbing and shaping someone else's writing for the purpose of the task is a Higher tier reading skill.

- Write down what you understand ⓕ to be the main points of this news item, in your own words as far as possible. (Use quotations only when there is no alternative.)

- Analysing texts at Higher tier requires you ⓗ to consider more than one answer or point, so you should try to begin some sentences with phrases such as:
  This also means that... In addition... I also think that... Also... Another point is that... To examine this in detail, I...
- You should show in your writing that you have absorbed and shaped the material for the purpose of the task.

STEP 4: PLANNING AND DRAFTING

1   Think about the features of the two news reports. Look, for example, at:

- the writers' awareness of audience
- their method of helping the audience to understand scientific concepts and statistics
- the possibility of accessing further information
- their use of adjectives and adjective phrases to get across the magnitude and seriousness of the event
- their use of quotes
- their use of photographs (and moving images) and headlines

2   List the similarities between the two news reports.

3   List the differences between them.

4   Sequence the two lists by numbering them and adding *compare* words and phrases.

5   Write your answer, using the *compare* words and phrases in every paragraph.

STEP 5: WRITING TO ANALYSE, REVIEW AND COMMENT

Now try to use everything that you have learned in this unit to compare the two news reports.

STEP 6: SAMPLE ANSWER

Read this section from a sample answer which focuses on comparing the use of presentational devices in the two reports.

> ...Both of these reports use presentational devices, but these vary because the two news reports are in different media. They have different purposes and audiences, and therefore need to use different presentational devices.
>
> For example, the Daily Mail article uses devices such as ...., which you would expect to see in a national daily newspaper...

It is a big step forward when students realise that writers start off with a definite purpose and audience in mind: this student is obviously on the right lines.

Quick tip   Try to write about three aspects of each part of the question. That should give your answer plenty of detail.

Two thousand years of history...

In this unit you will:

- compare leaflets advertising historic buildings
- learn about the language and design of tourist leaflets
- compare different leaflets

This is part of a leaflet advertising Warwick Castle.

WARWICK CASTLE
A thousand years of history in the making

Come and take a look inside Warwick Castle - and step back in time!

Warwick Castle – with history, drama and excitement, it's a great day out for everyone!

Encounter over 1,000 years of mystery and intrigue at Warwick Castle. From the days of William the Conqueror to the splendour of the Victorian era, the Castle has been a mighty force in English history.

Experience the sights and smells of a mediaeval household in 'Kingmaker – a preparation for battle' or feel the weight of a sword in 'Death or Glory'. Take a step forward in time and marvel at the elegant splendour of the Great Hall, State Rooms and the Victorian 'Royal Weekend Party, 1898'.

Warwick Castle is a great day out for all the family, with plenty to see and do all year round – see our calendar inside for all our special events taking place throughout the year.

Food and drink facilities are available at the Castle from the Coach House and the Undercroft, where delicious hot meals, snacks, morning coffee, afternoon tea, children's meals, wine and beer are offered.

Visit our gift shops where you will discover Warwick Castle themed gifts, plus our more unique ranges. Turn your child into a fair maiden or deadly archer or treat yourself to one of our tapestries, books or jewellery sets.

Death or Glory

Our armoury attraction is home to some magnificent displays, all grouped into three distinct historical periods of the last 1,000 years. You'll get the chance to try on a helmet and discover the sheer amount of strength needed to lift a sword.

The Dungeon and Torture Chamber

Why not venture underground to the eerie silence of the Mediaeval Dungeon or enter into our grisly Torture Chamber.

Grounds and Gardens

With 60 acres of grounds and gardens, there's always plenty to see outside as well as in, whatever time of the year you visit. Wander around our beautiful Peacock Garden and enter our 18th century Conservatory, filled with an array of exotic plants. Then take a trip to our Victorian Rose Garden where the delicate English flowers bloom during late June.

Towers and Ramparts

Marvel at the impressive Towers and Ramparts and survey the panoramic views of the Castle grounds and Warwick Town. Initially used as mighty defence systems, the Towers were later converted into sumptuous apartments for affluent and powerful visitors, many of which can be viewed as part of our special events during January to March – see our calendar of events inside for further details.

Kingmaker

Witness a mediaeval household in 'Kingmaker – a preparation for battle'. The year is 1471 and preparations are being made for what will be Richard Neville's, Earl of Warwick, final battle.

See how weapons would have been made, watch the seamstresses hard at work, come face to face with the Earl's warhorse and feel the incredible weight of the armour worn.

Royal Weekend Party

Step back in time to the splendour of the Victorian period at Warwick Castle. Meet the beautiful Daisy, Countess of Warwick, preparing for one of her spectacular parties, with her impressive guest list consisting of royalty and future prime ministers. Watch as day passes to evening and witness the guests in twelve rooms of the former private apartments preparing for the celebrations. See and hear for yourself the British aristocracy at play.

Great Hall and State Rooms

Deep in the heart of the Castle, enter the grandeur of the Great Hall before stepping through into the State Rooms surrounded by superb collections of family treasures from around the world.

Ghost Tower

Enter our spooky Ghost Tower and hear the chilling tale of the murder of Sir Fulke Greville, whose restless soul is said to still haunt these rooms.

To book fast-track entry tickets or for further information please call 0870 442 2000 or book on-line at www.warwick-castle.co.uk

This is the inside of a leaflet advertising Tower Bridge in London.

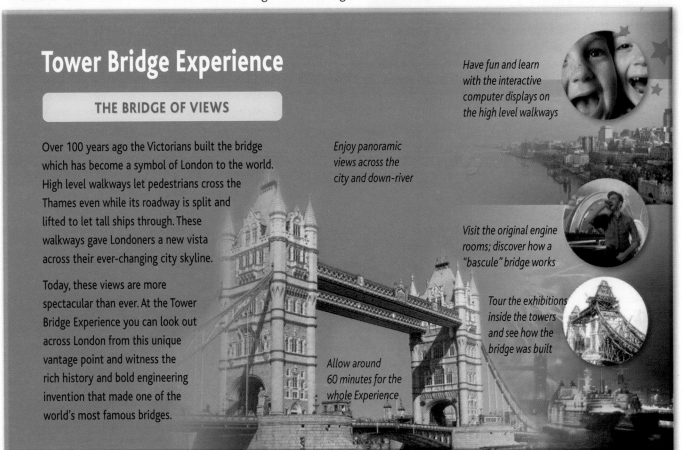

Tower Bridge Experience

THE BRIDGE OF VIEWS

Over 100 years ago the Victorians built the bridge which has become a symbol of London to the world. High level walkways let pedestrians cross the Thames even while its roadway is split and lifted to let tall ships through. These walkways gave Londoners a new vista across their ever-changing city skyline.

Today, these views are more spectacular than ever. At the Tower Bridge Experience you can look out across London from this unique vantage point and witness the rich history and bold engineering invention that made one of the world's most famous bridges.

Have fun and learn with the interactive computer displays on the high level walkways

Enjoy panoramic views across the city and down-river

Visit the original engine rooms; discover how a "bascule" bridge works

Tour the exhibitions inside the towers and see how the bridge was built

Allow around 60 minutes for the whole Experience

Station X was the name given to Bletchley Park, the home of the codebreakers in the Second World War. The leaflet below describes what visitors can see there today.

BLETCHLEY PARK

STATION X

COMMUNICATIONS THAT CHANGED THE WORLD

TOP SECRET

Home of the world's first programmable electronic computer - Colossus

Bletchley Park

Bletchley Park, also known as 'Station X', was home to the famous codebreakers of the Second World War and the birthplace of modern computing and communications. It is now a heritage site run by a charitable Trust, with historic buildings, exhibitions and tours for visitors, community activities and non-residential conference facilities.

The Mansion

Bought in 1883 by Sir Herbert Leon as his family home, the Mansion is the centrepiece of Bletchley Park. Its exterior reflects his changing tastes, each addition being a different architectural style, whilst the opulence of the wood-panelled interior and gilded ballroom is indicative of the status of a wealthy Victorian businessman.

The Mansion's first reprieve from demolition was its acquisition in 1938 by the Government Code and Cypher School. The wooden huts and brick blocks were added until over 12,000 people worked within the Park.

The extensive Churchill Memorabilia Collection, the Toy Museum and the Post Office famous for its First Day Covers are all located within the Park.

The 'Bombe' machine was devised by Alan Turing to assist in breaking 'Enigma' codes.

The Grounds

The Bletchley Park heritage site occupies 30 acres. Within this area there are a number of different exhibitions and displays covering, amongst others:

- Uniforms & WWII Memorabilia
- WWII aircraft recovery
- Wartime fire engines and historic vehicles
- US, German & British Re-enactment groups
- Wartime electronics and amateur radio station
- Model railway layouts
- Model boats (displays often take place on the lake)
- Military vehicles
- Historic cinema projectors

Displays frequently change so there is always something new to see.

Enjoy a picnic by the lake or a visit to the 'Hut 4' bar and café when you are ready to 'take a break'. Snacks available in the museum complex.

The Cryptology Trail

This fascinating experience enables you to follow the trail of a coded message from its interception to decode and interpretation. With its complex system of outposts and intercept stations, the wireless system was the forerunner of the Worldwide Web.

The need for speed, accuracy and secrecy was paramount, so very few knew the whole story. After following the Cryptology Trail you will know the secrets of Bletchley Park almost as well as those who worked here!

Enigma

The Enigma machine was the main decoding device for German armed forces and rail system. They believed its codes were unbreakable. Some of the finest brains in Britain were assembled at Bletchley Park for the sole purpose of breaking the Enigma codes.

One of the leading figures was Alan Turing, a brilliant mathematician considered to be the father of the modern computer. During your visit you will see working examples of Enigma and other coding machines, plus a replica of the 'Turing Bombe' deciphering device.

The Tour

No visit to Bletchley Park is complete without a guided tour. Experienced guides give you a real insight into the work that went on here and the secrecy surrounding it until just a few years ago.

The tours are optional and run at regular intervals. Your guide will first give you the background to the Park and then take you around the main buildings. Your guide will explain what went on at key locations and illustrate the story with a few amusing anecdotes of their own.

The tour takes about one hour.

The Internet

Take a virtual tour of Bletchley Park through our website at **www.bletchleypark.org.uk** This will help you get more out of your visit and also keep you up-to-date with many different special events taking place on Open Weekends.

Left and below are the front cover and the inside of a leaflet advertising the underground rooms used by the Cabinet during the Second World War.

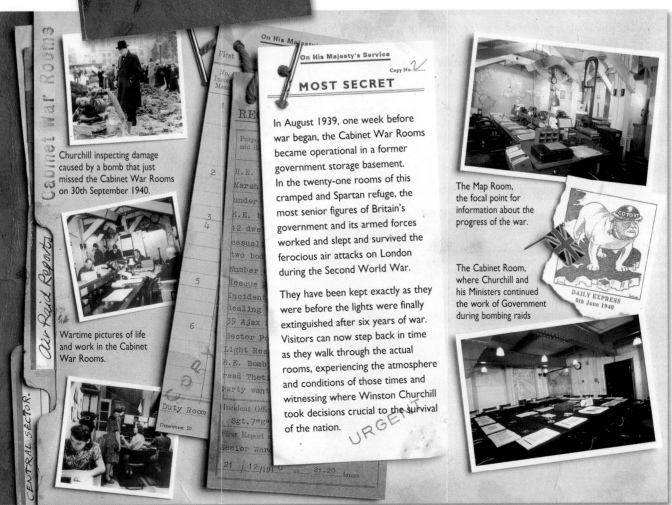

Churchill inspecting damage caused by a bomb that just missed the Cabinet War Rooms on 30th September 1940.

Wartime pictures of life and work in the Cabinet War Rooms.

MOST SECRET

In August 1939, one week before war began, the Cabinet War Rooms became operational in a former government storage basement. In the twenty-one rooms of this cramped and Spartan refuge, the most senior figures of Britain's government and its armed forces worked and slept and survived the ferocious air attacks on London during the Second World War.

They have been kept exactly as they were before the lights were finally extinguished after six years of war. Visitors can now step back in time as they walk through the actual rooms, experiencing the atmosphere and conditions of those times and witnessing where Winston Churchill took decisions crucial to the survival of the nation.

The Map Room, the focal point for information about the progress of the war.

The Cabinet Room, where Churchill and his Ministers continued the work of Government during bombing raids

The power of language

Key features of the leaflets are:

1 imperatives

2 vocabulary

3 the combination of text and image

1 IMPERATIVES

We use the **imperative** form of the verb when we want to give a command, issue a warning, make a request or persuade someone to do something.

Imperatives for persuasion

Imperatives are widely used in leaflets of this kind. Most often, they are used as a way of persuading you to visit the place being advertised: *Come* and *take* a look inside Warwick Castle – and *step* back in time!

a) Write down examples of imperatives used in:

- the left-hand panel of the Warwick Castle leaflet (*Warwick Castle – with history...*)
- the final section of the Station X leaflet (headed *The Internet*)
- the right half of the Tower Bridge leaflet

b) The Warwick Castle leaflet is full of imperatives. Reread the sections on page 51 headed *Kingmaker* and *Royal Weekend Party*. Make a note of all the imperatives, starting with *Witness...*

c) Write a paragraph to explain how effective the imperatives are in persuading the reader that there will be plenty of things to see and do on a visit to Warwick Castle.

2 VOCABULARY

Vocabulary is the term given to a writer's choice of words.

The vocabulary in these leaflets has been chosen with the aim of getting across certain ideas and associations. For example, the Tower Bridge leaflet contains the phrase *witness the rich history...*

- The **verb** *witness* is an example of an imperative (see section 1); it suggests that we will see something important and worth remembering.
- The **adjective** *rich* suggests the wealth of exciting and interesting things in our past.
- The **abstract noun** *history* is the 'product' that these tourist attractions are 'selling'.

An **adjective** is a word which gives us information about a noun or pronoun. A group of words which does this is called an **adjective phrase**.

a) Look at the Tower Bridge leaflet, which describes the attraction as *one of the world's most famous bridges*. Pick out the other adjectives and adjective phrases that describe the following nouns (listed in the order in which they appear in the text):

- the walkways (an adjective phrase)
- ships
- the vista across London
- the city skyline
- the views (an adjective phrase)
- the vantage point
- the views across the city

b) Each of the adjectives you have just found helps to describe the same feature. Which special attraction of Tower Bridge are they focusing on? Write a sentence or two to comment on the message that the writers of the leaflet were trying to convey with these adjectives. What in particular are they trying to 'sell'?

c) Write a paragraph commenting on the following adjectives and adjective phrases in the leaflet about the Cabinet War Rooms:

*this **cramped** and **Spartan** refuge... the **most senior** figures... the **ferocious** air attacks... the **actual** rooms... decisions **crucial** to...*

How do they help to convey:

- what the rooms must have been like to work in?
- what part the rooms played in the war?

> An **abstract noun** is the label we give to something we cannot touch, such as an emotion, feeling or idea.

d) Reread the section of the Station X leaflet headed *The Cryptology Trail*. The first half (up to *...Web*) contains the following abstract nouns:

experience, message, interception, decode (here an abstract noun, but more usually a verb), *interpretation, system, forerunner, Worldwide Web*

Find the abstract nouns in the rest of the section (down to *...worked here!*).

e) The section headed *The Cryptology Trail* is about three features of Station X:

- Station X's work with codes
- the system they built up
- the qualities which were most important to them

Divide the abstract nouns from *The Cryptology Trail* into three groups, showing how each noun helps us to understand one of these three features.

3 **TEXT AND IMAGE**

> Explanatory texts will often use a combination of **text** (words) and **image** (photographs and illustrations).

a) In pairs, talk about the following images. What message or messages does each one get across?

- The photograph of Station X at the top of the leaflet (what atmosphere does it conjure up?).
- The round photograph in the top right-hand corner of the Tower Bridge leaflet.
- The photograph at the top of the Warwick Castle leaflet.

b) Study the front cover and inside panels of the leaflet on the Cabinet War Rooms. Make notes on which ideas and facts are explained:

- through the **text** alone — look at the centre panel and the captions accompanying the photographs
- through the **illustrations** alone — look at the use of:
  - **realia** (the term given to real documents and historical objects), such as:
    - the photographs and newspaper cartoon from the Second World War
    - the labels
    - the leather file
  - modern **photographs**

c) Write a paragraph or two commenting on the ways in which the spread uses a combination of text and image in order to give us an idea of how interesting and important the Cabinet War Rooms are. In your writing, explain the choices made about the overall **design concept** (the main design idea which aims to get across a particular impression or message). Which central idea holds the whole design together?

Writing to analyse, review and comment

FOUNDATION TIER TASKS

 1 SUMMARISING THE ATTRACTIONS

Summarise in your own words what Bletchley Park (Station X) is and what its attractions are to visitors.

Planning and drafting

You could write a short paragraph on each of the following:

- why Station X is important
- what visitors can see and enjoy there
- the Enigma machine and its importance

Use the writing frame on the right as a guide.

You could start:

Bletchley Park was an important centre in the Second World War. It was also known as...

Paragraph	Which section to look at in the leaflet	Possible openers
Why Station X is important	**Bletchley Park**	*It was important because...*
		These days it is...
	The Mansion	*At the centre of Bletchley Park is the Mansion, which...*
What visitors can see and enjoy there	**The Grounds**	*In the 30-acre site, you can see...*
	The Cryptology Trail	*This is a fascinating experience, which...*
Its most important exhibit	**Enigma**	*The Enigma machine was...*

2 WRITING A LETTER

Write a letter to a friend in which you recommend her or him to visit a particular historic building.
You could choose:

- a site that you have visited yourself
- one of the buildings advertised in the leaflets on pages 50–3

Planning and drafting

In your letter, you could refer to:

- the building itself (look at the descriptions in the Cabinet War Rooms and Station X leaflets)
- the attractions (look at the Tower Bridge and Warwick Castle leaflets)
- visitor facilities (such as cafés, picnic areas and access for the disabled; look at the advertisements for *The Tour* and *The Internet* in the Station X leaflet)

Choose adjectives and abstract nouns (see pages 54–5) to make your letter sound enthusiastic, and to get across how dramatic and interesting your visit was.

You could start:

Dear ....,

Have you ever been to ....?

It's amazing! I suppose I had been expecting...

FOUNDATION & HIGHER TIER TASK

 COMPARING THE LEAFLETS

Write a comparison of the four leaflets. First describe which features they have in common, using examples to illustrate your points. Then explain which of the four is most effective in your opinion, again referring closely to the texts as you give your reasons.

(See pages 58–9 for 'the moderator's view' on how to tackle this question.)

HIGHER TIER TASK

 COMPARING WAR MUSEUM LEAFLETS

Compare the Cabinet War Rooms leaflet with this spread from a leaflet advertising the American Air Museum at Duxford, saying which you find more effective:

Planning and drafting

1 Think about the features you are going to compare. Look, for example, at:
- careful choice of vocabulary, particularly adjectives, abstract nouns and proper nouns (names of particular people, places or things)
- the combination of text and image
- the overall design concept

2 List the similarities between the two leaflets.

3 List the differences between them.

4 Sequence the two lists by numbering them and adding *compare* words and phrases.

5 Write your answer, using the *compare* words and phrases in every paragraph.

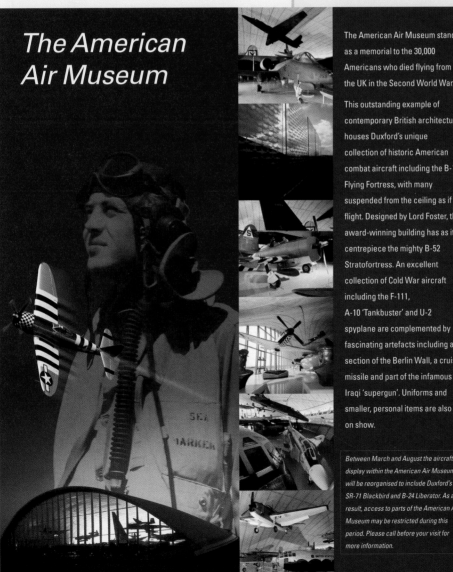

The American Air Museum

The American Air Museum stands as a memorial to the 30,000 Americans who died flying from the UK in the Second World War.

This outstanding example of contemporary British architecture houses Duxford's unique collection of historic American combat aircraft including the B-17 Flying Fortress, with many suspended from the ceiling as if in flight. Designed by Lord Foster, the award-winning building has as its centrepiece the mighty B-52 Stratofortress. An excellent collection of Cold War aircraft including the F-111, A-10 'Tankbuster' and U-2 spyplane are complemented by fascinating artefacts including a section of the Berlin Wall, a cruise missile and part of the infamous Iraqi 'supergun'. Uniforms and smaller, personal items are also on show.

Between March and August the aircraft display within the American Air Museum will be reorganised to include Duxford's SR-71 Blackbird and B-24 Liberator. As a result, access to parts of the American Air Museum may be restricted during this period. Please call before your visit for more information.

The moderator's view

> Write a comparison of the four leaflets. First describe which features they have in common, using examples to illustrate your points. Then explain which of the four is most effective in your opinion, again referring closely to the texts as you give your reasons.

STEP 1: READ THE TEXT

You could be asked this type of question either for your media coursework or in the reading section of Paper 1 in your English exam.

The task assesses how well you can write to analyse, review and comment, but it is based on the reading and comparing of several tourist leaflets. Reread the leaflets. As you read, make notes on similarities and differences between the leaflets. Think in terms of:

- purpose and audience
- use of language
- design

- Why was each leaflet written?
- Who is each leaflet aimed at?

- In your opinion, which leaflet fulfils its purpose most successfully? Explain how it does this.

STEP 2: PRESENTATIONAL DEVICES

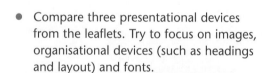

These leaflets use various presentational devices to help persuade the reader to visit their particular historical museum or site.

- Choose one presentational device from each leaflet and explain why you think it is effective. For example *The writer uses bright, primary colours and a variety of images. This very effectively attracts the reader's attention.*

- Compare three presentational devices from the leaflets. Try to focus on images, organisational devices (such as headings and layout) and fonts.
- Evaluate which is the best presentational device or design feature in your opinion, and explain why you think it is particularly effective.

STEP 3: THE USE OF LANGUAGE

Students rarely do themselves justice when comparing the use of language in non-fiction texts such as leaflets. There are always some features that you can comment on and compare:

- Identify and comment on the **person** that the writers choose – the first person (*I, we*), the second person (*you*) or the third person (*he, she, they, it...*)
- Do the writers write in the past, present or a combination of the two?

- Explain how the writers' choice of **person** influences the reader's response.
- Explain how the writers' choice of past or present **tense** influences the reader's response.

STEP 4: PLANNING AND DRAFTING

In describing the features of the leaflets, explain the effectiveness of:

- the widespread use of **imperatives**
- careful choice of vocabulary, particularly **adjectives** and **abstract nouns**
- the combination of **text** and **image**
- the overall **design concept**

In comparing the effectiveness of the four leaflets, ask yourself which ones use the above features most successfully to:

- describe the overall site clearly, so that you know exactly what is there
- focus on something particularly attractive or interesting, such as the views from Tower Bridge or the Enigma machine at Station X
- explain what facilities there are for visitors

STEP 5: WRITING TO ANALYSE, REVIEW AND COMMENT

You are now going to use all of the skills that you have practised in this unit to write to analyse, review and comment.

Remember to use these steps when comparing:

- choose an aspect of the leaflets that you are going to compare
- explain how the leaflets are similar
- explain how the leaflets are different
- use *compare* words and phrases to show where you are making comparisons

STEP 6: SAMPLE ANSWER

Read these extracts from a sample answer.

> All of the leaflets have certain language features in common. For example, they all use the imperative, because they are all telling the reader that they should visit their particular site or museum. An example of the use of the imperative in the first leaflet is when we are 'told' to "Come and take a look inside Warwick Castle – and step back in time."...
>
> Although there are many similarities in the use of language in the four leaflets, there are various differences in the presentation. For example, the Cabinet War Rooms leaflet uses a clever design which...

This student has looked at both language and presentation, and has identified both a similarity (*they all use...*) and a difference (*Although...*). You will need to do all of these things to get a good grade.

! Quick tip Remember to use the question as a planning and structuring tool for your response.

A message from the president

In this unit you will:

- compare two speeches
- examine the language of argument
- write a speech arguing a particular case

In 1863, at a time when America was being torn apart by a civil war between the North and South, President Abraham Lincoln made a speech. It has come to be known by the name of the battlefield on which the Confederate Southern army had just been defeated – the Gettysburg Address. This is what he said.

THE GETTYSBURG ADDRESS

Fourscore and seven years ago our fathers brought forth on this continent a new nation, conceived in liberty, and dedicated to the proposition that all men are created equal.

Now we are engaged in a great civil war, testing whether that nation, or any nation so conceived, can long endure. We are met on a great battlefield of that war. We have come to dedicate a portion of that field as a final resting place for those who here gave their lives that that nation might live. It is altogether fitting and proper that we should do this.

But, in a larger sense, we cannot dedicate – we cannot consecrate – we cannot hallow – this ground. The brave men, living and dead, who struggled here have consecrated it far above our poor power to add or detract. The world will little note nor long remember what we say here, but it can never forget what they did here. It is for us, the living, rather, to be dedicated here to the unfinished work which they who fought here have thus far so nobly advanced. It is rather for us here to be dedicated to the great task remaining before us – that from these honored dead we take increased devotion to that cause for which they gave the last full measure of devotion; that we here highly resolve that these dead shall not have died in vain; that this nation, under God, shall have a new birth of freedom; and that government of the people, by the people, for the people, shall not perish from the earth.

| consecrate/hallow | make holy or sacred |

In December 2001, Bill Clinton, former President of the United States, delivered the annual Richard Dimbleby Lecture, named after the distinguished BBC broadcaster. The speech took place in the midst of the bombing of Afghanistan, and only three months after terrorists had flown two airliners into the World Trade Centre in New York on 11 September 2001. After a brief introduction, Bill Clinton began to talk about three issues facing the modern world, saying 'Let me take each of these issues quickly in turn...'.

THE STRUGGLE FOR THE SOUL OF THE 21ST CENTURY

First, terror. The deliberate killing of non-combatants has a very long history. No region of the world has been spared it and very few people have clean hands. In 1095, Pope Urban II urged the Christian soldiers to embark on the first
5 crusade to capture Jerusalem for Christ. Well, they did it, and the very first thing they did was to burn a synagogue with three hundred Jews; they then proceeded to murder every Muslim woman and child on the Temple Mount in a travesty that is still being discussed today in the Middle
10 East. Down through the millennium, innocents continued to die, more in the twentieth century than in any previous period. In my own country, we've come a very, very long way since the days when African slaves and native Americans could be terrorised or killed with impunity, but
15 still we have the occasional act of brutality or even death because of someone's race or religion or sexual orientation. This has a long history.

Second, no terrorist campaign apart from a conventional military strategy has ever succeeded. Indeed the purpose
20 of terrorism is not military victory, it is to terrorise, to change your behaviour if you're the victim by making you afraid of today, afraid of tomorrow and, in diverse societies like ours, afraid of each other. Therefore, by definition, a terror campaign cannot succeed unless we
25 become its accomplices and, out of fear, give in.

The third point I want to make is that what makes this terror at the moment particularly frightening, I think, is the combination of universal vulnerability and powerful weapons of destruction... Now, in any new area of conflict,
30 offensive action always prevails in the beginning. Ever since the first person walked out of a cave millennia ago with a club in his hand, and began beating people into submission, offensive action prevails. Then after a time, someone figured out, well, I could put two sticks together and
35 stretch an animal skin over it and I would have a shield, and the club wouldn't work on me any more. All the way through to the present day, that has been the history of combat – first the club, then the shield; first the offence, then defence; that's why civilisation has survived all this
40 time even in the nuclear age. So it is frightening now because we are in the gap, and the more dangerous the weapons, the more important it is to close quickly the gap between offensive action and the construction of an effective defence...

45 We're gonna win this fight – then what? The reason September 11th happened – and it was shocking to Americans, because it happened on our soil – is that we have built a world where we tore down barriers, collapsed distances and spread information. And the UK and America
50 have benefited richly – look at how our economies have performed, look at how our societies have diversified, look

at the advances we have made in technology and science. This new world has been good to us; but you can't gain the benefits of a world without walls without being more
55 vulnerable. September 11th was the dark side of this new age of global interdependence. If you don't want to put those walls back up – and I don't think you do, and we probably couldn't if we tried ... and if you don't want to live with barbed wire around your children and grandchildren
60 for the next hundred years, then it's not enough to defeat the terrorist. We have to make a world where there are far fewer terrorists, where there are fewer potential terrorists and more partners. And that responsibility falls primarily upon the wealthy nations, to spread the benefits and shrink
65 the burdens...

But what are the burdens of the twenty-first century? They are also formidable. Global poverty – half the people on Earth are not part of that new economy I talked about. Think about this when you go home tonight. Half the
70 people on Earth live on less than two dollars a day. A billion people, less than a dollar a day. A billion people go to bed hungry every night and a billion and a half people – one quarter of the people on Earth – never get a clean glass of water. One woman dies every minute in childbirth. So you
75 could say 'don't tell me about the global economy; half the people aren't part of it; what kind of economy leaves half the people behind?'

...So we now live in a world without walls that we have worked hard to make. We have benefits, we have burdens;
80 we have to spread the benefits and shrink the burdens.

non-combatants	people involved in a war who are civilians, rather than military personnel
travesty	a mockery of their original intentions
with impunity	without being punished
universal vulnerability	the fact that no country, anywhere in the world, is now safe from attack

The power of language

Key features of the texts are:

1 structure

2 the language of speeches

3 the language of argument

---

1 STRUCTURE

> The **structure** of a text is the way in which it is put together in sections.

a) The most obvious way in which to structure a written speech is in paragraphs (see page 105). Write down appropriate topic headings for each of the six paragraphs in the extract from Bill Clinton's speech. For example, the first one might be *Terrorism throughout history*.

b) What are the four or five main points that Clinton makes in the paragraph beginning *First, terror*? Write them down, in note form, in your own words. The first one might be: *There have always been civilian casualties in wars through the ages.*

c) Both Clinton and Lincoln open each of their longer paragraphs with punchy sentences. For example, Clinton opens one paragraph with *But what are the burdens of the twenty-first century?* Pick one example (from either speech) and write two or three sentences to explain why it is particularly effective. Think about the following questions:

- How does it grab the listener's attention? What is special about the language?

- What point does it make?

- How does it help to introduce the paragraph's main topic?

> **Tense** is the name given to the form of the verb which shows when something happens: the past, the present or the future.

One idea that unites both speeches is that of the violent past, the troubled present and the hoped-for future.

d) In pairs, look at the three paragraphs of Abraham Lincoln's speech. Discuss what you notice about the three different tenses of the following main verbs:

Paragraph 1: *our fathers **brought forth**...*

Paragraph 2: *Now we **are engaged**...*

Paragraph 3: *government of the people, by the people, for the people, **shall not perish** from the earth.*

Now look at these quotations from Clinton's speech. Again decide which tense each of the verbs is in and compare the arrangement of tenses with those in the Gettysburg Address:

Paragraph 1: *they **proceeded** to murder...*

Paragraph 3: *what **makes** this terror at the moment particularly frightening...*

Paragraph 4: *We're **gonna** win this fight...*

e) Write a short paragraph headed *Tenses in speeches by Lincoln and Clinton*. In your paragraph, explain:

- how the two speakers use tenses to give their speeches a structure

- how the arrangement of tenses in this particular structure helps us to understand the speakers' arguments

2 THE LANGUAGE OF SPEECHES

> Speakers aim for particular effects when they are composing important speeches. These effects are achieved through the use of **rhetorical language**.

Rhetorical language includes structures such as **lists** and **repetition**.

Three-part lists

One structure which has been popular with public speakers for centuries is the **three-part list**.

Three-part lists are frequently used in everyday speech (*lock, stock and barrel*; *Tom, Dick and Harry*), but they can be very effective in formal situations such as speeches.

a) Find the three-part lists in the second and fourth paragraphs of Bill Clinton's speech. Write a sentence or two about each one, commenting on the ways in which they help to get across the important points in paragraphs two and four.

b) Abraham Lincoln's Gettysburg Address concludes with one of the most famous of all three-part lists: *government of the people, by the people, for the people.*

Find the three-part list at the opening of Lincoln's third paragraph. Write down in your own words the point that Lincoln is getting across and explain how it is developed in the sentences which follow.

Repetition

Speech-makers can achieve some very powerful effects from repetition: think of Winston Churchill's famous wartime declaration in 1940: *...we shall fight on the beaches; we shall fight on the landing grounds; we shall fight in the fields and in the streets; we shall fight in the hills; we shall never surrender.*

c) Find three examples of repetition in each speech.

In pairs, discuss which of the repetitions you find most, and least, effective, explaining why. Think about the point that the speaker is attempting to get across with each example and its purpose within the argument as a whole.

3 THE LANGUAGE OF ARGUMENT

> Speakers who hope to get across a strong **argument** or message pay close attention to language. They choose particular language features to serve different **purposes**.

a) The following grid lists some of the language and content features used by Lincoln and Clinton to get their points across. Each feature serves a particular purpose. Copy the grid and then complete it by filling in the empty boxes with examples. Two have been filled in to start you off. (You are asked to find examples from both speeches. For the first feature, for example, find two from Lincoln and two from Clinton.)

Features	Their purposes	Examples
Powerful conclusions to paragraphs	to emphasise the main point of the paragraph	AL 1 *...all men are created equal* AL 2 BC 1 BC 2
Examples from recorded history	to illustrate and add authority to the argument	BC 1 BC 2
Parallels with humankind's earlier history	to show that things have always been the same	BC
Striking images	to...	BC *walls ... barbed wire*
Statistics	to...	BC

Writing to argue

FOUNDATION TIER TASKS

 **SUMMARISING THE MAIN POINTS**

Read the first three paragraphs of Bill Clinton's speech again. Summarise the main points he makes about the three issues facing the modern world.

Use your own words as far as possible.

 EXAMINING THE SPEAKERS' LANGUAGE

Reread Abraham Lincoln's Gettysburg Address and paragraphs 4, 5 and 6 of Bill Clinton's speech. Explain:

- what has to be done, in each speaker's opinion, to make the world a better place
- how the speakers use language to get their arguments across

---

Planning and drafting

Use these points in order to make preparatory notes.

the three issues facing the modern world

Look at:

- the history of terrorism (paragraph 1)
- the purpose of terrorism (paragraph 2)
- terrorism at the moment (paragraph 3)

You could start:

Bill Clinton begins by making the point that there is nothing new about terrorism...

Planning and drafting

The task asks you to look at two features of the texts: content and language.

- As you make notes on the language, list examples like this:

  Examples of repetition in the two speeches:

  Abraham Lincoln (all from paragraph 3)
  what we say here ... what they did here
  It is for us, the living, rather, to be ... It is rather for us here to be...
  devotion ... devotion
  shall not have died ... shall not perish

  Bill Clinton
  look at... (paragraph 4)
  half the people... (paragraph 5)
  benefits ... burdens (paragraph 6)

Use the writing frame below as a guide.

Paragraph	Look at	You could start...
What has to be done		
1	'finishing the work' *the new birth of freedom...* (Lincoln, paragraph 3)	*Both writers address the question of what has to be done to make the world a better place. Abraham Lincoln believes that...*
2	'closing the gap' (Clinton, paragraph 3)	*Bill Clinton talks about 'closing the gap' between...*
3	'shrinking the burdens' (Clinton, paragraphs 4, 5 and 6)	*He then goes on to...*
How they use language to get these points across		
4	paragraphs: • structure • openings and conclusions tenses	*The speakers' choice of language is essential in getting these points across. For example...*
5	rhetorical language: • three-part lists • repetition	*Three-part lists are a striking feature of the rhetorical language used by both speakers. Lincoln, for example...*

FOUNDATION & HIGHER TIER TASK

 ## COMPOSING A SPEECH

Compose your own speech on an issue which interests you. Choose your own structure or follow the example of Lincoln and Clinton: look back to a difficult past, consider a troubled present, and make recommendations for a better future.

This could be on a major global issue (such as the mistreatment of animals or the problem of drugs), or a question which affects your local community (such as racism or street crime).

(See pages 68–9 for 'the examiner's view' on how to tackle this question.)

HIGHER TIER TASK

 ## COMPARING THE SPEECHES

Read both speeches again. Explain how the writers convey their arguments in similar ways, through the content and use of language.

> ### Planning and drafting
>
> The question asks you to look at two features of the speeches: content and language. You are also asked to point out similarities between the two speeches. Use these points in order to make preparatory notes.
>
> 1 *List the similarities in the content of the two speeches*
>
> Look at the use of:
>
> - examples from recorded history (Lincoln, paragraph 1; Clinton, paragraph 1)
> - parallels with humankind's earlier history (Clinton, paragraph 3)
> - statistics (Clinton, paragraph 5)
>
> 2 *List the similarities in the language*
>
> Look at:
>
> - tenses
> - paragraphs:
>   - structure
>   - openings and conclusions
> - rhetorical language:
>   - three-part lists
>   - repetition
>
> 3 Sequence the two lists by numbering them and adding *compare* words and phrases.

> **You could start:**
>
> *The two speakers use a variety of methods to get their arguments across. Both, for example, refer to events from history...*

The examiner's view

Compose your own speech on an issue which interests you. Choose your own structure or follow the example of Lincoln and Clinton: look back to a difficult past, consider a troubled present, and make recommendations for a better future.

STEP 1: READ THE QUESTION CAREFULLY

The writing section of the English exam (Paper 1, Section B) asks you to answer one of four questions. A question testing your ability to write to argue will always be one of the options. In the exam, you will have 45 minutes for this task, which counts for 15% of your total mark for English.

In order to gain a grade C for this type of question, you will be expected to:
● confidently use rhetorical devices such as repetition, lists and exclamations
● integrate discourse markers (see page 115) into your writing

STEP 2: A WRITING PROCESS

Whether you are taking the Foundation or Higher tier paper, adopting the following **writing process** will help you work efficiently under exam conditions:

1 **Read** the question and identify your purpose and audience, and choose an appropriate form (letter, article, speech etc).
2 **Brainstorm** for ideas.
3 **Sequence** your argument into the best order for your purposes. At this stage, you should add discourse markers and rhetorical devices such as examples of repetition.
4 **Write** your response referring to your plan regularly. Two sides of normal-sized handwriting should be plenty.
5 **Check** for errors and that you have included everything in your plan.

STEP 3: THE USE OF LANGUAGE

You cannot succeed in your writing to argue if you don't show evidence of the skills that you have learned in this unit. You do not gain more marks in an exam simply by writing more: you gain more marks by using more skills.

After you have gone through the reading and brainstorming parts of the writing process, include the following in your plan.

● a three-part list
● an example of repetition

● three short, punchy sentences that you could use to open or close a paragraph
● three discourse markers to link your paragraphs

STEP 4: PLANNING AND DRAFTING

When planning your answer, think about:

- the past, the present and the future
- particular examples from recent and earlier history
- paragraphs to underline the structure of the argument
- Your writing should be clearly identified as a speech by its purpose, audience, layout and choice of person (mainly first person in this case).
- Try to **integrate** rhetorical devices into your work – so that it reads smoothly like the speeches on pages 60–3.

STEP 5: WRITING TO ARGUE

You are now going to use all of the skills that you have learned in this unit to write your speech. Remember to focus on purpose and audience: **why** are you writing this speech and **for whom**?

STEP 6: SAMPLE ANSWER

Read this introduction from a sample answer.

> Good afternoon ladies and gentlemen. Today, I am going to argue that racism in football needs to be stamped out: in Britain, in Europe, and throughout the whole footballing world. We are no longer part of a world where footballers are predominantly white and European; we cannot accept the sort of behaviour shown by some so-called football 'fans'; so we must look forward to a world where racism has no place.
>
> My first argument is that black footballers have brought such a lot to football, that the game would be a far poorer place without them...

This student has used a three-part list at the outset which immediately gives shape to the speech. You will need to include rhetorical devices like this in order to get a B grade.

! Quick tip   Remember that *skills* get you marks, not length.

Save the rainforest!

In this unit you will:

- read and compare three texts, all to do with rainforests
- examine the language of writing to persuade
- create a page of a leaflet or brochure

This text, an example of writing to **persuade**, is one side of a leaflet encouraging people to visit The Living Rainforest, near Newbury in Berkshire.

THE LIVING RAINFOREST

Our mission

Bringing the Rainforest to Life

The Living Rainforest's mission is to explore the relationship between humanity and the world's rainforests through education and research. The Living Rainforest provides a hands-on rainforest experience to many thousands of visitors. Throughout its work, an emphasis is placed on being engaging, down-to-earth and innovative.

A visit to the Living Rainforest is a rare and valuable opportunity to see some of the wonderful plants and wildlife that the world is losing as rainforests disappear.

The Living Rainforest is committed to providing an opportunity for as many people as possible to experience an authentic rainforest environment, without having to travel thousands of miles for the privilege.

A Living Learning experience

To walk in a rainforest is to experience a different world. Every year, thousands of visitors are delighted by the sights, sounds and smells of a living rainforest environment – without leaving England.

Over 10,000 school children visit The Living Rainforest each year. School tours are linked to the National Curriculum.

Special workshops aim to enhance and expand the visitor experience. Day, night and school tours give different perspectives on the rainforest world. Please call (01635) 202444 for a programme of events geared to all ages.

NATIONAL LOTTERY CHARITIES BOARD

In 1998 the National Lottery Charities Board granted over £108,000 for a Special Needs Education Project to improve access and learning opportunities at the rainforest. Come and see the difference this money is making, particularly for people with physical, mental or sensory difficulties.

This advertisement for Rainforest Concern is encouraging people to sponsor acres of threatened rainforest in Ecuador, South America.

DON'T LET IT GO TO PIECES

Frustrated and tired of hearing about the disappearing rainforests? Well here's your chance to do something positive about it – by protecting areas of rainforest forever.

The world's rainforests represent a vast reservoir of knowledge and hold potential for the discovery of new medicines and foods. There is no doubt that large-scale deforestation alters the climate – intensifying droughts in the dry season and floods in the rainy season. The result being fewer animal and plant species, soil erosion, an unreliable water supply and poorer health for the local people.

Photograph: ARDEA London Ltd

Within these forests live an amazingly high number of endangered species, many of which are found nowhere else on earth. This is why the region has been classified as one of the world's "biodiversity hotspots".

You will be helping to secure the survival and culture of the Awa and Cayapas indigenous people who still live in harmony with their natural environment. These forests are also home to exotic animals such as jaguars, pumas, tapirs, sloths and monkeys, hundreds of species of birds and thousands of species of plants.

We are two thirds of the way to achieving our objective of completing the Choco-Andean Corridor, so please help this dynamic conservation project by completing the coupon now or, if you prefer, telephone us. All currencies will be accepted when paying by credit card.

Your sponsorship will be a wonderful gift for your children, their children and the Earth itself.

direction of Corridor

protected areas

What can you do to help?
By joining Rainforest Concern and sponsoring acres of threatened rainforest for the Choco-Andean Rainforest Corridor in Ecuador, South America, you will be protecting one of the world's most important ecological areas.

YOU CAN MAKE A DIFFERENCE – THERE IS STILL TIME IF WE ACT QUICKLY!

indigenous people   people who are native to a particular area or region

Many students decide to spend a year working and travelling abroad between leaving school and starting higher education. This has become known as a 'gap' year. The page below is from a magazine called *Go Global!*, published by Gap Activity Projects, which organises gap year placements.

conservation

GAPpers (left to right) Chris Palmer from Stocksfield and Charlotte Berry from Abingdon in the Northern Territories, Australia

Getting involved in conservation with GAP means getting out there with groups of like-minded people. You'll see the real difference you can make to the environment, as you work on ongoing projects. It's a great way to appreciate the natural world and the mod cons which you'll have to do without!

The work in Australia and the rainforests of Latin America is more land management and heritage refurbishment than the protection of endangered species, although there is often the scope for surveys of flora and fauna, which will be of ecological value. Conservation can be hard physical work, so you'll need to be prepared to get stuck in. You could be working alongside volunteers from all over the world and you'll be able to see the results of all that hard work! As your project develops, you'll be looked upon as an experienced volunteer, having been trained for each particular job, be it coppicing, laying tracks or restoring old buildings. You'll come home with skills you never thought yourself capable of, and a new group of international friends. Steve Chapman from Leeds describes settling in at Iracambi Rainforest & Research Centre in Brazil.

"The work is hard and physical, in temperatures of above 35°C and in hot sun, and the diet is very healthy. Tonight I hope to catch some fish from our lake, it's small yet there are 8000 fish in it apparently! Our diet consists of fish, veg, rice and pasta. The lack of a TV, shower, or anything hi-tech merely stands to make them seem insignificant. The river is far more fun than any shower and without TV, people actually talk — the people here are great.

"The interaction is fantastic, and the general experience is life changing. My views on the world have changed already! The most fun part is the improvisation. Using a foam box as a freezer (with ice packs), using the river as a fridge. It brings a new meaning and diversifies your thoughts. Also, the little things like waking up to a humming bird at 7:30 and the noise of crickets as you go to sleep."

"the general experience is life changing"

Other Opportunities . . .

GAP has some projects that don't fall easily into the previous categories.

Currently these other opportunities include things like research posts in the Falkland Islands and Community Centre work in Fiji. These options can be discussed at your interview.

Kerry Dinsmore from County Antrim, Northern Ireland, volunteered on a conservation project in Australia:

"We soon learned the way our project operated. Rocklea was our home, our base that we came back to each weekend, and during the week we got sent off in a team of usually about six to pretty much anywhere in South Queensland that needed help in protecting the environment. We built fences to protect Bilbys — strange-looking marsupials that were like overgrown mice with rabbit ears and baby pouches — in Currawinga. We built paths through Brisbane Forest Park, and planted hundreds of thousands of trees just about everywhere."

VSO welcomes the contribution of GAPpers to building a more equitable world.

A Duke of Edinburgh's Award is always good preparation for your GAP project. Furthermore, your experiences with GAP can count towards the service or residential sections of the award, through the Award's Access Scheme. It doesn't matter if you haven't started the Award Scheme before — it's open to everyone. For more information, contact GAP House.

medical

This is a great opportunity to get real experience of living and working in a hospital, and will be useful if you intend to study medicine or nursing. There will be different tasks and challenges to adapt to as you move around different wards with patients with different conditions, you will also gain administrative experience as well as a good range of general skills. You don't have to be planning a career in medicine, but a GAP medical project will certainly help if you are. GAPpers work with the Red Cross or local organisations.

Clare Bradley from Hertfordshire volunteered at Kitami Red Cross Hospital, Hokkaido, Japan:

Amy Done, GAPper from Wolverhampton, on her project at Wakayama Red Cross Hospital, Japan

"My work included basic stuff like making beds, cleaning wheelchairs and collecting supplies. At mealtimes we would feed the patients and we'd have to wheel patients around the hospital for X-rays, appointments in other departments, and to collect lab results.

"Kitami is a well-supplied modern hospital, and we had a four-day induction touring both the town and the hospital. We met the hospital Director and had lessons in calligraphy and ikebana. I did actually learn to speak a bit of Japanese although it was necessary to learn not to care if you sounded silly or made mistakes!"

"team building, climbing towers, water sports, high ropes and archery"

Outdoor Activities

There are a variety of outdoor activities – you could be farming in the Falklands or orienteering in Ohio. You will need to enjoy being out in all weathers and working with other people towards a shared aim. Outdoor work can seem repetitive and physically draining, but the rewards will be obvious and you'll know you've achieved something as you learn new skills. Think about the climate that appeals to you.

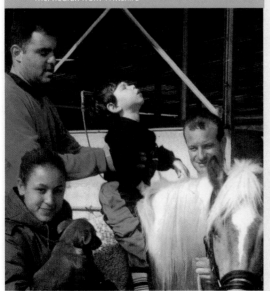

GAPper Jessica Apps from Kent on her outdoor activities project. Photo: Jessica's GAP partner, Amy McPhedran from Wiltshire

Jessica Apps from Kent describes her outdoor project at the Therapeutic Riding School, Israel:

"Our work was divided into three main areas – Hippo therapy uses the horse's movement to physically help the riders' healing process, and gives vital movement to muscles that are not generally worked daily. The horses also provide the ideal opportunity to help autistic children or those with behavioural problems, as they learn discipline and concentration. The final therapy is recreational – sports riding is undertaken by riders with many different problems, and can provide confidence, exercise and independence from the confines of a wheelchair or crutches."

Craig Argent from Stafford volunteered at YMCA Camp Becket, Massachusetts, USA:

"During the busy season we led, instructed and assisted in team building, climbing towers, water sports, high ropes and archery. Evenings included campfire songs and skits, night hikes and square dances, plus quieter moments for office and admin work. When the snow arrived, programmes switched to snow sports, tracking, hibernation and survival studies, and indoor activities like arts and crafts.

"All groups on camp have to be prepared for, fed, cared for and cleaned up after. GAPpers take part in nearly every part of running the camp."

check it out

www.gap.org.uk

The power of language

Key features of the texts are:

1 the language of persuasive texts

2 writing for a purpose

3 the use of presentational devices

 THE LANGUAGE OF WRITING TO PERSUADE

> Writing to **persuade** focuses on presenting a case and influencing the reader. This kind of writing is found, for example, in leaflets (e.g. for places to visit), advertisements (including those for charities and campaigns) and brochures (e.g. for organisations).

Adjectives and adjective phrases

> An **adjective** is a word which gives us information about a noun or pronoun. A group of words which does this is called an **adjective phrase**.

The leaflet advertising The Living Rainforest depends upon adjectives and adjective phrases to explain the centre's attractions.

a) Below are a number of quotations taken from the leaflet. They all contain adjectives and adjective phrases:

- *Living* Rainforest
- *hands-on rainforest* experience
- being *engaging, down-to-earth* and *innovative*
- *rare and valuable* opportunity
- *wonderful* plants and wildlife
- an *authentic rainforest* environment
- to experience a *different* world
- *Special* workshops
- *different* perspectives
- *physical, mental* or *sensory* difficulties

Write three short paragraphs to show how these adjectives and adjective phrases help to get across the main themes of the text, that:

- a visit to The Living Rainforest is an *active* experience
- this particular conservation centre offers a chance to see first hand some of the remarkable vegetation that is under threat
- the experience is geared to the needs of schools and also people with particular difficulties

Abstract nouns

> An **abstract noun** is the label we give to something we cannot touch, such as an emotion, feeling or idea.

b) The writers of the Rainforest Concern advertisement have used abstract nouns to label key concepts — starting with the idea of *concern* itself. They include the following (in the order in which they appear):

areas, knowledge, potential, discovery, deforestation, climate, season, result, species, erosion, supply, health, number, hotspots, survival, culture, harmony, environment, objective, project, sponsorship, difference, time

Find where these abstract nouns appear in the text. Then copy out the grid below and place the abstract nouns into four groups, according to the message they are helping to convey. Some have been inserted to start you off.

Message	Abstract nouns
Rainforests are a source of very important scientific information and future discoveries.	*knowledge*
They are home to a huge variety of plants and animals.	*species*
Cutting down the rainforests is therefore doing great damage.	*climate*
Your money is needed to help protect rainforest in Ecuador and support the Awa and Cayapas people who live there.	*sponsorship*

2 PURPOSE

Whatever we write – whether it is a shopping list or a short story – we should always have a **purpose** in mind.

In all three of these texts the writers have had a major purpose: **to persuade**. But writers usually have more than one purpose in mind when they create a text – they might be aiming to persuade while they are offering **advice**, for example, or they might be **arguing** in order to persuade you.

a) Copy the grid below and fill it in with examples of the different kinds of writing found in the texts on pages 70–3: to persuade, to argue and to advise. A short quotation will do for each example. Three have been filled in to start you off. Remember that purposes overlap; so, when you have completed the grid, compare your entries with other people and talk about your decisions.

3 PERSUASIVE PRESENTATIONAL DEVICES

A successful leaflet or brochure will usually use one or more **persuasive presentational devices** to help get its message across. Examples are the combination of **text** (words) and **image** (photographs and illustrations), the **use of colour**, and striking **headings** and **slogans**.

a) Write three paragraphs to show how the designers of each extract have effectively combined text and image. In the Rainforest Concern advert, for example, think about the effect of combining:

- the two photographs at the top, juxtaposed (placed next to each other) with the text beneath
- the jigsaw puzzle shape with its slogan

Text and purpose for writing	Example
The Living Rainforest	
Writing to persuade	
Writing to argue	*...the difference this money is making, particularly for people with physical, mental or sensory difficulties.*
Writing to advise	
Rainforest Concern	
Writing to persuade	*Your sponsorship will be a wonderful gift...*
Writing to argue	
Writing to advise	
GAP: Go Global!	
Writing to persuade	
Writing to argue	
Writing to advise	*It doesn't matter if you haven't started the Award Scheme before...*

Writing to persuade

  SUMMARISING THE INFORMATION

Reread the advertisement for Rainforest Concern. Then summarise what it says about:

- the threats to the rainforest environment
- the steps that are being taken to protect rainforests

Use your own words as far as possible.

Planning and drafting

The question is in two parts. Use these points in order to make preparatory notes.

Part 1: the threats to the rainforest environment

Look at:

- the paragraphs which begin *The world's rainforests...* and *Within these forests...*

Part 2: the steps that are being taken to protect rainforests

Look at:

- the paragraphs which begin *What can you do to help?, You will be helping...* and *We are two thirds...*

You could start:

The advertisement begins by listing some of the threats to the rainforest environment. It says that...

  WRITING A LETTER

Write a letter to a newspaper arguing that people in this country should care about what happens to the rainforest and should support attempts to protect it. Don't include addresses or the date, as you would normally in a letter: just start *Dear Sir*, or *Dear Madam*, and end *Yours faithfully,*

Planning and drafting

First, to get some ideas, reread the Rainforest Concern advertisement.

Then plan your letter. You might find this writing frame useful to start you off.

Paragraph and contents	Possible phrases	Language features to use
1 introduce the subject	*I wonder how many of your readers are aware that...*	second person
	I have recently become extremely concerned about...	first person
	The world's rainforests are under threat...	third person
2 explain the problem	*Deforestation – large scale destruction of trees – is causing a number of problems...*	abstract nouns
	The results are...	adjectives and adjective phrases
3 suggest what can be done	*If readers of this newspaper were willing to sponsor...*	
4 explain why this will help	*This will help to secure the survival of...*	
	Sponsorship will aid the work that has already been done...	

FOUNDATION & HIGHER TIER TASK

 ### CREATING YOUR OWN LEAFLET

Create a leaflet to persuade parents to bring their children to a tourist attraction near to where you live.

(See pages 78–9 for 'the examiner's view' on how to tackle this question.)

HIGHER TIER TASK

 ### EXAMINING THE LANGUAGE OF PERSUASION

This is part of a leaflet advertising an exhibition at the Natural History Museum, London, called *Predators*. Explain how the creators of the leaflet, through their choice of content and use of language, persuade us to visit the exhibition.

Planning and drafting

Look, for example, at the use of:

- persuasive language to do with (a) the creatures represented and (b) the ways of exhibiting them
- slogans and catchphrases
- powerful ends of paragraphs
- imperatives
- questions
- abstract nouns
- adjectives and adjective phrases
- combination of text and image

Predators try to eat ...
Prey try to escape ...
Every meeting is
a battle of life
and death ...

Survival is the aim

From great white sharks to tiny but lethal spiders, the natural world is full of sophisticated killers. They use an amazing range of weapons and strategies to hunt and kill. But their prey are far from helpless. They too fight for survival using cunning defences, from lightning speed to camouflage and armour. The outcome of each battle for life is never certain.

Eat or be eaten

Predators, a major new exhibition at the Natural History Museum, is ideal for families with children aged 7–12. Dynamic displays include three huge moving models: a life-size shark, a man-size spider and a chameleon you can control. Operate its eyes and sticky tongue to see if you could eat enough to survive – or test your skills against others in a high-speed interactive game. Before you leave, dare you touch the giant spider's sprung steel web?

Museum specimens and stunning photography give a powerful insight into the drama behind the 'evolutionary arms race', and show the delicate balance that exists between hunter and hunted.

Create a leaflet to persuade parents to bring their children to a tourist attraction near to where you live.

STEP 1: READ THE TEXT

Although this section is about writing to persuade, you may be asked to show that you can appreciate how another writer has written persuasively in Paper 1, Section A – the reading section of Paper 1.

Read the leaflet on page 77 about what's on offer at the *Predators* exhibition. Before you look at some possible examination tasks, read the text, paying special attention to the following points:

- the purpose and audience
- the use of language
- persuasive presentational devices

STEP 2: PURPOSE AND AUDIENCE

Write down the answers to the following questions:

- Why was this leaflet written?
- Who is the leaflet aimed at?

- Explain how you have identified the purpose and audience of this leaflet.

STEP 3: THE USE OF LANGUAGE

The *Predators* leaflet uses adjectives and adjective phrases very effectively to describe the exhibition's attractions.

- Write down the adjectives and adjective phrases used in the left-hand column to describe:

  spiders   killers   their prey
  the range of weapons used by predators
  the prey's defences   their speed

- Choose three adjectives or adjective phrases and explain how each helps to persuade the reader to visit the *Predators* exhibition.

STEP 4: PERSUASIVE PRESENTATIONAL DEVICES

The leaflet uses a lot of presentational devices to help to persuade the reader to visit the exhibition.

- Choose three presentational devices and explain how each one tries to persuade,
  e.g. *The writer uses bright colours to attract the reader's attention.*

- Compare the use of presentational devices in the leaflet with the use of presentational devices in The Living Rainforest leaflet on page 70.

STEP 5: WRITING TO PERSUADE

You are now going to use all of the skills that you have practised in this section to produce your own piece of persuasive writing.

You should aim to write about two pages and use at least one example of each of the following:

- **adjectives and adjective phrases**, e.g. *amazing*, *tiny but lethal*
- **abstract nouns**, e.g. *strategies, survival, defences*
- **an effective short paragraph** (perhaps at the beginning of the leaflet)
- **presentational devices**, e.g. *headings* and *slogans*

STEP 6: SAMPLE ANSWER

Read this opening from a sample answer.

Are you stuck about what to do with the kids this weekend? Are you sick of going to the cinema? How about keeping the whole family happy and paying a visit to The Lowry?

Voted in the Top Ten UK Outings of the Year!

Art   Local Heritage   History   Performance   Architecture

Find all of this and more at the Lowry Centre with the NEW Imperial War Museum of the North and the NEW designer retail outlet.

What more do you need to keep the whole family happy?

This student uses abstract nouns, adjectives and adjective phrases well; the answer also shows strong and confident use of paragraphs. The student is heading for at least a B grade.

! Quick tip Remember why you are writing and who you are writing for: purpose and audience are the keys to success.

Crimestoppers

In this unit you will:

- study pages from a crime prevention booklet
- examine the language of advice texts
- create a page of an advice leaflet

Many local police forces publish booklets and leaflets offering advice on how to protect yourself against crime. Here are four extracts from a publication issued by Thames Valley Police.

Bogus Callers

①

Strangers at your door

Do not be fooled by bogus callers. When anyone calls at your home and claims to be an official of any organisation or local authority department, here's what you should do:

The Doorstep Code
Our advice is to follow these simple rules:

Be prepared. Have a door chain and spyhole fitted.

Ensure you know what to say and do when someone unexpected calls.

Secure your door chain before opening the door.

Ask all suspicious callers for identification and keep the door chain on while you check it.

Feel confident in being able to say no if someone wants to come in without showing their ID.

End up feeling safe rather than sorry. If you're suspicious don't let them in; if you're worried call the police.

DON'T BE SORRY... BE SAFE
In an emergency always dial 999

Personal Safety

The chances that you or a member of your family will be a victim of violent crime are low. However, the fear of becoming a victim is very real for many people, and if an attack does occur it can have a major impact on our lives, so it makes sense to take some simple precautions to keep ourselves and those close to us as safe as possible.

Transport

When using a taxi always sit in the back.

Only use a reputable taxi company (ask around your friends if you don't know one).

If you are being picked up by a Private Hire vehicle, ask the driver who he is there to collect. Remember! Private Hire taxi drivers are not allowed to tout for business on the street and should be pre-booked. (Don't jump in the first car that pulls up.)

If you are unhappy with the conduct of the driver make a note of the licence plate number (this should be displayed clearly inside the taxi) and report the matter.

Don't engage in conversation that lets the driver know you live alone.

When you arrive at your destination, be prepared: have your fare ready and your keys to hand.

If you are travelling a long distance, ensure you agree a fare before setting off.

On buses and trains sit near to other people or the driver.

If you are pestered by someone, report it to the driver or guard.

Never be tempted to hitch or accept a lift from someone you don't know and trust completely. If you go out for the night make sure you save enough money to get you home.

Whenever possible, share a taxi with a friend, it is safer and cheaper!!

Street Robbery

Whilst intimidation and robbery is rare, always be on your guard and don't take risks.

The following advice will help ensure your safety:

Always try to avoid carrying large amounts of cash.

When using cashpoints put the money and your card safely in your pocket or bag before walking away from the machine.

Avoid using cashpoints on your own late at night.

Don't carry your pin number with your card. Try to memorise it or write it down in code.

If someone approaches you and demands money or property, hand it over. Your safety is worth more than cash.

Do not keep cheque books and cards together.

If your credit cards are lost or stolen, tell the credit card companies immediately.

Be extra careful with your belongings in crowded places. Pickpockets operate in crowded shops and bars.

Never let your bag, purse or wallet out of your sight. Always report incidents to the Police.

Locks and bolts

For advice and installation of locks for your home consider contacting a member of the Master Locksmiths Association. You will find members of this will display the logo in their advertising – check out your local telephone directory.

Shed and garden equipment theft

Burglary of garden sheds and theft of garden equipment is one of the fastest growing crimes in the country.

What can you do to prevent it?

Perimeter fencing walls and gates should ideally be of uniform height (approximately 2 metres) and be in a good state of repair.

There should be no climbing aids alongside them. A trellis on which spiteful plants are growing will provide additional security at the perimeter. Shrubs, hedges and large plants should be cut back to enable intruders to be seen.

Install security lighting to illuminate your gardens. Sensors can switch lights on when a moving body is detected.

Ensure your shed is in a good state of repair to stand up to a security test. If not, then take steps to improve it and remove valuable property.

Fit two substantial padlocks to your shed door at equal spacing. Hasps, staples and hinges should be secured with coach bolts and backing plates.

Any windows should have a grille fixed to steel plates inside the shed. Windows are an easy target. At the very least consider fitting reinforced glass and a good lock if the window opens.

Postcode all property such as lawnmowers and strimmers. Also note all serial numbers of such items. Chain valuable items to the superstructure of the building. Keep your shed secure at all times and never leave items unattended in the back garden. It only takes a minute to commit a crime.

Encourage your neighbours to keep an eye on your property.

Fire Prevention

4

Smoke alarms save lives – have you got one? Is it working?

A fire strikes when you least expect it, often during the night. If you are asleep when a fire starts and you do not have a smoke alarm to wake you, the chances of you and your family surviving are zero. Smoke suffocates quickly, and you'll be dead before the flames reach you.

ACTION

- If you do not have a smoke alarm **FIT ONE**.
- If you do have a smoke alarm **TEST IT**.

Smoke alarms are not an early warning they are your ONLY warning!

Escape Plan

Fitting a smoke alarm will give you the vital moments to alert everybody in the house and escape. The next step is to have a FIRE ACTION PLAN so everyone knows exactly what to do if there's a fire. Key points of the plan should be:

- Take all persons in your home into account including children and elderly or disabled people.
- Choose the best escape route and another way out just in case the normal way is blocked. Keep all routes clear.
- Tell every member of the household the plan including the location of door and window keys.

Remember – If a fire should start in your home.

GET OUT – and get others out, but don't risk your own life.

GET THE FIRE BRIGADE OUT – **Go to the nearest phone and dial 999.**

STAY OUT – do not go back inside for anything.

For free advice on any fire safety matter please contact your Community Fire Safety Team – please see our advertisement opposite.

The power of language

Key features of the text are:

1 imperatives and directives

2 adverbials

3 conditional sentences

---

1 IMPERATIVES AND DIRECTIVES

> We use the **imperative** form of the verb when, for example, we want to give a command, issue a warning, or make a request. The imperative form is used in **directives** – sentences which ask/tell someone to do something.

a) Here are some directives of different kinds, all of which use the imperative form of the verb. Copy the grid and add at least two of your own examples in each box in the right-hand column:

Type of directive	Example, using the imperative form of the verb	Further examples
command	*Take this.*	
request	*Please be on time tomorrow.*	
warning	*Watch out!*	
offer	*Have a sandwich.*	
plea	*Help!*	
invitation	*Come out with me this evening.*	
instruction	*Take the third on the left.*	
expression of good wishes	*Have a great birthday!*	

b) Write down the imperative verbs in *The Doorstep Code* on page 80. (To start you off, there are two in the first rule: *Be prepared* and *Have … fitted*.) Which kind of directive (from the eight listed in the grid above) are the rules in *The Doorstep Code*? For example, are they commands, offers, invitations…?

c) In advice leaflets like this one, imperative sentences (directives) will be used to tell you – or strongly advise you – either *to do* something or *not to do* something.

Pick out and write down three examples of each use:

- imperative sentences telling you *to do* something
- imperative sentences telling you *not to do* something

(Avoid the examples you looked at in question b.)

d) *The Doorstep Code* is an example of an **acrostic** (a form in which the first – or sometimes the last – letter of each line goes to form a key word or phrase). The key phrase in this case is BE SAFE.

Make up your own acrostic, based on a different key word or phrase, to offer pieces of advice on an important topic. (You might opt for something to do with school, such as 'safety in the laboratory'.) Remember that each line should be an imperative sentence.

2 ADVERBIALS

> **Adverbials** are words or phrases which usually add information to a sentence. They can help us to answer questions such as When? How? and Where?

For example, the following sentence – *When using a taxi, sit safely in the back.* – contains three common types of adverbial:

- **time adverbials** answer the question **When?**
  When using a taxi,…
- **manner adverbials** answer the question **How?**
  …(sit) safely…
- **place adverbials** answer the question **Where?**
  …in the back.

a) In the first two columns of the following grid are the three common types of adverbials: time, manner and place. Next to each type are two examples from the advice booklet. Copy the grid and write down three further examples of each type, also taken from the texts on pages 80–3.

Type of adverbial	Examples from the booklet	Three further examples from the booklet
Time adverbials (answer the question **When?**)	● *When you arrive at your destination, be prepared* ● *Keep your shed secure **at all times**.*	● ● ●
Manner adverbials (answer the question **How?**)	● *Avoid using cashpoints **on your own*** ● *write it down **in code***	● ● ●
Place adverbials (answer the question **Where?**)	● *always sit **in the back*** ● *Pickpockets operate **in crowded shops and bars**.*	● ● ●

 CONDITIONAL SENTENCES

> A **conditional sentence** is a sentence in which one thing depends upon another. The **conditional clause** in the sentence will usually begin with the words *if* or *unless*.

Conditional clauses are **adverbials**, because they add information to the sentence: they tell us the *condition* under which something can or cannot happen.

Here are two examples of conditional sentences with the conditional clauses highlighted:

If someone calls to read the meter, ask to see some identification.

*Do not open the door **unless they show you some identification**.*

a) Write down three conditional sentences from the Personal Safety page of the police booklet, underlining the conditional clauses in each one. For example:

<u>*If you are being picked up by a Private Hire vehicle*</u>*, ask the driver who he is there to collect.*

b) Conditional sentences are widely used in all sorts of advice texts. Invent and write down two examples of conditional sentences which might be found in each of the following advice texts. For each text, make up an *if...* sentence and an *unless...* sentence. Two have been completed to start you off:

● a booklet about safety in the home: e.g. *Never touch electrical wiring **unless you have switched off the power at the mains**.*

● a book on how to care for a pet: e.g. ***If your pet becomes overweight**, ask the vet about diet and exercise.*

● a leaflet about healthy eating

● a letter from school on how to prepare for exams

● a guide on getting the best out of a visit to a museum

Writing to advise

FOUNDATION TIER TASKS

 1 **SUMMARISING THE MAIN POINTS**

Read the first two extracts from the booklet again. Summarise the main points it makes about personal safety.

Use your own words as far as possible.

Planning and drafting

Use these points in order to make preparatory notes.

Look at:

- the *Doorstep Code* (*Bogus Callers* section)
- what to do in taxis and buses (*Personal Safety* section, under the heading *Transport*)
- how to avoid being robbed (*Personal Safety* section, under the heading *Street Robbery*)

You could start:

The booklet makes a number of important points about personal safety. To begin with, it advises...

2 **EXAMINING THE LANGUAGE OF THE BOOKLET**

Explain how the writers use language to advise readers about crime prevention.

Remember to put quotation marks round any words or phrases taken from the passage.

Planning and drafting

Look at the use of:

- imperatives and directives
- adverbials
- conditional sentences

Use the writing frame below as a guide.

Paragraph	Language features	You could start...
imperatives and directives		
1	directives telling you to do things (and not to do things) such as the instruction *always sit in the back*	*The booklet is full of instructions which take the form of directives. For example...*
2	the *Doorstep Code* acrostic	
adverbials		
3	time adverbials: e.g. *when a moving body is detected...*	*Adverbials are used throughout to add helpful pieces of information...*
	manner adverbials: e.g. *clearly* place adverbials: e.g. *in crowded places*	
conditional sentences		
4	*if* sentences: e.g. *If you are travelling a long distance...*	*Advice booklets often contain a large number of conditional sentences...*
	...if the window opens	

FOUNDATION & HIGHER TIER TASK

CREATING YOUR OWN ADVICE LEAFLET

Use the police booklet as a model to create a page from an advice leaflet of your choice. For example, it could be on *How to survive your first day of work experience*, or *Things you should and should not do at a party*. It will help to study other advice booklets.

(See pages 88–9 for 'the examiner's view' on how to tackle this question.)

HIGHER TIER TASK

EXAMINING THE LANGUAGE OF THE BOOKLET

Look at the section of the police booklet on page 83, which gives advice about fire prevention. Explain and comment on the ways in which the writers have expressed warnings and offered advice.

> **Planning and drafting**
> Use these points in order to make preparatory notes.
>
> Consider the points about:
> - smoke alarms
> - escape plans
> - what to do after leaving the building
>
> Look at the use of:
> - imperatives and directives
> - conditional sentences
>
> (the two bullets under ACTION are examples of both)
> - adverbials (such as *when you least expect it*)
>
> **You could start:**
> *The* Fire Prevention *page covers a number of different areas. The first...*

Use the police booklet as a model to create a page from an advice leaflet of your choice. For example, it could be on *How to survive your first day of work experience*, or *Things you should and should not do at a party*. It will help to study other advice booklets.

STEP 1: READ THE QUESTION CAREFULLY

As with other types of writing, it is vital to pay special attention to purpose and audience when writing to advise. You should have a very clear notion of who will be reading your advice (the expected audience) and the reason you are giving it (the purpose).

It is also important that you adopt the **tone** of someone who knows the answers, without lecturing your audience.

STEP 2: PRESENTATIONAL DEVICES

Your leaflet should include presentational and organisational devices to help draw the reader's attention to the advice you are giving. Although this task is preparing you for an English, not an Art and Design, exam, neat and clear presentation is important.

- Think of a catchy, alliterative title for your leaflet (e.g. *Party Problem Page*).
- Write down sub-headings for each of the subjects that you have brainstormed.

- Think of and write down sets of three bullet points that you will be able to use in your leaflet. Using bullet points in groups of three will help to give structure and coherence to your work.

STEP 3: THE USE OF LANGUAGE

Plan to use what you have learned about in this unit.

- Write an acrostic (see page 84) that you could use in your leaflet.
- Make a list of some directives – things to do and things not to do either during work experience or at a party.

- Write down three adverbials to include in your leaflet.
- Write down three conditional sentences to include in your leaflet.

STEP 4: PLANNING AND DRAFTING

When planning, you should decide on a clear structure. For example, the *Fire Prevention* extract on page 83 is made up of three sections:

- smoke alarms
- escape plans
- what to do after leaving the building

Try to use:

- imperatives and directives
- adverbials
- conditional sentences

STEP 5: WRITING TO ADVISE

You are now going to use all of the skills that you have learned in this section to produce your own piece of writing to advise. Keep the following points in mind:

- Use a **writing process** (see page 68).
- Consider what **tone** would be appropriate for the advice you are giving. The crime prevention information in this unit uses a practical and serious tone to convey the nature of the advice it is giving. However, in the sample answer below, a light-hearted, humorous tone is used effectively.

STEP 6: SAMPLE ANSWER

Read this introduction from a sample answer.

PARTY ANIMAL OR PARTY POOPER?

In the following leaflet, I want to give you advice on:

- what to do at parties
- what not to do at parties
- what's what at parties

If you're the sort of person who can never decide what to wear, when to arrive, how to behave, or who to talk to, then this is the right leaflet for you. I'm going to tame the wildest party animal and give licence to the palest party pooper.

Firstly, let's look at the most important issue of all:

WHAT TO WEAR

You say more about yourself in the way you dress for parties than in what you talk about. Loud clothes mean a loud personality, so you should spend some time deciding what to wear:

<u>Do</u> – make the most of the clothes you've got.

<u>Don't</u> – try to show off by spending too much money for a one-off occasion.

> This student is beginning to pile up the skills and show off what they can do. In this introduction, they have used a conditional sentence and directives. In addition, the presentation is clear and easy to follow.

! Quick tip You shouldn't include pictures or diagrams in your exam work; simply draw a box and label it with details of the image you wish to present.

Snow monster

In this unit you will:

- read two articles about the Bigfoot
- examine the language of information texts
- write an information article

The following articles give information about the mysterious creature known in different parts of the world as the *yeti, abominable snowman, Sasquatch* or *Bigfoot*.

Bigfoot of North America

by Lee Krystek

If the Himalayas of Asia has its Yeti, the Pacific Northwest of America has its Bigfoot: a hairy, ape-like biped that stands seven to nine feet tall and weighs between 600 and 900 pounds.

Bigfoot, or as it's often called in Canada, the Sasquatch, is mentioned in several native American legends. In fact, the term 'Sasquatch' is Indian for 'hairy giant'. The first sighting of a Sasquatch by a white man apparently came in 1811 near what now is the town of Jasper, Alberta, Canada. A trader named David Thompson found some strange footprints, fourteen inches long and eight inches wide, with four toes, in the snow…

Rumours about the Sasquatch continued through to the end of the century. Then, in 1910, the murder of two miners, found with their heads cut off, was attributed to the creatures, though there was little supporting evidence that the killing wasn't human in origin. In any case, the place of the murders, Nahanni Valley, in Canada, was changed to Headless Valley, because of the incident.

The year 1924 turned out to be a banner year in Bigfoot history… According to a Canadian lumberjack named Albert Ostman, he had been prospecting near Tobet Inlet when he was captured

The Unnatural Museum – Bigfoot

by a family of Bigfoots. The father and daughter guarded him while the mother and son prepared the meals…

Interest in Bigfoot began to pick up in the United States in 1958 when a bulldozer operator named Jerry Crew found enormous footprints around where he was working in Humboldt County, California. Crew made a cast of the footprint. A local newspaper ran the story of Crew and his footprint with a photo. The story was picked up by other papers and ran throughout the country. It was the picture of Crew holding the 'Bigfoot' that made the name stick.

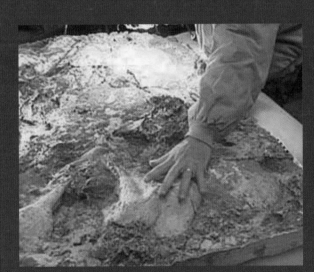

In 1967 Roger Patterson and Bob Gimlin, Bigfoot buffs, announced they'd captured Bigfoot with a movie camera. They filmed a few seconds of an ape-like creature, apparently female, moving across a clearing near Bluff Creek in northern California. While the film is not perfectly clear, there is no mistaking the creature in the film for a common animal. The movie shows either a real Bigfoot, or a man in a clever costume…

www.unmuseum.org/bigfoot

Bigfoot, Sasquatch, Yeti...

by **Paul Stonehill**

During the 1900s, the Colonist newspaper in Victoria, British Columbia, ran several stories about people spotting 'monkey-men' in remote wooded areas.

In the 1920s, British Columbia schoolteacher J. W. Burns wrote extensively in newspaper and magazine articles about reports of giant hairy creatures. Burns's writings were responsible for popularising the term 'Sasquatch', which he identified as a derivation from the language of the Coast Salish Indians. Sasquatch quickly became known among the general public of western Canada, long before tales of such a creature ever found notoriety in the United States.

Sasquatch sightings

Following the publicity surrounding Eric Shipton's 1951 photograph of a Yeti footprint, interest in Sasquatch increased dramatically. John Green, a newspaper publisher in British Columbia, began reporting Sasquatch sightings in 1955... Green became genuinely captivated by the creature, and his extensive compilation of stories and sightings made him the leading Sasquatch authority of his day.

One Sasquatch spotter Green interviewed was William Roe, a trapper, who claimed to have had a close encounter with a female of the species in 1955, while

hunting on British Columbia's Mica Mountain. 'The thought came to me that if I shot it I would probably have a specimen of great interest to scientists the world over,' Roe said. But he couldn't bring himself to pull the trigger on his rifle. 'Although I have called the creature "it", I felt now that it was a human being, and I knew I would never forgive myself if I killed it,' he said.

The publication of Roe's account would later inspire another man to step forward with his own Sasquatch experience, which he said had happened more

than thirty years before. Albert Ostman, a 64-year-old retired lumberman from British Columbia, went public in 1957 with a tale he had kept to himself since 1924, for fear of being ridiculed. Ostman's story was the most dramatic report ever in the history of Bigfoot studies: a first-person account of abduction by Sasquatch.

While on a camping trip near Vancouver Island, Ostman found that something had disturbed his supplies and food on two nights in a row…

Carried away

Then one night Ostman was shaken awake to find himself being indelicately carried away inside his sleeping bag. The opening of the sleeping bag was held shut, and Ostman had no choice but to be dragged along the forest ground for what he estimated to be 25 miles, nearly suffocating.

After what seemed like a three-hour ordeal, he was thrown to the ground in a heap, and emerged to find himself in the company of four Sasquatches. Ostman described them as a family, with a father and a mother and their pair of offspring, one male and one female. He indicated that the adult male, his kidnapper, was over eight feet tall and powerfully built, covered in dark hair all over. The children, though smaller, were still about seven feet tall.

Prospective mate

Ostman said the Sasquatches chattered amongst themselves in a seemingly intelligent language, and although they did not hurt or threaten him, they were determined not to let him leave. Their lair was inside a small valley enclosed by cliffs, and the adult male stood guard at the only apparent entry passage. Ostman suggested that he may have been selected as a prospective mate for the young female.

Ostman claimed that he was held captive for a period of six days. In that time he formed a tentative bond with the younger male, who became fond of sampling Ostman's snuff. That gave Ostman an idea. He offered his snuff to the adult male, which impulsively dumped the entire container into his mouth. The tobacco rush incapacitated the big Sasquatch in short order, making him writhe on the ground in overwhelming discomfort. Ostman seized the opportunity to escape…

www.n2.net/prey/bigfoot

in short order   very quickly

- a chapter on volcanoes in a school Geography textbook
- a write-up of a Science experiment in school
- an entry in a personal diary
- a police report on a road accident
- a newspaper report of an Olympic long-jump event
- a newspaper column headed *Yesterday in Parliament*
- a booklet giving timetables for a rail network

The power of language

Key features of the texts are:

1. chronological writing
2. parenthesis
3. active and passive

1 CHRONOLOGICAL WRITING

> **Chronological writing** organises events in the order in which they happened.

a) Reread both extracts and note down all the stages in the history of Bigfoot sightings and reports. Then draw up a **timeline** and enter dates and sightings from both extracts **in chronological order**.

- As the articles do not record sightings by native Americans, start off with David Thompson's in 1811.
- Albert Ostman's story could have two entries: one for when it took place, another for when he made it public.

b) Rate the different kinds of writing listed below on a scale of 1 to 5 (1 lowest), according to how far they would organise their material **chronologically**. Add a comment to explain your decision in each case. For example, a television and radio listings magazine like the *Radio Times* might have some sections arranged chronologically, and others not. You might therefore give it the following grading and comment:

Kind of writing	1–5	Comment
a television and radio listings magazine (e.g. *Radio Times*)	4	*Although each day's programmes are listed chronologically, some of the magazine is devoted to articles and features.*

- an encyclopedia article on eclipses
- a chapter on the First World War in a school History textbook

2 PARENTHESIS

> A **parenthesis** is a word, phrase or clause inserted into a sentence to provide additional information.

A parenthesis can be placed between **commas**, **dashes** or **brackets** (which are themselves sometimes known as **parentheses** – the plural form of the word).

Parenthesis is common in information texts like the two extracts about Bigfoot. It is used to add different kinds of information, such as:

- a more specific descriptive detail: *Jones, **a retired police officer**, was the first to spot the escape vehicle.*
- a time or date: *Two years later, **in the middle of January**, it suddenly collapsed.*
- an interesting fact: *The team, **known locally as 'the Terminators'**, is not noted for its skill.*

a) Use the two extracts to write a paragraph explaining and illustrating some of the uses that parenthesis can have in an information text. Look, for example, at the following sentences:

Lee Krystek

Bigfoot, or as it's often called...	(paragraph 2)
Then, in 1910...	(paragraph 3)
In any case, the place...	(paragraph 3)
In 1967 Roger Patterson...	(paragraph 6)
They filmed a few seconds...	(paragraph 6)

Paul Stonehill

John Green, a newspaper...	(lines 25–8)
One Sasquatch spotter...	(lines 33–9)
Albert Ostman, a 64-year-old...	(lines 55–60)
He indicated that...	(lines 87–90)

b) Write a brief (100 word) report for a local newspaper on a sporting event. Use parenthesis to add:

- specific descriptive details: *Rutherford, who usually plays in the back four, was substituted after...*
- times: *Then, ten minutes into the second half, came the moment...*
- interesting facts: *The Borough manager, whose sister captains the Northern Counties eleven, then took the bold step of...*

3 ACTIVE AND PASSIVE

> In an **active** sentence, the subject performs the action; in a **passive** sentence, the subject is on the receiving end of the action.

For example:

The Sasquatch **dragged** Ostman through the forest. (active)

The Sasquatch **was affected** by the snuff. (passive)

The passive enables the writer to describe an action without stating who the subject is. It can be used, for example:

- when the receiver of the action is more important than the doer (e.g. *she was struck by a car*)
- when the doer is not known (e.g. *the house was burgled during the night*)
- when the writer does not want to reveal who the doer is (e.g. *the handle was turned slowly from the inside*)
- when the doer is unimportant (e.g. *bicycles must not be left in the entrance hall*)
- when the doer is obvious (e.g. *Lincoln was re-elected*)
- in scientific writing which needs to be impersonal (e.g. *the substance was subjected to a battery of tests*)

a) Write down why you think the passive might have been used in each of the following sentences from Lee Krystek's article. For each sentence, think about the six reasons listed above and decide which ones apply.

*Bigfoot, or as **it's often called** in Canada, the Sasquatch, **is mentioned** in several native American legends.*

*Then, in 1910, the murder of two miners, found with their heads cut off, **was attributed** to the creatures*

*In any case, the place of the murders, Nabanni Valley, in Canada, **was changed** to Headless Valley, because of the incident.*

*The story **was picked up** by other papers and ran throughout the country.*

Writing to inform

FOUNDATION TIER TASKS

1 SUMMARISING THE BIGFOOT HISTORY

Use the two extracts to summarise the sightings and reports of Bigfoot.

Use your own words as far as possible.

Planning and drafting

Use these points to help you plan your summary.

- Base your summary on the timeline that you created for question 1a on page 94.
- Begin with David Thompson in 1811.
- Do not go into too much detail about Albert Ostman's experience.

You could start:

Although several legends of the native Americans contain stories of Bigfoot, the first recorded discovery of Bigfoot prints was in 1811...

2 WRITING AN ACCOUNT

Rewrite the account of Albert Ostman's abduction by Sasquatches as it might appear in his autobiography, *Abducted by Sasquatches*.

You could use the writing frame below as a guide.

Paragraph	Language and ideas	You could start...
1	Write in the first person.	*In 1924 I was on a camping trip near Vancouver Island...*
2	Use the facts from Paul Stonehill's account.	*Suddenly I was awoken by someone shaking me...*
3	Add details of your own to make the account dramatic and gripping.	*My back was severely bruised by the journey...*
4	Let the reader know how you felt.	*Imagine my horror when it dawned on me that I might have been selected as a prospective mate for the young female...*

FOUNDATION & HIGHER TIER TASK

 ### WRITING AN INFORMATION ARTICLE

Write an article for a magazine entitled *Does Bigfoot Exist?*

First read the account below by Paul Stonehill about Bigfoot enthusiast Roger Patterson. Having written a book about Bigfoot, Patterson set off to film one.

(See pages 98–9 for 'the examiner's view' on how to tackle this question.)

HIGHER TIER TASK

 ### ANALYSING THE LANGUAGE

Explain how both writers, through their content and use of language, inform us about the history of Bigfoot.

> **Planning and drafting**
> Refer among other things to:
> - the use of chronological writing
> - parenthesis
> - the mixture of active and passive sentences
>
> **You could start:**
> *The two writers use a number of different methods to inform us about Bigfoot. Lee Krystek, for example…*

Bigfoot captured on film

On October 20, 1967, Patterson and his friend Bob Gimlin were riding on horseback in the wilds of California's Bluff Creek valley, with Patterson carrying a rented 16mm camera to shoot some atmospheric footage for his planned film. He ended up filming a lot more than just scenery. Patterson and Gimlin spotted a huge, dark-furred, bipedal creature hunched over in the middle of a creek. The beast rose to a full height that Patterson estimated at seven feet, four inches, and began walking toward the woods. Thrown to the ground after his horse reared up in fright, Patterson anxiously yanked the movie camera from his saddlebag and began shooting. The day's filming had left him with only 28 feet of film in the camera, but he managed to record the alleged Bigfoot's image briefly before it fled from view…

In the ensuing three decades, the 952 frames of Patterson's Bigfoot film have been submitted to all manner of examination and analysis… The creature has been classified as female, because of its apparent breasts… the exact way in which it moves its neck, and its unusual method of distributing its weight as it strided, have led many to conclude that this could not be a man in a suit.

But many others feel certain that Patterson's Bigfoot was a fake. Being established in the "Bigfoot business," Patterson stood to profit from fabricating film footage of the creature. Bigfoot expert John Napier pointed out that the footprint casts were physiologically inconsistent with the height of the creature and the length of its stride as shown in the film. If the creature was a fake, everyone agrees that it was a remarkably skilful one. The only known source of such a high quality of costume and makeup in 1967 was the movie special effects industry, and in fact there is strong evidence that this Bigfoot came from Hollywood.

After lengthy investigations and interviews, journalist Mark Chorivinsky has found that the consensus among the movie-effects industry professionals is that the film depicts a prankster in a skilfully crafted costume. In fact, many state that the falsity of the Patterson film has been common knowledge in the business for years.

The examiner's view

★ **Write an article for a magazine entitled *Does Bigfoot Exist?***

STEP 1: READ THE QUESTION CAREFULLY

In Paper 2, Section B (worth 15% of your total mark for English) you will have to answer one of four questions. A question testing **writing to inform** will always be one of the options.

> There are many skills in this unit which will help you in other areas of your English assessments. For example, you will be able to use what you have learned about the passive voice when writing about language in the reading section of Paper 1. There are many other areas which you will be able to write about when comparing the use of language in two texts. For example:
>
> - the use of the first, second or third person
> - the use of direct speech
> - the use of adverbials
>
> Very few students say anything other than the most obvious points about language under exam conditions, so use what you have learned in this book.

STEP 2: SEQUENCING

Sequencing is an important part of the writing process which allows you to manipulate the chronological order of a story you are telling. Control over a story's structure: placing part of the story out of chronological order to create a particular effect, is a Higher tier writing skill.

- Brainstorm ideas to include in your article.
- Sequence your ideas in a way that will help make your article gripping.

- Think of and write down five discourse markers which will show that you have sequenced your writing. For example *The first point… Next I will… In addition…*

STEP 3: THE USE OF LANGUAGE

Using parenthesis is a Higher tier writing skill. You should plan to use at least one example of parenthesis in your writing to inform.

- Write a simple sentence for your article about whether Bigfoot exists.
- Add another part to the sentence, using commas for parenthesis. For example:
  In my opinion Bigfoot does not exist.
  > In my opinion, after reading the article, Bigfoot does not exist.

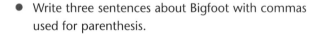

- Write three sentences about Bigfoot with commas used for parenthesis.

STEP 4: PLANNING AND DRAFTING

Your article could contain:

- a history of claimed Bigfoot sightings (perhaps based on the timeline you drew up for question 1a, page 94)
- a summary of the Patterson story and the arguments which followed
- your conclusions, based on the evidence, as to whether Bigfoot exists

Consider using:

- active and passive
- parenthesis

STEP 5: WRITING TO INFORM

Now use the skills you have practised in this unit to write your magazine article. Remember, you are not telling a story – aim to inform your audience about other people's Bigfoot stories.

STEP 6: SAMPLE ANSWER

Read these concluding paragraphs from a sample answer.

> To summarise, although many of us would like to believe in Bigfoot, the fact remains that there is very little hard evidence to prove its existence. The legend survives on a few highly improbable stories and a 'sighting' (the Patterson/Gimlin film) that is apparently known throughout Hollywood to be a fake.
>
> So, that's what I think about the Bigfoot phenomenon. It's a good story and has obviously made a lot of money for a lot of people. However, could it have happened anywhere but the United States of America?
>
> Now the Loch Ness Monster, or Nessie to her friends, is a real monster, isn't she?

There's a real sense of control in this writing, with the writer controlling the reader's response. Note the use of three sentences of equal length in the penultimate paragraph, and the use of irony in the very last sentence.

Quick tip Always use your reading skills in your writing and your writing skills in your reading: the two inform and support each other.

Mysteries of the dead

In this unit you will:

- read two newspaper articles
- examine the language of journalism
- write an explanatory news article

The following article appeared in the *Guardian* on 21 March 2002.

How Oetzi the Iceman was stabbed in the back and lost his fight for life

Rory Carroll in Rome

Scientists have discovered that Oetzi the Iceman, the world's oldest and best preserved mummy, was engaged in hand-to-hand combat shortly before perishing in the Alps 5,300 years ago.

Two wounds to his right hand and wrist show he was stabbed while trying to defend himself with a dagger against an attacker, bolstering theories that bronze age tribes waged war on mountain peaks. The discovery scotches claims that Oetzi was a human sacrifice and suggests instead that he was a warrior or the victim of an ambush who fought hard to save his life.

Researchers revealed the findings last night from the archaeological museum in the northern Italian town of Bolzano which keeps the mummy in a refrigerated room.

"This is very exciting. It tells us that Oetzi was involved in a battle, or at least in hand-to-hand combat of some kind," Eduard Egarter Vigl, the main caretaker for the corpse, told the *Guardian*.

A sharp object, possibly a flint-tipped spear or dagger, punctured the base of his thumb, shredding skin and muscle right to the bone, and a second blow damaged a bone on his wrist. The thumb wound had no scar, meaning it was fresh when the Iceman died.

It is the latest piece of a jigsaw which started in 1991 when two German hikers found a corpse in an Alpine glacier bordering Italy and Austria. Eleven thousand feet above sea level, it caused a sensation as the astonishing state of preservation held secrets about pre-history.

It is known that he was 46 and in a valley on the Italian side hours before ascending the glacier with an unfinished bow, arrows and a dagger.

Forensic scientists and archaeologists have become detectives, conceiving and discarding theories about why and how he died. The discovery last year of an arrow blade in

'This reinforces evidence that neolithic times were quite violent. From the bones in the Alps it appears there were battles'

scotches	puts an end to
forensic scientist	a scientist who uses his or her scientific knowledge to help solve police investigations or decide court cases
hypothermia	extreme drop in body temperature
appease	satisfy, pacify
neolithic	the last period of the Stone Age
scapula	shoulder-blade

his left shoulder showed his death was
55 violent, not the result of drowning,
hypothermia or a fall.

Researchers speculated he was a willing
sacrifice to appease the gods or the victim
of an accident or a long-range ambush. The
60 injured hand shows instead that Oetzi
knew he was in danger and had time to
defend himself.

One of the German hikers, Alois
Pirpamer, has revealed that Oetzi's dagger
65 was not beside the corpse, as previously
thought, but in his right hand, suggesting
the killer was close. That detail emerged
when the makers of a Discovery Channel
documentary to be broadcast next month
70 introduced Mr Pirpamer to Dr Egarter Vigl.
The clue prompted the scientist to re-exam-
ine the hand, revealing a 15mm-deep zig-
zag wound.

"This reinforces evidence that neolithic
75 times were quite violent because from the
bones found in the Alps it appears there
were battles up there," said Brando Quilici,
who directed the documentary.

It is thought Oetzi bled to death after
80 the arrow shattered the scapula and damaged nerves and blood vessels before lodg-
ing near the lung.

**Work on the body of Oetzi the Iceman
suggests that, rather than being
sacrificed, he died defending himself
from a knife-wielding attacker**

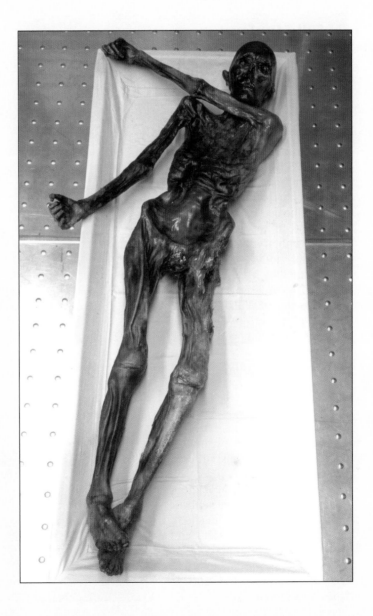

This article from the *Daily Mail* appeared on 20 March 2002.

Nearly 60 years on, a final chapter in the intriguing tale of The Man Who Never Was

By **Bill Mouland**

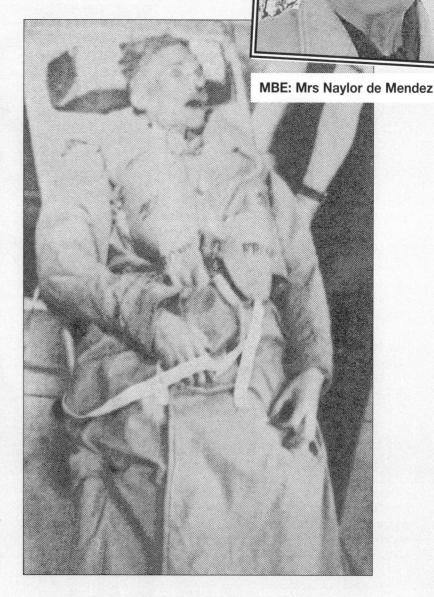

MBE: Mrs Naylor de Mendez

HE was perhaps the most unlikely hero of the Second World War.

In life, Glyndwr Michael was
5 a decrepit down-and-out who killed himself by drinking rat poison.

But in death, he helped save thousands of Allied lives and
10 speeded the end of the war.

In one of the greatest con-tricks in military history, the 34-year-old's body was secretly appropriated by MI5.

15 Michael was given a new identity – that of William Martin, an acting major in the Royal Marines – and dumped in the sea off Spain.

20 Fake documents on the corpse fooled Hitler over the intended focus of the Allies' invasion of Italy.

With Nazi forces massed
25 elsewhere, Allied troops met lit-tle resistance and thus suffered far fewer casualties.

The tale of the deception, codenamed Operation Mince-
30 meat, became a best-selling book and classic film – The Man Who Never Was – while the body of 'Major Martin' was laid to rest at the Cemetery of Solitude outside
35 Huelva, southern Spain.

For 50 years, his true identity was unknown. Yet red flowers were regularly laid on the grave.

In 1996, both these mysteries were solved. Amateur historian Roger Morgan discovered Glyndwr Michael's name in files at the Public Record Office in Kew, West London.

'He helped save many lives'

He is convinced MI5 used the body without the knowledge of the dead man's family.

However, agents in charge of Operation Mincemeat always insisted that the family gave permission on condition the identity of the corpse would never be revealed.

It also emerged that the flowers had been laid on the grave by British-born Isabel Naylor de Mendez.

Last night in Huelva, in possibly the final chapter to the story, Mrs Naylor de Mendez, 69, was made an MBE for tending the war graves at the cemetery.

She received her award from the British ambassador to Spain, Peter Torry.

She told how her father first put flowers on the grave of 'Major Martin' in 1946. He asked her to take on the task shortly before he died in 1966.

'My father told me that this man, whoever he might have been, saved many lives in the war and it was a sort of duty for us to keep his grave tidy,' Mrs Naylor de Mendez said.

Of her MBE, she added: 'I feel very honoured. I don't think I deserve it. It's been a great surprise and I'm very grateful.'

Mr Morgan said yesterday: 'I think it's jolly good that Mrs Naylor de Mendez is getting the MBE. She and her father had put flowers on the grave since 1946, and that had always been a bit of a mystery as well.'

The Commonwealth War Grave Commission has added Michael's name to that of the Major on the gravestone.

Mr Morgan said: 'Operation Mincemeat was a very successful tactical deception.

'Even after the war there were still highly ranked Germans who believed Major Martin was real.' Operation Mincemeat was drawn up in the spring of 1943.

With Churchill planning to invade Italy through Sicily, a ruse was needed to make the Germans believe the attack would take place elsewhere.

Intelligence agents conceived the idea of planting false papers on an officer and making it look as if he had died in a plane crash at sea.

London coroner Bentley Purchase provided them with the body of Michael, the illegitimate son of illiterate parents from a Welsh mining village, who had been found dead in a warehouse.

The cadaver was kept in cold storage while preparations continued in the minutest detail. Michael was given military papers, including a pass to Combined Operations Headquarters, identifying him as Acting Major William Martin, an expert in amphibious warfare.

To make it as convincing as possible, there was also a letter from his father, a warning about his overdraft from his bank manager, bills for an engagement ring and a shirt, theatre ticket stubs and a letter from his solicitor.

Finally, there were love letters and a photograph of his fiancee, 'Pam' – in reality Jean Gerard Leigh, who worked as a clerk for MI5.

Michael's body was dressed in the uniform of a Royal Marines officer and the personal effects were put in a briefcase – chained to his wrist – with 'plans' showing how the Allies would invade Italy via Sardinia and Greece.

'Very successful deception'

'Major Martin' was packed in dry ice, driven to Scotland and put on a submarine.

Off the Spanish coast, the submarine captain read Psalm 39 before the body, kept afloat by a life jacket, was slipped into the sea along with an upturned life raft.

Although Spain, under the fascist control of Franco, was officially neutral, MI5 knew the information would be passed on to the Germans.

When the 'Major' was found, German agents excitedly reported the contents of the briefcase to Berlin.

Hitler poured reinforcements into Sardinia and Greece, leaving Sicily poorly defended.

In 1956 the story was made into a film starring Clifton Webb and Gloria Grahame.

b.mouland@dailymail.co.uk

MI5	the secret service
MBE	an award: Member of the Order of the British Empire
cadaver	corpse
amphibious	both on land and in the sea
Psalm 39	from the Bible, often read at funerals

The power of language

Key features of the articles are:

1 photograph, headline and intro

2 paragraphs

3 pyramid writing

 1 **PHOTOGRAPH, HEADLINE AND INTRO**

> The **photograph** can be a key feature of a newspaper article.

a) Look at the photographs which accompany the two articles. Write a paragraph to explain what part they play in:

- attracting the reader's attention (What is there about each of the photos that makes you want to read the article?)
- adding to the interest of the story (What can the photo do that the text cannot do?)
- providing extra information (What details can you see in the photos which are not fully explained in the texts?)

> Apart from the photograph, the **headline** is usually the first feature of a newspaper article to capture the reader's attention.

Headlines are often brief and eye-catching:

117 PEGS ON MY ED

(*Sun*)

RANGERS IN CUP OF CHEER

(*Daily Express*)

b) The headlines to the two articles on pages 100–3 are much longer than the examples from the *Sun* and *Daily Express*. Write a paragraph to explain how these two headlines (*How Oetzi...* and *Nearly 60 years on...*) succeed in capturing the reader's interest. Think about:

- the ways in which each one provides key facts of the story which follows
- their dramatic language (*stabbed in the back... final chapter...*)
- the element of mystery (*How Oetzi... The Man Who Never Was*)

> Newspaper articles are structured so as to gain the reader's attention and then keep it. An important part of this structure is the opening, called the **intro**.

The intro will often contain a dramatic and attention-grabbing fact. For example:

Crazy Edward McKenna is facing up to stardom as a record holder after sticking 117 clothes pegs to his head...
(*Sun*, 18 March 2002)

c) Reread the intros to the two articles (*Scientists ... 5,300 years ago* and *He was ... end of the war*). Write a paragraph commenting on the way in which the writers have grabbed the reader's attention with the intros. For example:

- Which dramatic facts have been introduced?
- What is there about each intro that makes you want to read on?

2 PARAGRAPHS

> A **paragraph** is a block of sentences linked together by one main idea or subject.

Paragraphs in **tabloid** newspaper articles tend to be shorter than paragraphs in many other kinds of writing. (The tabloids are the popular, small-format newspapers such as the *Daily Mail*, the *Mirror* and the *Sun*.) This is done in order to keep the reader's attention, and is important in articles written to explain something. For example, some paragraphs in the article on The Man Who Never Was contain no more than a single sentence each.

a) The article about Oetzi the Iceman is divided into eleven paragraphs. Each one can be given a **topic heading**: a brief title which summarises the content. For example, the first paragraph might be headed: *Discovery about how Oetzi died*.

Write a topic heading for each of the other ten paragraphs. Compare your ten topic headings with a partner and talk about any differences between your two lists. Have you focused on different ideas within particular paragraphs, for example?

b) Bill Mouland's article on The Man Who Never Was is divided into many more paragraphs than the Iceman report.

- Join some of the paragraphs together so as to reduce the total number of paragraphs to eight, with the following possible topic headings:

  1 *Who was he?*
  2 *The 'con-trick' and its legend*
  3 *Solving the mystery*
  4 *Who tended the grave?*
  5 *The success of Operation Mincemeat*
  6 *The original idea*
  7 *The result in Spain and Germany*
  8 *The film*

- List your eight new paragraphs by writing down the opening and closing phrases only. (For example, if you were doing this with the Iceman article, the opening paragraph would be written as *Scientists have discovered ... 5,300 years ago*.)

- Finally, write a sentence or two about each new paragraph to explain what it contains. (For example, if you were writing about the Iceman article, you might say: *The opening two paragraphs contain the important new discovery about how Oetzi died; they introduce the account by presenting the key facts.*)

3 PYRAMID WRITING

> Journalists often use a method of structuring newspaper articles known as **pyramid writing**. This involves putting the most striking or important information at the beginning of the article.

It is called pyramid writing because, of all the readers who read an article's headline, only 70 per cent will read to the end of the intro, and only 50 per cent will carry on to the end of the third or fourth paragraph. This situation can be represented in an upside-down pyramid outline:

Percentage of people who read different sections of a newspaper article

Headline 100% of readers

Intro 70% of readers

2nd, 3rd or 4th paragraphs 50% of readers

a) Write two or three paragraphs analysing the ways in which the writers of the two explanatory articles have used pyramid writing. Quote from the articles to show how the writers have:

- created an attention-grabbing headline

- included the most dramatic facts in the intro

- included the slightly less dramatic facts in the next few paragraphs

- left the more technical, or least interesting, details until the end

Writing to explain

FOUNDATION TIER TASKS

 WRITING A NEWSPAPER ARTICLE

Imagine you are a journalist who has just interviewed Albert Ostman about his capture by a Sasquatch (Bigfoot) – you can find the account of his experience on pages 92–3. Use the notes you have taken (below) to write an article for your tabloid newspaper.

NOTES TAKEN DURING INTERVIEW WITH ALBERT OSTMAN

1. Ostman – 64-year-old retired lumberman from British Columbia
2. was on camping trip near Vancouver Island
3. found that something had disturbed his supplies and food on two nights in a row
4. one night was shaken awake to find himself being carried away inside his sleeping bag
5. the opening of the sleeping bag was held shut – Ostman dragged along the forest ground for maybe 25 miles, nearly suffocating – journey took 3 hours
6. he was thrown to the ground in a heap, and emerged to find himself in the company of four Sasquatches
7. a family: father, mother and pair of offspring – one male, one female
8. adult male over eight feet tall and powerfully built, covered in dark hair all over
9. the children, though smaller, were still about seven feet tall
10. the Sasquatches chattered amongst themselves in a seemingly intelligent language
11. did not hurt or threaten him, but were determined not to let him leave
12. their lair inside a small valley enclosed by cliffs – adult male stood guard at the only apparent exit
13. Ostman may have been selected as a prospective mate for the young female
14. held captive for six days – formed bond with the younger male, who became fond of sampling Ostman's snuff
15. Ostman's escape: he offered his snuff to the adult male, which dumped the entire container into his mouth – then writhed on the ground in great discomfort. Ostman ran off

Planning and drafting

First reread Albert Ostman's story in the article on pages 92–3. When you plan your article, remember the rules of pyramid writing:

- think up an attention-grabbing headline
- draft a dramatic intro
- leave the least important or least interesting details to the end

Quotes from Ostman will help bring the report to life, e.g. *'To my horror I realised that something was shaking me awake,' said the terrified 64-year-old…*

You are writing for a tabloid newspaper, so the paragraphs will be short. Add a rough sketch of a photo which could accompany the article.

Your article could begin:

A retired lumberman told yesterday about his nerve-wracking six-day ordeal – abducted by a family of Sasquatches!

2 SUMMARISING THE ARTICLE

Reread Bill Mouland's article about The Man Who Never Was.

Imagine you were a member of wartime intelligence. You have just been informed by an agent working under cover in Spain that Operation Mincemeat has been a total success.

Write a report for your Commanding Officer, explaining what happened. Remember that you need only summarise the main facts.

You could use the following eight points in the writing frame as a guide (reread the lines listed in the middle column).

Main points	Reread lines...	You could start...
1 Why the operation was necessary and what they hoped to achieve	100–4: *With Churchill planning...*	*As you know, when we were still planning to invade Italy through Sicily, the Prime Minister asked us to find a way of...*
2 When it was planned	95–9: '*Even after the war...*	*So, in the spring of this year...*
3 The idea	105–9: *Intelligence agents conceived...*	*MI5 came up with the idea of...*
4 Who the body was	4–7 and 110–15: *In life... London coroner Bentley Purchase...*	*The London coroner, Bentley Purchase, provided the body of...*
5 The first steps	11–19: *In one of the greatest... Michael was given...*	*Michael was given a new identity...*
6 The fake evidence planted on the body	116–43: *The cadaver was... To make it... Finally, there were... Michael's body was...*	*After keeping the body in cold storage...*
7 The journey by submarine	144–51: '*Major Martin' was... Off the Spanish coast...*	*Now called 'Major Martin', the body was...*
8 The enemy is fooled	152–63, 8–10 and 24–7: *Although Spain... But in death... With Nazi forces...*	*When Spanish forces found the body...*

FOUNDATION & HIGHER TIER TASK

 WRITING AN ARTICLE

Write an article for a tabloid newspaper, based on any story from history, legend or fiction.

(See pages 108–9 for 'the examiner's view' on how to tackle this question.)

HIGHER TIER TASK

 COMPARING THE ARTICLES

Write a comparison of the two articles on pages 100–3, showing how each one has succeeded in capturing and maintaining the reader's interest.

> ### Planning and drafting
> In your answer you should refer to each writer's use of:
> - pyramid writing
> - quotes
> - paragraphing
> - photographs
>
> **You could start:**
> *The two articles are linked by the common theme of 'mysterious bodies' and the writers have fully exploited the dramatic potential of their stories...*

Write an article for a tabloid newspaper, based on any story from history, legend or fiction.

STEP 1: READ THE QUESTION CAREFULLY

In Paper 2, Section B (worth 15% of your total mark for English) you will have to answer one of four questions. A question testing **writing to explain** will always be one of the options.

You should always highlight important words in the question before you start to plan. For example, in this question you are asked to write an article for a **tabloid** newspaper. This should give you an idea of what style and tone to use.

STEP 2: BRAINSTORMING

Brainstorming is an important stage in the process of writing. If you don't brainstorm, you risk either repeating yourself or not covering all of the relevant points.

- Write down five ideas for your article.
- Add discourse markers to show links between paragraphs.

- Identify your most interesting/important point and write a dramatic opening line to capture your reader's interest.
- Sequence your remaining ideas in the most interesting possible way (see the information on pyramid writing on page 105).

STEP 3: THE USE OF LANGUAGE

Tabloid newspapers are instantly recognisable as they usually use the following presentational features:

- striking colour
- images/photographs
- short paragraphs
- headlines, sub-headings and straplines

- Write a short sub-heading for each paragraph in your article – to help guide your reader.
- Find a photograph/image to use in your article.

- Include an example of alliteration in your headline.
- Link your image to the text with a caption.

STEP 4: PLANNING AND DRAFTING

You could choose a story from:

- **history**, for example the execution of Mary Queen of Scots
- **legend**, for example the fall of Troy or Arthur pulling the sword out of the stone
- **fiction**, for example Dr Frankenstein's creation of the monster, or the story of the Hound of the Baskervilles

Remember the rules of pyramid writing:

- think up an attention-grabbing headline
- draft a dramatic intro
- leave the least important or least interesting details to the end

You should also make sure that you:

- include quotes from eyewitnesses or other people involved
- keep the paragraphs short
- add a rough sketch of a photo which could accompany the article

STEP 5: WRITING TO EXPLAIN

Now use all of the skills you have practised in this unit to write your news article. Remember:

- you are writing for a tabloid newspaper – use an appropriate style
- this is an explanatory article

STEP 6: SAMPLE ANSWER

Read this introduction from a sample answer.

> Mary Queen of Scots is dead. Even to her very last gasp, she proved what a crowd puller and crowd pleaser she was. The lips of the dead queen moved up and down for a quarter of an hour yesterday after her head had been severed by axe-man Richard Tyrrell.
>
> HEARTBREAK
>
> Crowds wept from the moment she came into view, but this wailing was nothing to the crescendo of cries that echoed around the block at this most ghastly of sights. Blood spattered the garments of those closest to this melancholy event, but this did not deter her loyal subjects from starting to pray and plead for her soul.
>
> AXE-MAN
>
> However, as soon as she stopped moving, Richard Tyrrell left the scene a broken man. Strangely, it has been reported that Mary was mouthing prayers and exhortations directed at her bloody killer. One of the onlookers told our reporter that...

The short paragraphs in this piece of writing help to keep it clear and easy to follow. The writer has also used a discourse marker (*However*).

Quick tip Never write in columns when writing an article. This will slow you down in an exam and they can be mistaken for paragraphs.

The finger of fate

In this unit you will:

- read a newspaper article
- examine the language of description and report
- write a report

This article by Michael Hanlon appeared in the *Daily Mail* on 14 January 2002.

The finger of fate

Their end, when it came, was very different from that of their victims: swift and relatively painless. On the morning of May 23, 1905, Albert Stratton and his brother Alfred were taken to the gallows and blindfolded by the hangman.

Witnesses described Albert's death as instantaneous, his body becoming limp straight after the drop through the trapdoor.

In Alfred's case, according to a newspaper report, 'there was some muscular movement afterwards'.

Gruesome deaths, perhaps, but merciful compared with the savage butchery the brothers had inflicted just three weeks previously.

One Monday morning, a sales assistant called William Jones had turned up for work only to find the door to the shop – a paint suppliers in Deptford High Street, South London – locked.

The shop's elderly manager, Thomas Farrow, would normally have opened up a couple of hours earlier.

Puzzled, Jones broke in and discovered a horrific scene. Farrow lay face-down, his body crumpled in a bloody pile, his skull staved in by a crowbar. Upstairs, his wife Ann lay dying, her wounds also the result of a sustained bludgeoning with a metal implement.

Later that morning, when Scotland Yard's assistant commissioner Melville Macnaghten joined the policemen in the shop, he noticed a greasy smudge on the shop's empty cash box. Immediately, he had it sent to the Yard's Fingerprint Branch.

Meanwhile, a witness, Ellen Stanton, told police she had seen

It was the case that made history... the first time that a fingerprint had been used to catch a killer. But behind it lay a story of intrigue and bitter jealousy

by
Michael Hanlon

Alfred Stratton, a well-known petty criminal, and another man tearing at high speed away from the shop.

The Stratton brothers were arrested, and Detective Inspector Charles Collins of the Fingerprint Branch subsequently discovered that Alfred's right thumbprint matched the print on the cash box.

Though fingerprints had never been used before as evidence in a murder trial, Macnaghten decided to commit the case to prosecution.

The key question was: would a jury be willing to send two men to the gallows on fingerprint evidence?

Forensic evidence was still widely mistrusted. Until then, convictions for murder had relied on sworn testimonies from the witness box that placed the accused at the scene of the crime.

No one saw the Strattons commit the murder; eyewitnesses had merely seen them near the shop.

It took just two hours' deliberation for the jury to find the brothers guilty – and to change legal history for ever. The Strattons became the first men in England to be hanged for murder on the evidence of a fingerprint.

The perseverance of a few dedicated scientists and policemen in getting the new-fangled forensic techniques accepted, first by the lawmen and then by the public, is one of the great tales in the history of law enforcement.

It was not until the 17th century that scientists realised

everyone has hundreds of tiny ridges on their fingertips which form a unique pattern. With the invention of the microscope, people began to study them systematically.

It was Dr Nehemiah Grew, a physician and microscopist born in Warwickshire in 1641, who stumbled upon the ridge patterns on his fingertips, and he observed that 'upon these ridges stand the pores ... every pore looks like a little fountain, and the sweat may be seen to stand therein, as clear as rock water.'

When a fingertip touches an object, this sweat is left behind in the pattern of the ridges, like an ink impression made on paper with a rubber stamp.

It was in the late 19th century that two Britons, one living in India and one in Japan, independently stumbled on the practical use of fingerprinting as a means of identification. Henry Faulds, a temperamental, ambitious Scottish missionary to Japan, began studying the ridge patterns on primates and men because he believed the shared characteristic might have implications for Charles Darwin's new theory of evolution.

When Japanese police found a fingerprint at the scene of a crime, they asked Faulds to use it to determine the guilt of their suspect. Thus, Faulds became the father of fingerprints – or so he thought. But unknown to Faulds, William Herschel, a British magistrate in India, had been using fingerprints in place of signatures on contracts for 20 years.

It was all very well taking unique impressions of a person's fingertips, but how could those impressions be cross-referenced with fingerprints already on file without searching through the entire registry every time?

Henry's method classified fingerprints by the form of the ridge patterns: the arch, the loop, the tent and the whorl. Simply by looking at a man's fresh fingerprints, an expert could deduce where in the registry a set like it would be filed. Henry returned to Britain and founded the Metropolitan Police's Fingerprint Branch in 1902. The purpose of the branch was initially to use fingerprints to identify repeat offenders who gave false names in court.

They had tremendous success, making 632 identifications in

the first year. Det Insp Charles Collins, also of the Fingerprint Branch – which by now had 900,000 prints on file – wanted to get fingerprinting accepted by the courts. The Stratton murder presented him with a perfect opportunity.

When he received the cash box from Thomas Farrow's shop, Collins went straight to his laboratory, where he dipped his camel-hair brush into a small jar of lampblack – fine carbon soot.

Gently, he whisked his powder-covered brush across the box. As the dust stuck to whatever residue fingers had left upon it, a number of ridge patterns developed.

Carefully, Collins photo-graphed each of the patterns, and compared them with the fingerprints he had taken from people known to have touched the box.

One pattern of ridges, a right thumb print, belonged to an unidentified person – the murderer. It contained 12 identifiable characteristics, and

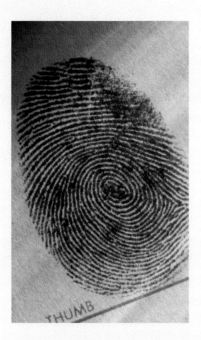

Alfred Stratton's right thumb print matched every one.

The trial of the Strattons began at the Old Bailey on May 5,

195 1905. Victory for the prosecution would mean fingerprints would be accepted as a legal tool in a murder conviction.

200 But failure would consign the technique to quackery – and the Fingerprint Branch had its enemies. One was sitting at the Strattons' defence table: Henry Faulds.

205 In an act of bitter revenge at failing to win recognition for his contribution to fingerprinting, Faulds planned to help the defence team argue that the Yard's system was misconceived.

210 He said that prosecuting a man on the basis of a mere fingerprint was folly.

The trial was gripping. The police were desperate to secure a

215 conviction; then, as now, there was extreme public disquiet about their seeming inability to stem the rising tide of crimes, while the Press rained vitriol on

220 the 'incompetent' Met.

After a mammoth court battle, the jury made it clear that fingerprint evidence was sufficient to win a conviction.

225 Justice had been done – but not to the reputation of Henry Faulds. For the rest of his long life, he fulminated against the forensic establishment. He died

230 in March 1930, aged 86.

It wasn't until 1987, when two researchers stumbled upon his grave in Stoke-on-Trent, that Faulds's reputation was finally

235 secured. The British Fingerprint Society officially recognised Faulds's contribution, and now pays for the upkeep of his grave.

The only people who have no

240 cause to thank the cantankerous Scot are the thousands of men and women who have been convicted on the evidence of his technique.

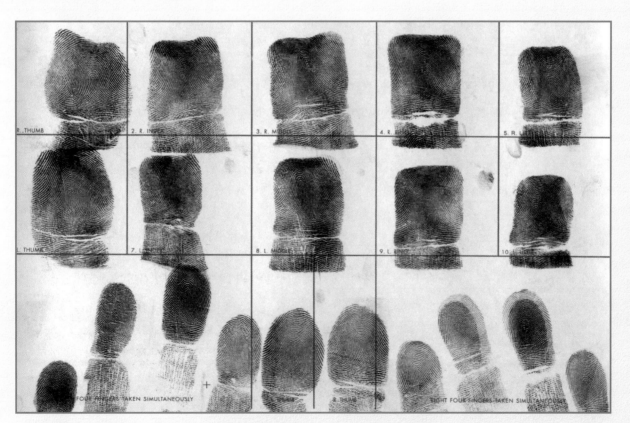

The power of language

Key features of the text are:

1 non-chronological writing

2 adverbials

3 adjectives

---

1 NON-CHRONOLOGICAL WRITING

Non-chronological writing organises events in a different order from the one in which they happened.

Look back at page 94 to remind yourself of *chronological* writing.

a) The article describes a crime and its aftermath in the following **non-chronological** order:

Paragraph	Events
1–2	the execution of the Stratton brothers
3	a newspaper report of the execution
5–7	William Jones's discovery of the crime
7	the injuries inflicted on the victims
8–9	the police investigation
10	the arrests
11–14	preparing the prosecution
15	the trial

- Re-organise these eight sections chronologically – in other words, so that the events are described in the order in which they happened.
- Write a paragraph to explain what effect Hanlon achieves by his non-chronological account.

  For example:
  - Why might he have opened the article with an account of the execution?
  - Why do you think he leaves describing the trial until the end?

---

2 ADVERBIALS

Adverbials are words or phrases which add important information to a sentence. They can help us to answer questions such as When? How? and Where?

For example, the following sentence from the article contains three common types of adverbial:

*Meanwhile, a witness, Ellen Stanton, told police she had seen Alfred Stratton … tearing **at high speed away from the shop**.*

- **time adverbials** answer the question **When?**
  Meanwhile…
- **manner adverbials** answer the question **How?**
  …at high speed…
- **place adverbials** answer the question **Where?**
  …away from the shop.

Adverbials can be:

single words	*Immediately, he had it sent…*
phrases	*One Monday morning, a sales assistant called William Jones had…*
whole clauses	*Though fingerprints had never been used before as evidence in a murder trial, Macnaghten decided…*

Manner adverbials and place adverbials

a) In the first column of the following table are two of the three common types of adverbials: **manner adverbials** and **place adverbials**. Next to each type are two examples from the extract. Copy the grid and write down three more examples of manner adverbials and place adverbials, also taken from the extract.

Type of adverbial	Examples from the extract
Manner adverbials (answer the question How?)	• *Farrow lay **face-down**…* • *…tearing **at high speed**…*
Place adverbials (answer the question Where?)	• ***Upstairs**, his wife Ann lay dying…* • *…tearing … **away from the shop**.*

Time adverbials

b) Most of the adverbials in the extract are **time adverbials**.

- Pick out the time adverbials in the phrases and sentences beginning:
  - *On the morning of...* (lines 4–8)
  - *there was some muscular...* (14–15)
  - *the savage butchery the brothers had...* (17–19)
  - *One Monday morning...* (20–5)
  - *The shop's elderly manager...* (26–9)
  - *Later that morning...* (38–43, there are two time adverbials in this sentence)
  - *and Detective Inspector Charles Collins...* (53–7)
  - *Until then, convictions for murder...* (67–71)
  - *and to change legal history...* (77–8)

- Write a paragraph or two to explain why time adverbials should be so useful in a *non*-chronological description like this one. Quote examples to show their importance. (For example, if the account starts with the executions, it is important to let the reader know that the murders were committed *just three weeks previously*.)

> **Adverbials** and other phrases which help to structure a text (e.g. *Firstly, On the other hand, However*) are sometimes known as **discourse markers**.

3 ADJECTIVES

> An **adjective** is a word which gives us information about a noun or pronoun. A group of words which does this is called an **adjective phrase**.

Adjectives play an important part in Michael Hanlon's description of the crime and its aftermath. For example, he writes about *gruesome* deaths, *savage* butchery, a *horrific* scene.

a) Pick out:

- the adjectives from the opening four paragraphs (lines 1–19). Two of them have been quoted in the sentence above.
- the one adjective which describes the manager, Thomas Farrow (in the paragraph beginning *The shop's...*, line 26)
- the four adjectives from the description of what William Jones discovered upon entering the shop (in the paragraph beginning *Puzzled, Jones broke in...*, line 30)

b) Write a paragraph to explain how the adjectives you found in question 3a are used to draw a contrast between the savagery of the attack upon an innocent man and the law's treatment of the murderers.

To do this, compare:

- adjectives in the section from *The shop's...* to *...metal implement.*

with

- adjectives in the opening four paragraphs

c) There are fewer adjectives in the next section of the article, but they play a key role.

For example, look at the following two sentences

Forensic evidence was still widely mistrusted. (lines 66–7)

The Strattons became the first men in England to be hanged for murder on the evidence of a fingerprint. (lines 78–81)

- Pick out the adjective in each sentence.
- Write a paragraph to explain how these two adjectives are essential in summing up one of the main points of the article.

Writing to describe

FOUNDATION TIER TASKS

1 RETELLING WHAT HAPPENED

Retell the first part of Michael Hanlon's account (up to line 81) in chronological order.

Use your own words as far as possible.

> **Planning and drafting**
>
> Retell the account in the order in which the events actually happened:
>
> - the robbery and the injuries inflicted on the victims (lines 30–7)
> - William Jones's discovery of the crime (20–37)
> - the police investigation (38–51)
> - the arrests (52–7)
> - preparing the prosecution (58–74)
> - the trial (75–81)
> - the execution of the Stratton brothers (1–12)
> - newspaper reports of the execution (13–19)
>
> **You could start your account:**
>
> *One morning in May 1905, two brothers, Albert and Alfred Stratton, attacked and robbed Thomas Farrow, the elderly manager of a paint suppliers in Deptford High Street, south London...*

2 WRITING AN ARTICLE

Write a newspaper report of a crime which was solved using fingerprints. To make it different from *The finger of fate*, choose any crime but murder.

> **Planning and drafting**
>
> Base your report on a crime which could be solved through the evidence of fingerprints, such as burglary, arson or handling stolen goods.
>
> Use the writing frame below as a guide.

Include paragraphs on...	You could start...
1 details of the crime (What happened? Who were the victims? Were they harmed?)	*On the morning of 23 May, 2003...*
2 the discovery of the crime	*At 8.45, a young sales assistant, Ginny Foster...*
3 the police investigation (How did fingerprints help police to solve the crime?)	*The police took three days to inspect the premises. Then...*
4 the arrests	*That evening, X and Y were drinking in the King's Arms...*
5 the trial (What was said? What sentence were the criminals given?)	*Speaking for the first time in public...*

FOUNDATION & HIGHER TIER TASK

 WRITING A NON-CHRONOLOGICAL REPORT

Write a non-chronological newspaper report of any episode from history, legend, mythology or fiction.

(See pages 118–19 for 'the examiner's view' on how to tackle this question.)

HIGHER TIER TASK

 ANALYSING THE LANGUAGE

Explain how Michael Hanlon, through his content and use of language, creates a gripping and informative article.

Planning and drafting

First, consider the subject matter. Why does it capture our interest? What makes it:

● important historically?

● dramatic?

Then think about the language. Comment on his use of:

● non-chronological writing

(Why does he open with the execution, do you think?)

● adverbials

(Why are time adverbials so important here?)

● adjectives

(How have they been used to get across the essential points the writer wants to make?)

You could start:

In choosing to write an article on the history of fingerprinting, Michael Hanlon has found a subject guaranteed to capture our interest...

The examiner's view

⭐ Write a non-chronological newspaper report of any episode from history, legend, mythology or fiction.

STEP 1: READ THE QUESTION CAREFULLY

A question testing **writing to describe** is one of three choices on Paper 2, Section B in the English exam, and is worth 15% of your overall mark for English.

Writing to describe is very different from writing to inform or writing to explain, because it requires the writer to use language that appeals to the senses and show more control over imagery. There are specific aspects of this type of writing that you need to address:

- using adverbials and adjectives to help to build up a picture in words
- appealing to each of the senses in order to bring your description to life

The following notes refer to an answer describing Macbeth's rise and fall; however, the same ideas apply to any piece of descriptive writing.

STEP 2: USING ADVERBIALS

Adverbials can be used to help paint a vivid picture in the reader's mind. Read the first part of Act 4 Scene 1 of *Macbeth* (up to Macbeth's entrance), then:

- Imagine and describe how Macbeth moves when he is approaching the witches.
- Imagine and describe how the witches move and behave when Macbeth arrives in their midst.

- Add time adverbials to the description of Macbeth.
- Add place adverbials to the description of the witches.

STEP 3: APPEALING TO THE SENSES

You can help to bring your description to life by using adjectives that appeal to all of the senses. Try to describe sounds and smells as well as things you can see.

- Describe one sound and one sight at the scene on the heath. For example:
  As Macbeth approached the scene he heard a wild wailing and saw three gruesome shapes circling a blazing fire.

- Describe one smell at the scene on the heath. For example:
  Macbeth approached the threesome with a sense of growing dread, only heightened when he smelt the unmistakable stench of putrid animal.

STEP 4: PLANNING AND DRAFTING

- Write out the main events of your report (in note form) in chronological order. For the story of Macbeth, you might write:
  - The witches are seen on the heath chanting spells.
  - Macbeth approaches the witches.
  - Macbeth talks to the witches.
- Plan a gripping, non-chronological order of events, choosing a dramatic moment with which to open your report.

STEP 5: WRITING TO DESCRIBE

Now write your report – aim to show evidence of the following:

- an awareness of your purpose and audience
- a variety of organisational and structural devices (e.g. non-chronological paragraphing)
- a variety of sentence types and lengths
- a sophisticated choice of vocabulary (e.g. effective use of adjectives and adverbs that appeal to the senses)

STEP 6: SAMPLE ANSWER

Read this opening from a sample answer.

The severed head spiked on the gatehouse of Dunsinane Castle today is dramatic evidence that the bloody reign of King Macbeth is finally over.

As more and more details of this story emerge, one wonders at the recklessness of the man who murdered his way to the throne.

But this is no 'simple' story of treachery. I have unconfirmed reports that Macbeth had spoken with a group of three witches on more than one occasion. There seems little doubt that dark and mysterious forces were at work here.

One can only imagine the bizarre scene as Macbeth, future King of Scotland, approached the three black-clad creatures across a desolate heath, as they gyrated around a blazing fire and uttered unearthly wails...

> The beginning of your report needs to show control of structure and tone. This student has chosen a good point to start; their introduction grips us and makes us want to read on.

Quick tip
Writing to describe gives you an opportunity to show off your writing skills to the examiner.

The vulture woman

In this unit you will:

- read an extract from a novel
- learn about narrative craft and ways of telling stories
- write an episode from a novel in a chosen genre

This extract comes from *The Amber Spyglass*, the third novel in Philip Pullman's trilogy, *His Dark Materials.* Lyra and Will have travelled to the land of the dead, accompanied by Tialys and Salmakia, two Gallivespians — tiny warriors who ride on the backs of dragonflies.

The Amber Spyglass

They stood still and listened. The only sound was an endless drip-drip-drip of water from the leaves, and as they looked up they felt one or two drops splash coldly on their cheeks.

"Can't stay here," said Lyra.

They moved off the wharf, keeping close together, and made their way to the wall. Gigantic stone blocks, green with ancient slime, rose higher into the mist than they could 5 see. And now they were closer, they could hear the sound of cries behind it, though whether they were human voices crying was impossible to tell: high mournful shrieks and wails that hung in the air like the drifting filaments of a jellyfish, causing pain wherever they touched.

"There's a door," said Will, in a hoarse strained voice. 10

It was a battered wooden postern under a slab of stone. Before Will could lift his hand and open it, one of those high harsh cries sounded very close by, jarring their ears and frightening them horribly.

Immediately the Gallivespians darted into the air, the dragonflies like little war-horses eager for battle. But the thing that flew down 15 swept them aside with a brutal blow from her wing, and then settled heavily on a ledge just above the children's heads. Tialys and Salmakia gathered themselves and soothed their shaken mounts.

The thing was a great bird the size of a vulture, 20 with the face and breasts of a woman. Will had seen pictures of creatures like her, and the word *harpy* came to mind as soon as he saw her clearly. Her face was smooth and unwrinkled, but aged beyond even the age of the 25 witches: she had seen thousands of years pass, and the cruelty and misery of all of them had formed the hateful expression on her features. But as the travellers saw her more clearly, she became even more repulsive. Her eye-sockets were clotted with filthy slime, and the redness of her lips was caked and crusted as if she had vomited ancient blood again and again. Her matted, filthy black hair hung down to her shoulders; her jagged claws gripped the stone fiercely; her powerful dark wings were folded along her back, and a drift of putrescent stink wafted from her every time she moved. 30

Will and Lyra, both of them sick and full of pain, tried to stand upright and face her. 35
"But you are alive!" the harpy said, her harsh voice mocking them.
Will found himself hating and fearing her more than any human being he had ever known.
"Who are you?" said Lyra, who was just as repelled as Will.
For answer the harpy screamed. She opened her mouth and directed a jet of noise right in their faces, so that their heads rang and they nearly fell backwards. Will clutched 40 at Lyra and they both clung together as the scream turned into wild mocking peals of laughter, which were answered by other harpy-voices in the fog along the shore. The jeering hate-filled sound reminded Will of the merciless cruelty of children in a playground, but there were no teachers here to regulate things, no one to appeal to, nowhere to hide. 45

He set his hand on the knife at his belt and looked her in the eyes, though his head was ringing and the sheer power of her scream had made him dizzy.
"If you're trying to stop us," he said, "then you'd better be ready to fight as well as scream. Because we're going through that door." 50
The harpy's sickening red mouth moved again, but this time it was to purse her lips into a mock-kiss.
Then she said, "Your mother is alone. We shall send her nightmares. We shall scream at her in her sleep!" 55
Will didn't move, because out of the corner of his eye he could see the Lady Salmakia moving delicately along the branch where the harpy was perching. Her dragonfly, wings quivering, was being held by Tialys on the 60 ground, and then two things happened: the lady leapt at the harpy and spun around to dig her spur deep into the creature's scaly leg, and Tialys launched the dragonfly upwards. In less than a second Salmakia had spun away and leapt off the branch, directly on to 65 the back of her electric-blue steed and up into the air.
The effect on the harpy was immediate. Another scream shattered the silence, much louder than before, and she beat her dark wings so hard that Will and Lyra both felt the wind, and staggered. But she clung to the stone with her claws, and her face was suffused with dark-red anger, and her hair stood out from her 70 head like a crest of serpents.
Will tugged at Lyra's hand, and they both tried to run towards the door, but the harpy launched herself at them in a fury and only pulled up from the dive when Will turned, thrusting Lyra behind him and holding up the knife.

121

The Gallivespians flew at the harpy at once, darting close at her face and then darting away again, unable to get in a blow but distracting her so that she beat her wings clumsily and half-fell on to the ground.

Lyra called out, "Tialys! Salmakia! Stop, stop!"

The spies reined back their dragonflies and skimmed high over the children's heads. Other dark forms were clustering in the fog, and the jeering screams of a hundred more harpies sounded from further along the shore. The first one was shaking her wings, shaking her hair, stretching each leg in turn and flexing her claws. She was unhurt, and that was what Lyra had noticed.

The Gallivespians hovered, and then dived back towards Lyra, who was holding out both hands for them to land on. Salmakia realized what Lyra had meant, and said to Tialys: "She's right. We can't hurt her, for some reason."

Lyra said, "Lady, what's your name?"

The harpy shook her wings wide, and the travellers nearly fainted in the hideous smells of corruption and decay that wafted from her.

"No-Name!" she cried.

"What do you want with us?" said Lyra.

"What can you give me?"

"We could tell you where we've been, and maybe you'd be interested, I don't know. We saw all kinds of strange things on the way here."

"Oh, and you're offering to tell me a story?"

"If you'd like."

"Maybe I would. And what then?"

"You might let us go in through that door and find the ghost we've come here to look for, I hope you would, anyway. If you'd be so kind."

"Try, then," said No-Name.

And even in her sickness and pain, Lyra felt that she'd just been dealt the ace of trumps.

"Oh, be careful," whispered Salmakia, but Lyra's mind was already racing ahead through the story she'd told the night before, shaping and cutting and improving and adding: *parents dead; family treasure; shipwreck; escape…*

"Well," she said, settling in to her story-telling frame of mind, "it began when I was a baby, really. My father and mother were the Duke and Duchess of Abingdon, you see, and they were as rich as anything. My father was one of the king's advisers, and the king himself used to come and stay, oh, all the time. They'd go hunting in our forest. The house there, where I was born, it was the biggest house in the whole south of England. It was called –"

Without even a cry of warning the harpy launched herself at Lyra, claws outstretched. Lyra just had time to duck, but still one of the claws caught her scalp and tore out a clump of hair.

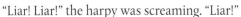

"Liar! Liar!" the harpy was screaming. "Liar!"

She flew around again, aiming directly for Lyra's face; but Will took out the knife and threw himself in the way. No-Name swerved out of reach just in time, and Will hustled Lyra over towards the door, because she was numb with shock and half-blinded by the blood running down her face. Where the Gallivespians were, Will had no idea, but the harpy was flying at them again and screaming and screaming in rage and hatred: 125

"*Liar! Liar! Liar!*"

And it sounded as if her voice was coming from everywhere, and the word echoed back from the great wall in the fog, muffled and changed, so that she seemed to be screaming Lyra's name, so that *Lyra* and *liar* were one and the same thing. 130

Will had the girl pressed against his chest, with his shoulder curved over to protect her, and he felt her shaking and sobbing against him; but then he thrust the knife into the rotten wood of the door, and cut out the lock with a quick slash of the blade.

Then he and Lyra, with the spies beside them on their darting dragonflies, tumbled through into the realm of the ghosts as the harpy's cry was doubled and redoubled by others on the foggy shore behind them. 135

The power of language

Key features of the writing are:

1 genre

2 comparisons

3 language that appeals to the senses

 1 **GENRE**

> **Genre** is the name given to a particular kind of writing with its own typical features.

a) *The Amber Spyglass* can be placed in the **fantasy** genre. In pairs, brainstorm the titles of books and films which belong to each of the following popular fiction genres: **fantasy**, **horror**, **crime** and **science fiction**. Think up four or five titles for each genre heading.

b) Each genre has its own recognisable features to do with characters, plot, themes and language. Copy the table below and, using the list you have just made, add examples of the characteristic features of each genre. Features of *The Amber Spyglass* and *The Lord of the Rings* by JRR Tolkien have been inserted as examples of the fantasy genre.

c) The first book of Tolkien's *The Lord of the Rings* trilogy opens with the following paragraph. In pairs discuss how you would guess that it was the introduction to a fantasy.

When Mr Bilbo Baggins of Bag End announced that he would shortly be celebrating his eleventy-first birthday with a party of special magnificence, there was much talk and excitement in Hobbiton.

d) Write a similar opening to a book in a different genre such as horror, crime or science fiction. Include as many features of the chosen genre as you can.

FEATURES	GENRES			
	FANTASY	HORROR	CRIME	SCIENCE FICTION
	examples *The Amber Spyglass, The Lord of the Rings*			
characters	including imagined creatures with strange powers: e.g. *Gallivespians, orcs, wizards*			
settings	other worlds with their own 'rules': e.g. *parallel universes, Middle-earth*			
plots	journeys, quests: e.g. *to destroy the One Ring*			
events	encounters with terrifying creatures: e.g. *the harpy, the balrog*			
themes	major themes: e.g. *innocence and experience, Good v Evil*			
language	strange names: e.g. *Salmakia, Gandalf*			

2 COMPARISONS

Fantasy writers use familiar language in order to describe the unfamiliar. **Comparisons** help the reader to picture the scene.

These might be:

- **literal comparisons:** *Will's face was like his father's...* or
- **impressions:** *his features brought to mind an old, lined map...*

They might also be:

- **similes:** *it glowed as brightly as a holly berry in the dimness...* or
- **metaphors:** *her face lit up...*
  her eyes were dark pools of mystery...

(A **simile** is a means of comparing things in an unusual or unexpected way in which the writer creates an image in the reader's mind. A simile uses the words *like* or *as*. A **metaphor** serves the same purpose, but does not involve the use of *like* or *as*: the person or object is described as though they *really were* something else.)

a) In pairs, find the following lines in the extract. Then discuss what kind of comparison each one is (not all of them are clear-cut), and how effective it is in the context of the description:

wails that hung in the air...

like the drifting filaments of a jellyfish, causing pain wherever they touched.

like little war-horses eager for battle.

the word harpy *came to mind as soon as he saw her clearly.*

as if she had vomited ancient blood again and again.

reminded Will of the merciless cruelty of children in a playground...

and her hair stood out from her head like a crest of serpents.

b) Write a short description of a landscape in a fantasy or science fiction novel, using all four types of comparison.

3 LANGUAGE THAT APPEALS TO THE SENSES

A writer will call on a variety of language skills in order to create powerful descriptions. In this extract Philip Pullman uses **language that appeals to our senses**.

Philip Pullman's descriptions of landscape and character are not just visual descriptions: he also asks us to use our senses of hearing, touch and smell.

a) Write down the following quotations from the extract. Next to each, state which of our senses is being appealed to.

they felt one or two drops splash coldly on their cheeks.

one of those high harsh cries sounded very close by, jarring their ears and frightening them horribly.

and a drift of putrescent stink wafted from her every time she moved.

b) Using the three quotations above, and others that you can find, write a paragraph about the effect that Philip Pullman achieves in his description by appealing, not only to the sense of sight, but to the senses of hearing, touch and smell.

Writing to imagine

FOUNDATION TIER TASKS

 1 WRITING ABOUT THE NOVEL

Write a short description in two sections, describing:

- the harpy's appearance and behaviour
- Lyra's and Will's reactions to it

Use the writing frame below as a guide.

Para	Look at...	You could start...
Part 1: describe the harpy's appearance and behaviour		
1	the creature's first appearance *The thing was … time she moved.* lines 20–34	*Their first impression was that the creature was a cross between a vulture and a woman…*
2	its reaction to being spoken to by the children *For answer … nowhere to hide.* 39–45	*It screamed…*
3	its reaction to Will's threats *The harpy's sickening … her sleep!* 51–5	*In response to Will's threat, the harpy…*
4	its response to being attacked by Lady Salmakia *The effect on the harpy … serpents.* 67–71	*As soon as it realised that it had been attacked…*
Part 2: describe Lyra's and Will's reactions to the harpy		
5	the children's first reactions at seeing the creature *Will and Lyra … repelled as Will.* 35–8	*The children felt sick at the sight of the harpy…*
6	their reactions to the harpy's scream *Will clutched … nowhere to hide.* 40–5	*The jet of noise had a powerful effect on the children…*
7	Will's thoughts about using the knife *He set his hand … that door.* 46–50	*Will thought about using the knife to…*
8	what they learn after the harpy is attacked by Lady Salmakia *She was unhurt … for some reason.* 82–6	*Studying the harpy's reaction to the attack, they realised that…*

2 WRITING YOUR OWN FANTASY EXTRACT

Write an extract from a fantasy story, beginning:

As they approached the massive iron gates, they were aware of a shadow...

Planning and drafting

Remember that you are writing an *extract* from a story – not the complete story.

You could follow the structure of the extract from *The Amber Spyglass*:

- description of the characters arriving in a new and frightening place
- sudden appearance of a terrifying creature or human figure
- the characters' reactions to the creature's behaviour and appearance

You might want to use:

- comparisons (look back at page 125):
  literal comparisons, impressions, similes, metaphors
- language which appeals to different senses (page 125)

FOUNDATION & HIGHER TIER TASK

 ### WRITING YOUR OWN EXTRACT IN A CHOSEN GENRE

Write an extract from a novel in a particular genre.

(See pages 128–9 for 'the moderator's view' on how to tackle this question.)

You could start with any of the quotations on this page.

Western
'I don't like it. It's too quiet,' whispered Jed, reloading his Winchester and squinting up at the ridge...

Crime
'The explanation is simple,' said Battersby, lighting his pipe. 'Only one person had a cast-iron alibi...'

Horror
The thing which crawled from the coffin bore no resemblance to the body which had been placed in it...

Fantasy
Eldan felt old: even for a wizard, eleven hundred years was an advanced age...

Romance
His voice, when at last he spoke, was husky and surprised. 'You're... you're beautiful,' he whispered, gazing down into the blueness of her eyes...

Supernatural
The candles flickered and she felt a sudden drop in temperature...

Science fiction
'Anxiety is illogical,' declared Zarn, reading her thoughts. 'These are merely different life-forms...'

HIGHER TIER TASK

 ### WRITING ABOUT THE NOVEL

What are your impressions of this extract from *The Amber Spyglass*?

Write about:

- the feelings this extract arouses in you
- what might be found frightening or horrifying in it

Support your answer by reference to details from the text.

Remember to put quotation marks round any words or phrases from the story that you have used.

You could start:
My first response to this extract was...

The moderator's view

★ **Write an extract from a novel in a particular genre.**

STEP 1: READ THE QUESTION CAREFULLY

This is the type of task you could submit for your original writing coursework (which counts for 5% of your total mark for English). The task tests your ability to write to imagine, explore and entertain and focuses on how well you can interest a reader when you tell a story. You will be assessed on how well you can:

- use elements of your chosen genre effectively
- organise your ideas into sentences and paragraphs
- use a range of sentence structures effectively with accurate punctuation and spelling

STEP 2: SENTENCE STRUCTURE

An important assessment objective for all of your writing is the ability to use sentence structure effectively. This is very useful when writing to imagine, explore and entertain.

- Write a long descriptive sentence where (F) you describe the setting of your story.
- Write a short sentence which draws attention to the arrival of a new character.

- Write a paragraph in your chosen genre which includes a variety of sentence types. The sentence length should help the reader to appreciate whether this is an exciting or descriptive part of your story.

STEP 3: THE USE OF LANGUAGE

Try to imagine your characters in as much detail as possible. What do they look and sound like? How do they move?

Describe one of the main characters in your story using each of the following:

- a simile
- a metaphor
- language which appeals to two of your senses

- Describe one of the main characters H in your story using literal comparisons, impressions, similes and metaphors.
- Describe the character in a way that will appeal to your reader's senses of sight, hearing, touch and smell.

STEP 4: PLANNING AND DRAFTING

Choose a genre that you enjoy. Look back at page 124 to remind yourself about the typical features of your chosen genre in terms of:

- characters
- language
- plots
- events
- settings
- themes

STEP 5: WRITING TO IMAGINE, EXPLORE AND ENTERTAIN

You are now going to use the skills you have practised in this unit to write an extract in your chosen genre. Remember, you are writing an extract; you don't need an introduction, a middle and an ending. Instead, concentrate on bringing *part* of a story vividly to life. You should:

- remember the genre you are writing in throughout
- use comparisons and language which appeals to the senses
- use vocabulary which is appropriate for your chosen genre
- use sentences and paragraphs effectively
- present your work accurately and neatly

STEP 6: SAMPLE ANSWER

Read this introduction from a sample answer.

> Eldan felt old: even for a wizard, eleven hundred years was an advanced age. His skin was so thin that you could see his veins quite clearly, as if through crazed glass. Crazed glass covered his forehead which pulsed with ancient fury that his land had been taken. His land had been taken and he was the only survivor.
>
> Eldan felt cold: even for a wizard, the wind atop this promontory was extreme.
>
> And he had to wait for Gerfin.
>
> Instantaneously, the cap of the promontory rose: Gerfin appeared in a shower of molten lava and groaned, 'Eldan, you're ...'

> This student is showing clear control of genre and structure. The choice of names helps to keep a sharp focus on this particular genre: fantasy. You don't gain more marks by simply writing more; you gain more marks by showing your teacher or examiner your writing skills. This student has shown lots of skills in only a few lines. You can gain an A* grade for 3 sides of writing, so concentrate on control.

! Quick tip   Keep the genre and structure in mind at all times.

Outsiders

In this unit you will:

- compare two extracts about childhood
- examine the language of biography and autobiography
- write a biographical article and some autobiography

The two extracts which follow are both about childhood in the middle of the twentieth century.

Billy

Billy is a biography of the Scottish comedian and actor Billy Connolly, written by his wife Pamela Stephenson. In this extract she describes a period in the early 1950s when Billy was nine and had joined the Scouts.

Later on, when Billy graduated to becoming a Scout, he found the boys were divided into patrols that had animal names. He had fancied himself as a Cobra or a Buffalo and was embarrassed
5 to be placed among the Peewits. However, being a Scout gave him a love of the outdoors that has never left him. Billy still jokes about the novelty of a country visit for Glasgow city children of the time: 'They take you to the countryside once a year. It's
10 supposed to be good for you. The teachers say: "See that green stuff over there? Grass. See the brown things walking about on it? Cows. Don't break them and be back here in half an hour."'

Scouts had their own campground with a real
15 totem pole at Auchengillan, near Loch Lomond, but Wolf Cubs went on day trips to nearby jamborees and threw themselves into the annual bob-a-job fund-raiser, doing jobs for neighbours for a shilling a time. Billy loved having the chance to visit
20 strangers' houses and observe their lives. He was particularly curious about people who seemed to be different from him. The social differences in people and the rigidity of class divisions were just now becoming apparent to him. Not yet imbued with
25 working-class pride, or fury at those born into more advantageous stations in life, he was intrigued by the variety in society and comfortably embraced people of all classes.

He had one great customer, a wonderful
30 upper-class man in Byres Road. To his amazement, this gentleman wore a sports jacket, flannels and tie around the house, and warmly welcomed Billy whenever he appeared. 'Oh, is that you? Come in, sit down!'

35 Billy's task was to polish all his shoes, and he had an enormous collection, brown brogues with curved designs on them, and black Oxfords. All the polishes and brushes were laid out, and the two of them would sit on either side of the fire. Billy would
40 go to work on his shoes, and the gentleman would tell him all about his early life in the Caribbean. Nowadays Billy has a ridiculously large collection of shoes and boots (73 pairs on my last count), several of which are brogues and Oxfords. Buying these
45 shoes and keeping them shipshape has very pleasant associations, for the gentleman's kind and appreciative treatment of Billy was rare and very meaningful for him. 'Do you collect stamps?' the man would ask. 'Well, I've got some for you ... from
50 Trinidad and Tobago!'

Billy's great affection for many 'upper-class' people seems to stem from the great kindness he received as a Wolf Cub. He has often been
55 criticized for such friend- ships, as if he were somehow betraying his roots. As a 'classless'

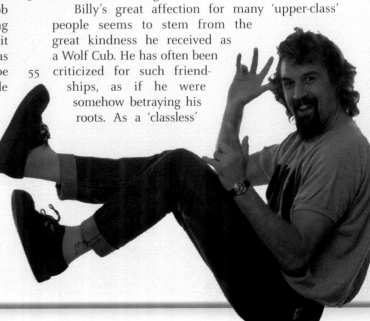

60 Australian, I have always been astounded by all that hoo-ha. Fortunately, Billy's attitude is a sensible one: 'What am I supposed to say? ... "I can't come to dinner with you because I'm working-class"? I'd look such a prick.'

65 Sometimes Billy's bob-a-job task would involve cleaning out the cellars of wealthy folk who lived at the top of the hill. As he sorted out tents and climbing boots, fishing rods and skis, he thought, 'God, it must be brilliant being a toff! You can just take off and do these amazing things all the time!'

70 When he wasn't being a Wolf Cub, Billy spent his spare time with a number of close pals who lived near his house. Mrs Magee's grandson Gerald lived on the ground floor of his tenement, and opposite him lived Robert Alexander. Ronnie and Billy Meikle 75 were upstairs, along with Jimmy and Kay Whitelaw. Ian Meikle lived behind them in the next street and Billy could hear him through the wall, practising his pipe-band drums. Billy had a great time with this jolly gang of ruffians. They played rounders, kick-80 the-can, and an omni-directional form of cricket. They had chalk-drawn a set of wickets on the wall with 'LBW' (Leg Before Wicket) written above. Naturally, the wickets could never fall, but they invented an ingenious way to get a player out: they 85 soaked the ball so it made a wet mark to show where it hit the wall.

Another game was a risky assault course, beginning at the Dumbarton Road fruit shop, and continuing fast around the corner into Hyndland Street, where the 90 fishmonger and the remnant shops were practically side by side. The object of the game was to avoid being caught. It was one of Billy's favourites and its name describes the rules. It was called 'steal an orange, slap a fish, and spit on a remnant...

95 ...It was such a relief to be able to escape from home and visit his pals who lived in other towns. Billy McKinnel came from Bearsden, an up-market district in north-west Glasgow. It was absolute luxury to sit watching television on Mrs McKinnel's white-and-100 gold, floral sofa in its squeaky, plastic covering. The Glaswegian comedian Chic Murray, a hefty riot of a man with a tartan suit and a cloth cap, came on the box one day, telling a story about two men called 'Simmet' and 'Drawers' – 'simmet' means singlet in 105 Scotland and, of course, 'drawers' are underpants. Chic's tale was all wordplay and absolutely the funniest thing Billy had ever heard. Mr and Mrs McKinnel were roaring along with the boys. In the story, the Drawers' son had just announced to his

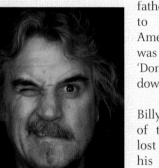

110 father that he wanted to go and live in America, and his father was admonishing him: 'Don't let the Drawers down!'

115 At that moment, Billy slid over the arm of the couch, for he lost all mastery over his body. He lay on 120 the floor completely convulsed, and Billy says he knew right then, without a shadow of a doubt, that he would spend his life being a funny man. The only comedians he'd previously heard 125 were radio stars like Ted Ray, who all had English accents. Chic Murray, and the variety theatre comic Jimmy Logan, had a profound effect on Billy because they spoke with Glaswegian accents and talked 130 about things that were familiar to him.

One afternoon in March 2001, spluttering laughter from a thousand mourners violates the sombre atmosphere of Glasgow Cathedral. Billy has stepped into the pulpit, nicely understated in a black 135 suit, with bright orange Buddha beads and a diamanté scarf. 'I bet you never thought you'd see me here!' He smirks at the largely Protestant congregation.

Billy glances down at Jimmy Logan's Saltire-draped coffin lying beneath him in the nave. 'I made 140 him laugh one lunchtime,' he boasts. 'There was ham on the menu so I told him, "You've been doing it for years, so you might as well have a bit!"'

admonishing	telling off
convulsed	creased up with laughter
diamanté	a brightly sparkling material
largely Protestant	Billy was brought up a Catholic
Saltire-draped	covered with the Scottish flag
ham	it can also mean overacting

MY PLACE

Australian writer and artist Sally Morgan wrote her autobiography *My Place* as a celebration of her aboriginal grandparents. In this extract she describes the moment at school when she first understood that the children in her class had different backgrounds, even though they were all from the same town of Manning.

It was early in Grade Three that I developed my infallible Look At The Lunch method for telling which part of Manning my class-mates came from. I knew I came from the rough-and-tumble part, where there were teenage gangs called Bodgies and Widgies, and where hardly anyone looked after their garden. There was another part of Manning that, before I'd started school, I had been unaware   5 of. The residents there preferred to call it Como. The houses were similar, only in better condition. The gardens were neat and tidy, and I'd heard there was carpet on the floors.

Children from Como always had totally different lunches to children from Manning. They had pieces of salad, chopped up and sealed in plastic containers.   10 Their cake was wrapped neatly in grease-proof paper, and they had real cordial in

a proper flask. There was a kid in our class whose parents were so wealthy that they gave him bacon sandwiches for lunch.   15

By contrast, kids from Manning drank from the water fountain and carried sticky jam sandwiches in brown paper bags.

The kids at school had also   20 begun asking us what country we came from. This puzzled me because, up until then, I'd thought we were the same as them.

If we insisted that we came from Australia, they'd reply, 'Yeah, but what about   25
ya parents, bet they didn't come from Australia'.

One day, I tackled Mum about it as she washed the dishes.

'What do you mean, "Where do we come from?"'

'I mean, what country. The kids at school want to know what country we
come from. They reckon we're not Aussies. Are we Aussies, Mum?'   30

Mum was silent. Nan grunted in a cross sort of way, then got up from the
table and walked outside.

'Come on, Mum, what are we?'

'What do the kids at school say?'

'Anything. Italian, Greek, Indian.'   35

'Tell them you're Indian.'

I got really excited, then. 'Are we really? Indian!' It sounded so exotic.

'When did we come here?' I added.

'A long time ago', Mum replied. 'Now, no more questions. You just tell them
you're Indian.'   40

It was good to finally have an answer and it satisfied our playmates. They
couldn't quite believe we were Indian, they just didn't want us pretending we
were Aussies when we weren't.

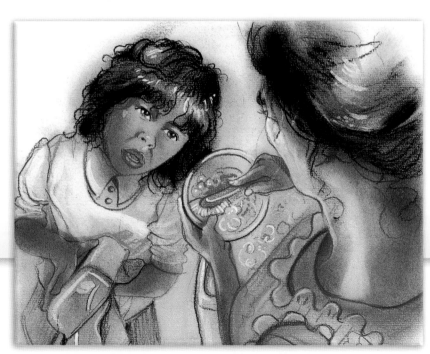

The power of language

Key features of the texts are:

 1 direct speech

2 juxtaposition

3 biographical and autobiographical writing

1 **DIRECT SPEECH**

There are two ways of reporting what somebody says: direct speech and indirect speech. **Direct speech** uses the speaker's actual words. In **indirect** (or **reported**) **speech**, the writer reports what the speaker has said but does not use the speaker's exact words.

For example: *'Write this down,' she said.* (direct speech)
She told us to write it down. (indirect or reported speech)

The writers of both extracts use direct speech, but the effects are different.

a) Find three examples of direct speech from different phases of Billy's life:

- his time in the Scouts
- an occasion in childhood when he watched television at a friend's house
- an episode in his adult life when he spoke at a funeral

b) Write a paragraph to explain why you think Pamela Stephenson decided to use direct speech in recounting these incidents. In other words, why was it important for us to read the speaker's exact words in each case?

Think, for example, about:

- the language used by the teachers and the instructions they issued
- the tone of the man from Byres Road's speech
- Billy's attitude to his friendships with upper-class people
- the wordplay in Chic Murray's tale
- Billy's wordplay at the funeral
- the fact that Billy has spent most of his adult life as a comedian

c) Reread the second section of the extract from *My Place*. Most of it is in direct speech. In groups of three, redraft the section from *The kids at school...* to *...tell them you're Indian* as though it were two short scenes from a television drama – scene one, the playground; scene two, the kitchen.

You could start:

Scene one: the playground

A group of children have gathered round Sally and her brother and sister.

CHILD 1 *So where d'ya come from?*

SALLY (*puzzled*) *Australia.*

CHILD 2 *Yeah, but what about...*

When you have completed the play script, act it out (don't feel that you have to imitate Australian accents). Then discuss how realistic the dialogue sounds.

d) Redraft the discussion in the kitchen (from *One day...*) wholly in *indirect* speech. You could start:

One day, when I tackled Mum about where we had come from, she asked what I meant...

e) Now write a paragraph to explain why direct speech is more effective than indirect speech at this point in Sally's story. Think about:

- the realistic sound of the schoolchildren's reply: *Yeah, but...*
- Sally's explanation that *Where do we come from?* means *What country?*
- her use of the word *Aussies*
- Nan's grunt and departure from the room
- Sally's insistence: *Come on, Mum, what are we?*
- Mum's brief reply: *Tell them you're Indian.*
- Mum's *Now, no more questions...*

2 JUXTAPOSITION

> **Juxtaposition** is the placing of one item next to another for particular effect.

Writers of biography and autobiography often juxtapose incidents or facts in order to make a particular point.

a) Write a paragraph to explain what point Pamela Stephenson is making when she juxtaposes the account of Billy watching television as a child with the funeral of the Scottish comedian Jimmy Logan. How does the juxtaposition help us to understand the kind of person Billy Connolly has become and the events that influenced him?

b) Juxtaposition can be used very effectively to point out a contrast. Look back at the first three paragraphs of the extract by Sally Morgan (*It was early … brown paper bags.*). Write a paragraph to explain how Sally Morgan contrasts the two neighbourhoods of Manning by juxtaposing descriptions.

For example, look at the contrasts she points out by juxtaposing:

- the account of her own neighbourhood (*I knew I came from…*) with the account of the other part of Manning (*The residents there…*) – think about names (*Bodgies, Como*), houses and gardens
- the descriptions of the children's lunches

3 BIOGRAPHICAL AND AUTOBIOGRAPHICAL WRITING

> In a **biography**, an author writes about someone else's life; an **autobiography** is an account of the writer's own life.

- Because biographies are accounts of someone else's life, they are written mainly in the **third person**: *Later on, when **Billy graduated** to becoming a Scout, **he found** the boys were divided into patrols that had animal names.*
- Autobiographies are written from the subject's own point of view and are therefore mainly in the **first person**: *I knew I came from the rough-and-tumble part…*

a) Write down three important sentences from *Billy*, written in the third person, and from *My Place*, written in the first person.

b) Biographies are not written wholly in the third person, and autobiographies are not wholly in the first. Find examples in *My Place* where Sally Morgan uses the third person in order to convey other people's feelings. For example, look at sentences about:

- the residents in the other part of Manning
- the children at school
- Mum
- Nan

Although Pamela Stephenson's biography is mainly in the third person, most of the account is told from Billy's **viewpoint**.

For example:

It was such a relief to be able to escape from home and visit his pals who lived in other towns.

c) Write down other examples of sentences which, although in the third person, give Billy's viewpoint. Look, for example, at accounts of:

- joining a Scout patrol
- visiting the countryside
- watching television on the McKinnels' sofa
- Chic Murray's tale and Billy's reaction to it

Writing biography and autobiography

FOUNDATION TIER TASKS

1 WRITING AN AUTOBIOGRAPHY

Write about an episode from your own life. Choose a single moment or incident in which something important happened.

> **Planning and drafting**
>
> Use the extract from Sally Morgan's autobiography as a model. For example, you could write about:
>
> - the moment when you realised something important about your school, your neighbourhood or your friends (as Sally Morgan does in paragraphs 1 to 3)
>
> - a time when you had an important conversation with your parents or other adults (as she does in the second section of the extract).
>
> Think about using:
>
> - direct speech; juxtaposition, to highlight contrasts (question 2b) and first- and third-person sentences, for variety (questions 3b and 3c)

2 WRITING A BIOGRAPHY

Write a short biography of a well-known person for a children's encyclopedia.

> **Planning and drafting**
>
> Pick a person you are interested in and know something about. For example, you could choose to write about someone who is historically important or a sports-person or someone from the world of entertainment.
>
> First make some notes. The writing frame below has examples of notes that you might make in preparation for writing an entry on Nelson Mandela.

> **You could start:**
>
> *It was in my third year at primary school that I first realised...*
>
> or
>
> *One day I decided to ask my grandmother why...*

Para	Notes	You could start...
1	• born 1918, at Umtata in the Transkei, South Africa • called Rolihlahla as a child – means 'stirring up trouble' • spent childhood herding cattle • sent away to school	*Nelson Mandela was born in 1918 at Umtata in the Transkei, South Africa. Nicknamed Rolihlahla – which means 'stirring up trouble' – he spent his childhood herding cattle, until being sent away to school...*
2	• married his first wife, Evelyn • qualified as a lawyer • became angry about the system of apartheid	*After marrying his first wife, Evelyn...*
3	• 1944: joined the African National Congress • 1952: put in charge of ANC's peaceful protests • thousands of ANC supporters arrested in the 1950s • 1956: tried for treason	*In 1944 Mandela...*
4	• 1960: after 69 protestors killed in the Sharpeville Massacre, he helped to form Umkhonto we Sizwe (Spear of the Nation) – secret organisation to plan sabotage against the government	*A turning-point came in 1960...*
5	• married his second wife, Winnie • 1962: arrested and sentenced to five years in prison • 1964: second trial – given life sentence	*Now married to his second wife...*
6	• became a worldwide symbol of resistance to apartheid	*In the three decades that followed...*
7	• 11 February 1990: released • 1991: end of apartheid • 1994: became first black President of South Africa	*Mandela was finally released from prison on...*

FOUNDATION & HIGHER TIER TASK

 WRITING BIOGRAPHY

Write a section from a full-length biography of a well-known person who interests you. You could choose a figure you have studied in the school curriculum, for example, or somebody from the world of sport or entertainment.

(See pages 138–9 for 'the moderator's view' on how to tackle this question.)

HIGHER TIER TASK

 ANALYSING THE LANGUAGE

Explain how Pamela Stephenson and Sally Morgan, through their content and use of language, provide insights into life as it was in 1950s Glasgow and 1960s Western Australia.

Planning and drafting

Think about the ways in which they provide local background details.

Refer, among other things, to their use of:

- direct speech (e.g. the instructions issued by Billy's teachers, and Sally's conversation with her mother)
- juxtaposition
- first- or third-person sentences

You could start:

Both writers have chosen to describe the experiences of people who, for different reasons, did not have easy childhoods. For example…

137

The moderator's view

> Write a section from a full-length biography of a well-known person who interests you. You could choose a figure you have studied in the school curriculum, for example, or somebody from the world of sport or entertainment.

STEP 1: READ THE QUESTION CAREFULLY

Biographical writing could be used for your original writing coursework. This counts for 5% of your overall mark for English. You are being assessed on your ability to write to imagine, explore and entertain by writing part of the biography of a well-known person who interests you. You will only be able to complete this task after you have done some background research.

In this piece of coursework, you should focus on:

- purpose and audience
- layout and structure
- choosing effective vocabulary for any direct speech
- accurate punctuation

Only one piece of coursework in your folder has to be in your own handwriting. The remainder, including this one, can be word-processed. Word-processing your work can help it look much clearer, especially if you have used direct speech.

STEP 2: PUNCTUATION

- Write down sentences with examples of the (F) following punctuation: full stops, commas, question marks, exclamation marks and speech marks.

- Reread the extract from *Billy* on pages 130–1. Find and explain three different uses of the comma.

- Write a paragraph that includes examples of: colons, semi-colons, apostrophes to show omission and apostrophes to show possession.

STEP 3: THE USE OF LANGUAGE

Try to make any direct speech that you use sound as realistic as possible. Think carefully about the person you are writing about – how would they speak in a particular situation?

- Try to think of as many variations as (F) possible for the word 'said'. For example: *'That is my best friend,' concluded the schoolboy.*

- Write a short section of dialogue using 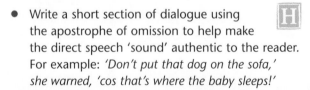 the apostrophe of omission to help make the direct speech 'sound' authentic to the reader. For example: *'Don't put that dog on the sofa,' she warned, 'cos that's where the baby sleeps!'*

STEP 4: PLANNING AND DRAFTING

Before planning your section of biography, think carefully about the person you want to write about. Pick an important moment in their adult life or an episode from childhood which has significance for the kind of person they were to become.

For example, you might choose to write about Nelson Mandela (see the details on page 136) and either:

- recount an episode from childhood which helped to give him the nickname Rolihlahla (showing how significant this was for someone who later 'stirred up trouble')

or

- describe his release from prison in 1990

STEP 5: WRITING TO IMAGINE, EXPLORE AND ENTERTAIN

You are now going to use all of the skills that you have learned in this unit to write your own piece of biographical writing. This task is based upon your research of a well-known person who interests you; communicate your interest by trying to **entertain** your audience.

STEP 6: SAMPLE ANSWER

Read this section from a sample answer.

> Having been informed that he and the other prisoners were to leave Robben Island, Mandela had a strange mixture of feelings: a sense of excitement at the task to come, thankfulness towards his supporters, a fear of the unknown and the oddest feelings of regret at leaving what had been his home for so many years.
>
> However, the prisoners initially only moved from one prison to another: from Robben Island, to Pollsmoor maximum security prison a few miles out of Cape Town. This prison's facilities were far better than they were used to, but it was a world full of concrete and ugliness...

Starting with a correctly punctuated list has given this student the opportunity to impress from the outset.

! Quick tip Never try to use punctuation marks which you are unsure about, and use the less common marks (colons and semi-colons) sparingly.

Poetry from different cultures

In this unit you will:

- read some poems from different cultures and traditions
- consider the different contexts in which they are set
- examine the ways in which the poets achieve their effects

Nothing's Changed

Small round hard stones click
under my heels,
seeding grasses thrust
bearded seeds
5 into trouser cuffs, cans,
trodden on, crunch
in tall, purple-flowering,
amiable weeds.

District Six.
10 No board says it is:
but my feet know,
and my hands,
and the skin about my bones,
and the soft labouring of my lungs,
15 and the hot, white, inwards turning
anger of my eyes.

Brash with glass,
name flaring like a flag,
it squats
20 in the grass and weeds,
incipient Port Jackson trees:
new, up-market, haute cuisine,
guard at the gatepost,
whites only inn.

25 No sign says it is:
but we know where we belong.

I press my nose
to the clear panes, know,
before I see them, there will be
30 crushed ice white glass,
linen falls,
the single rose.

Down the road,
working man's cafe sells
35 bunny chows.
Take it with you, eat
it at a plastic table's top,
wipe your fingers on your jeans,
spit a little on the floor:
40 it's in the bone.

I back from the glass,
boy again,
leaving small mean O
of small, mean mouth.
45 Hands burn
for a stone, a bomb,
to shiver down the glass.
Nothing's changed.

TATAMKHULU AFRIKA

Two Scavengers in a Truck, Two Beautiful People in a Mercedes

At the stoplight waiting for the light
        nine a.m. downtown San Francisco
a bright yellow garbage truck
        with two garbagemen in red plastic blazers
standing on the back stoop   5
        one on each side hanging on
and looking down into
        an elegant open Mercedes
      with an elegant couple in it
The man   10
     in a hip three-piece linen suit
        with shoulder-length blond hair & sunglasses
The young blond woman so casually coifed
        with a short skirt and colored stockings
on the way to his architect's office   15

And the two scavengers up since four a.m.
          grungy from their route
     on the way home
The older of the two with grey iron hair
          and hunched back   20
      looking down like some
          gargoyle Quasimodo
And the younger of the two
        also with sunglasses & long hair
    about the same age as the Mercedes driver   25

And both scavengers gazing down
         as from a great distance
    at the cool couple
as if they were watching some odorless TV ad
     in which everything is always possible   30

And the very red light for an instant
      holding all four close together
    as if anything at all were possible
          between them
    across that small gulf   35
      in the high seas
        of this democracy

LAWRENCE FERLINGHETTI

Half-Caste

Excuse me
standing on one leg
I'm half-caste

Explain yuself
5 wha yu mean
when yu say half-caste
yu mean when picasso
mix red an green
is a half-caste canvas/
10 explain yuself
wha yu mean
when yu say half-caste
yu mean when light an shadow
mix in de sky
15 is a half-caste weather/
well in dat case
england weather
nearly always half-caste
in fact some o dem cloud
20 half-caste till dem overcast
so spiteful dem don't want de sun pass
ah rass/
explain yuself
wha yu mean
25 when yu say half-caste
yu mean tchaikovsky
sit down at dah piano
an mix a black key
wid a white key
30 is a half-caste symphony/

Explain yuself
wha yu mean
Ah listening to yu wid de keen
half of mih ear
35 Ah lookin at yu wid de keen
half of mih eye

and when I'm introduced to yu
I'm sure you'll understand
why I offer yu half-a-hand
40 an when I sleep at night
I close half-a-eye
consequently when I dream
I dream half-a-dream
an when moon begin to glow
45 I half-caste human being
cast half-a-shadow
but yu must come back tomorrow
wid de whole of yu eye
an de whole of yu ear
50 an de whole of yu mind

an I will tell yu
de other half
of my story

JOHN AGARD

Island Man

*(for a Caribbean island man in London who still wakes
up to the sound of the sea)*

Morning
and island man wakes up
to the sound of blue surf
in his head
5 the steady breaking and wombing

wild seabirds
and fishermen pushing out to sea
the sun surfacing defiantly
from the east
10 of his small emerald island   groggily groggily
he always comes back

Comes back to sands
of a grey metallic soar
                  to surge of wheels
15 to dull North Circular roar

muffling muffling
his crumpled pillow waves
island man heaves himself

Another London day

GRACE NICHOLS

Not my Business

They picked Akanni up one morning
Beat him soft like clay
And stuffed him down the belly
Of a waiting jeep.
5   What business of mine is it
       So long they don't take the yam
       From my savouring mouth?

They came one night
Booted the whole house awake
10   And dragged Danladi out,
Then off to a lengthy absence.
       What business of mine is it
       So long they don't take the yam
       From my savouring mouth?

15   Chinwe went to work one day
Only to find her job was gone:
No query, no warning, no probe –
Just one neat sack for a stainless record.
       What business of mine is it
20   So long they don't take the yam
       From my savouring mouth?

And then one evening
As I sat down to eat my yam
A knock on the door froze my hungry hand.
25   The jeep was waiting on my bewildered lawn
Waiting, waiting in its usual silence.

NIYI OSUNDARE

---

from

Unrelated Incidents

this is thi
six a clock
news thi
man said n
5 thi reason
a talk wia
BBC accent
iz coz yi
widny wahnt
10 mi ti talk
aboot thi
trooth wia
voice lik
wanna yoo
15 scruff. if
a toktaboot
thi trooth
lik wanna yoo
scruff yi
20 widny thingk
it wuz troo.
jist wonna yoo
scruff tokn.
thirza right
25 way ti spell
ana right way
ti tok it. this
is me tokn yir
right way a
30 spellin. this
is ma trooth
yooz doant no
thi trooth
yirsellz cawz
35 yi canny talk
right. this is
the six a clock
nyooz. belt up.

TOM LEONARD

143

Language in context

The power of language

Key features of the poems are:

  context

2 meaning and language

3 first and third person

---

1 CONTEXT

> When we study a piece of writing it is important to bear in mind its **context**: the society, the historical period and the culture in which it was written.

A good example of this is Lawrence Ferlinghetti's *Two Scavengers in a Truck, Two Beautiful People in a Mercedes*. The poem ends with the phrase *...of this democracy*.

Politics: living in a democracy

a) In small groups:

- Agree on a definition of the word **democracy**. What makes a country **democratic**?

- Write down three examples of major democracies in different parts of the world. The United Kingdom is one example.

- In which democracy is Ferlinghetti's poem set? How do we know?

- What do you think made Ferlinghetti write this poem? Why does he end the poem with a reference to *this democracy*? What connection is he making between the four people and the fact that they live in a democracy?

History: living with apartheid

b) It is also important to understand at what point in a society's history a poem was written. In small groups, reread Tatamkhulu Afrika's *Nothing's Changed*.

- Discuss what you know about **apartheid** and **segregation**. When was apartheid in force and in which country? When did it officially end? What did segregation involve?

- How do we know that the poem is describing a society in which people are segregated? What are the effects of that segregation on the way people live?

- What does the speaker mean by *boy again* (line 42)? What special meaning does *boy* have in the context of apartheid?

- Was this poem written during or after apartheid? How can you tell? What does the title mean?

Comparing the poems

c) Make brief notes which will help you to compare the two poems *Two Scavengers...* and *Nothing's Changed*. What are the similarities and what are the differences? Look at:

- the contexts: the two political systems under which the poems were written

- the people featured

- the contrasts drawn within each poem

---

2 MEANING AND LANGUAGE

> Poets often choose **vocabulary** and **syntax** (sentence grammar) which are not from Standard English, because it suits the point they are trying to make. They might write in a non-standard **dialect** or represent a particular **accent**. Dialect is a variety of language used by a particular group of people, which has distinctive features of vocabulary and grammar. Accent is the term given to the way people pronounce words according to their regional or social background.

Both Tom Leonard and John Agard chose not to use Standard English when they wrote their poems *Unrelated Incidents* and *Half-Caste*.

Accent and dialect

a) In pairs, discuss how Tom Leonard uses a Scottish accent and dialect in the extract from *Unrelated Incidents*.

- Which words and phrases in particular help to bring out the Scottish voice? Find five or six examples.

- What point is the poem making? How does the non-standard dialect help to convey this point? (Look particularly at lines 30–8. What does he mean by *ma trooth* and what does it have to do with language?)

> **Pidgins** and **creoles** are languages which have developed to allow groups who do not understand each other's language to communicate. Pidgin languages grew up when European traders made contact with African or Asian language communities and they needed to exchange simple information. In time, when children were born who spoke the pidgin language as their mother tongue, it became a creole. In other words, a creole is a pidgin which has become the mother-tongue of a community.

John Agard was originally from Guyana, and his poem, *Half-Caste* has strong Guyanese creole influences. This can be seen in:

- the spelling of single words, e.g. *yuself* (instead of Standard English *yourself*, line 4)

- grammar, e.g. *dem cloud* (instead of *those clouds*, line 19)

b) Make a list of other examples of spellings and syntax which show influences of Guyanese creole in *Half-Caste*. For each one, write down the word or phrase and its Standard English equivalent.

c) Write a paragraph explaining why you think John Agard chose to write the poem in creole, rather than in Standard English. Think about:

- the connection between a creole language and the person who has been called a *half-caste*

- the fact that some people ignorantly think of creole languages as being 'bad' or 'corrupt' English, when in fact they are rule-based languages in their own right, just like English or French.

Comparing the poems

d) Make brief notes which will help you to compare the two poems *Unrelated Incidents* and *Half-Caste*. What are the similarities and what are the differences? Look at:

- the speakers of the two poems – what do they have in common?

- the language of the poems

- the way the language is part of the message in each case

3 FIRST AND THIRD PERSON

> When an author writes from their own viewpoint, using the pronouns *I*, *we* and *us*, they are using the **first person** of the verb. The **third person** is used to describe other people's actions.

There is more on the first and third person on page 135.

a) In pairs, reread the poems on pages 140–3 and write down which ones are in the first person and which are in the third person. Discuss why Tatamkhulu Afrika, Tom Leonard and John Agard might have chosen to write their poems in the first person. What powerful effect do the poems have which would be harder to achieve if they were written in the third person?

b) Reread Niyi Osundare's poem *Not my Business*. What do you notice about the person of the verb in the first three stanzas? For example, look at the verbs *They* **picked**, **Beat** *him*, **stuffed** *him*, *What business of mine* **is** *it...*, *they don't* **take**...

Writing about poetry drawn from different cultures and traditions

FOUNDATION TIER TASKS

 1 WRITING ABOUT THE PEOPLE IN THE POEMS

Choose two or three poems and write about the different people featured in them. Where are they from? How do they feel about things?

Planning and drafting

For example, you could choose to write about:

Nothing's Changed

- Who is describing the incident? What are they angry about (lines 15–16 and 45–7)?

Island Man

- What is his background? Where does he live now and what does he feel about his present way of life?

Two Scavengers...

- Describe the four people featured in the poem. What are the main differences between them?

from *Unrelated Incidents*

- What can you tell about the speaker? Where is he from? What does he feel about the way the BBC News is usually read?

Half-Caste

- What is the speaker's view of the term *half-caste*?

Not my Business

- What do we know about the society in which the speaker lives? How do they feel about what has happened to Akanni, Danladi and Chinwe?

You could start:

Each of these poems features a person. They live in different societies and each has their own story to tell...

2 COMPARING POEMS WHICH POINT OUT CONTRASTS

In *Island Man* the poet Grace Nichols describes the contrast between the man's memories of the Caribbean and the reality of waking up in London. Compare it with one other poem from pages 140–3 which points out a contrast. Say what the contrasts featured in each poem are, and explain how the poets' use of language helps to get them across.

Planning and drafting

You could compare *Island Man* with *Nothing's Changed* or with *Two Scavengers in a Truck, Two Beautiful People in a Mercedes*.

Use the writing frame below as a guide.

Para	Details and language...
Comparing *Island Man* with *Nothing's Changed*	
1	First write about the contrast Grace Nichols describes in *Island Man* between the sounds of the Caribbean and the sounds of London. • compare lines 3–7 with lines 12–16
2	Then compare another poem which describes a contrast: *Nothing's Changed*. Write about the atmosphere and surroundings of the inn and café. • compare lines 22–4 with 34–9
3	Then write about the contrast in the different types of food available. • compare lines 22 and 35
Comparing *Island Man* with *Two Scavengers...*	
1	See section 1 above on *Island Man*.
2	Then compare it with *Two Scavengers...* Look at the contrasts in: • the title of the poem, and the two couples' jobs, vehicles and clothes

FOUNDATION & HIGHER TIER TASK

 COMPARING CONTEXTS

Reread Tatamkhulu Afrika's *Nothing's Changed*. Compare it with another poem to show how important it is to know something about a poem's context. Explain what each poem is about and say why we need to understand the context in which it was written.

(See pages 148–9 for 'the examiner's view' on how to tackle this question.)

Para	You could start...
1	*In* Island Man, *a contrast is drawn between the man's dream-like memories of the Caribbean where he was born and the daily reality of living in London...*
2	*The person in* Nothing's Changed *describes the contrast between the inn and the café...*
3	*The meals are very different...*
1	
2	*In* Two Scavengers... *there is a stark contrast between the lifestyles of the garbagemen and the people in the Mercedes...*

HIGHER TIER TASK

 COMPARING DIFFERENT KINDS OF ENGLISH

The extract from Tom Leonard's *Unrelated Incidents* shows how effective it can be not to use Standard English. Compare it with another poem which is not written in Standard English and comment on the advantages of writing in a non-standard form. In what ways can this help to get the meanings across?

Planning and drafting

You could compare the extract from *Unrelated Incidents* with John Agard's *Half-Caste*.

1 *Unrelated Incidents*
- Describe the language. Give examples of the ways in which the accent is reflected in the spelling.
- Which words and phrases in particular help to bring out the Scottish voice in Tom Leonard's poem?

2 *Half-Caste*
- Describe the language. Give examples of the ways in which it differs from Standard English.

3 Explain in what ways the poets have been able to convey their meanings partly through their choice of a non-standard variety of English.
- Look back at question 2a and think about:
  - what point the poem is making
  - how the non-standard dialect helps to convey this point (look particularly at lines 30–8)
- Look back at 2c and think about:
  - the connection between a creole language and the person who has been called a *half-caste*
  - the fact that some people ignorantly think of creole languages as being 'bad' or 'corrupt' English

You could start:

Poets sometimes choose to write in something other than Standard English. Both Tom Leonard and John Agard have done this, and for comparable reasons...

The examiner's view

Reread Tatamkhulu Afrika's *Nothing's Changed*. **Compare it with another poem to show how important it is to know something about a poem's context. Explain what each poem is about and say why we need to understand the context in which it was written.**

STEP 1: READ THE TEXTS

You will be asked a question on poetry from different cultures and traditions in Section A of Paper 2 in the English exam. You will have 45 minutes to answer one question which is worth 15% of your overall mark for English.

Comparing poems under exam conditions is an important reading skill – you must make sure that you adopt a **reading process**:

- **Read** the question and identify what you are being asked to do.
- **Select** an appropriate poem to compare with the one you have been given.
- **Brainstorm** ideas for both poems.
- **Sequence** your ideas by writing a list of phrases to show similarity and difference.
- **Write** your answer, making sure that you keep to the question.

STEP 2: COMPARING POEMS

Comparing means that you are looking for similarities as well as differences. Remember that you should always support your points with examples.

- Write a list of similarities and differences between what is described in *Nothing's Changed* and *Two Scavengers...* Add *compare* words and phrases for each pair of items. For example:

  - racial inequality
    similarly
    social divisions

  - set in South Africa
    however
    takes place in America

- Write a similar list comparing how the poets use poetic devices and language. For example:

  - describes a scene
    likewise
    paints a vivid picture

  - short stanzas for effect
    whereas
    shape makes rhythm 'jerky'

- Now find and write down a quotation to support each of your points. For example *whites only inn./ No sign says it is:/ but we know where we belong.* would support a point about how *Nothing's Changed* discusses racial segregation.

STEP 3: THE USE OF LANGUAGE

You gain few or no marks for simply identifying a poetic device (such as simile or metaphor). You gain many more marks if you explain what effect the device has and why the poet has chosen to use it.

- Find one example of a poetic device in each of these two poems.
- Explain what effect each device has and how it helps to convey the meaning of the poem.

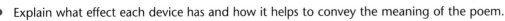

STEP 4: PLANNING AND DRAFTING

First make notes on the context of *Nothing's Changed*. Look back at question 1b on page 144. Think about apartheid and segregation. What does segregation involve? How does it affect people like the speaker? Which period is this poem describing?

You could compare it with *Two Scavengers...* or *Not my Business*.

Two Scavengers...
In which country is this poem set? What is it saying about democracy?

Not my Business
Who are *They*, referred to throughout the poem? Even though we may not know in which particular country the incidents in the poem took place, what can we tell about its political regime? What does the speaker say about each individual's responsibility in a society like that?

For each poem, discuss:

- in what ways the subjects of the poems are oppressed (e.g. through physical hardship, prejudice, being denied an equal chance in life...)
- who are the oppressors (e.g. other citizens, the state...)

STEP 5: COMPARING TWO POEMS

When answering this type of question, you will be assessed using these criteria:

- effective use of quotations
- your ability to highlight similarities and differences between the meaning and the techniques of two poems
- appreciation of what the poets set out to do
- your own understanding of the poems

> Already, this student has started to fulfil the assessment objectives for this task by quoting effectively, comparing each poem's context and appreciating the poets' purposes.

STEP 6: SAMPLE ANSWER

Read this introduction from a sample answer.

> The poem that I have chosen to write about in addition to 'Nothing's Changed' is 'Two Scavengers in a Truck, Two Beautiful People in a Mercedes' by Lawrence Ferlinghetti. It is important with both of these poems to understand their cultural contexts in order to appreciate what the poets are trying to say.
>
> The poems have many similarities, with both of them showing how groups of people can be alienated within a society. 'Nothing's Changed' is set against a background of inequality in post-apartheid South Africa where the disadvantaged voice of the poem says 'we know where we belong'. Similarly, in 'Two Scavengers...' the garbage collectors gaze down at the couple in the Mercedes 'across that small gulf'. The language used here emphasises how divided different social groups are in the United States.
>
> However, the poems are set in very different cultural...

Quick tip Back up your opinions using evidence from the poems.

The poetry of Seamus Heaney and Gillian Clarke

In this unit you will:

- read poems by Seamus Heaney, Gillian Clarke and Gerard Manley Hopkins
- examine the ways in which the poets achieve their effects
- compare their treatment of a particular theme

These three poems are by Seamus Heaney.

Death of a Naturalist

All year the flax-dam festered in the heart
Of the townland; green and heavy headed
Flax had rotted there, weighted down by huge sods.
Daily it sweltered in the punishing sun.
5 Bubbles gargled delicately, bluebottles
Wove a strong gauze of sound around the smell.
There were dragon-flies, spotted butterflies,
But best of all was the warm thick slobber
Of frogspawn that grew like clotted water
10 In the shade of the banks. Here, every spring

I would fill jampotfuls of the jellied
Specks to range on window-sills at home,
On shelves at school, and wait and watch until
The fattening dots burst into nimble-
15 Swimming tadpoles. Miss Walls would tell us how
The daddy frog was called a bullfrog
And how he croaked and how the mammy frog
Laid hundreds of little eggs and this was
Frogspawn. You could tell the weather by frogs too
20 For they were yellow in the sun and brown
In rain.
Then one hot day when fields were rank
With cowdung in the grass the angry frogs
Invaded the flax-dam; I ducked through hedges
25 To a coarse croaking that I had not heard
Before. The air was thick with a bass chorus.
Right down the dam gross-bellied frogs were cocked
On sods; their loose necks pulsed like snails. Some hopped:
The slap and plop were obscene threats. Some sat
30 Poised like mud grenades, their blunt heads farting.
I sickened, turned, and ran. The great slime kings
Were gathered there for vengeance and I knew
That if I dipped my hand the spawn would clutch it.

Digging

Between my finger and my thumb
The squat pen rests; snug as a gun.

Under my window, a clean rasping sound
When the spade sinks into gravelly ground:
5 My father, digging. I look down

Till his straining rump among the flowerbeds
Bends low, comes up twenty years away
Stooping in rhythm through potato drills
Where he was digging.

10 The coarse boot nestled on the lug, the shaft
Against the inside knee was levered firmly.
He rooted out tall tops, buried the bright edge deep
To scatter new potatoes that we picked
Loving their cool hardness in our hands.

15 By God, the old man could handle a spade.
Just like his old man.

My grandfather cut more turf in a day
Than any other man on Toner's bog.
Once I carried him milk in a bottle
20 Corked sloppily with paper. He straightened up
To drink it, then fell to right away

Nicking and slicing neatly, heaving sods
Over his shoulder, going down and down
For the good turf. Digging.

25 The cold smell of potato mould, the squelch and slap
Of soggy peat, the curt cuts of an edge
Through living roots awaken in my head.
But I've no spade to follow men like them.

Between my finger and my thumb
30 The squat pen rests.
I'll dig with it.

Blackberry-Picking

For Philip Hobsbaum

Late August, given heavy rain and sun
For a full week, the blackberries would ripen.
At first, just one, a glossy purple clot
Among others, red, green, hard as a knot.
5 You ate that first one and its flesh was sweet
Like thickened wine: summer's blood was in it
Leaving stains upon the tongue and lust for
Picking. Then red ones inked up and that hunger
Sent us out with milk-cans, pea-tins, jam-pots
10 Where briars scratched and wet grass bleached our boots.
Round hayfields, cornfields and potato-drills
We trekked and picked until the cans were full,
Until the tinkling bottom had been covered
With green ones, and on top big dark blobs burned
15 Like a plate of eyes. Our hands were peppered
With thorn pricks, our palms sticky as Bluebeard's.

We hoarded the fresh berries in the byre.
But when the bath was filled we found a fur,
A rat-grey fungus, glutting on our cache.
20 The juice was stinking too. Once off the bush
The fruit fermented, the sweet flesh would turn sour.
I always felt like crying. It wasn't fair
That all the lovely canfuls smelt of rot.
Each year I hoped they'd keep, knew they would not.

These poems and 'The Field-Mouse' opposite are by Gillian Clarke.

Cold Knap Lake

We once watched a crowd
pull a drowned child from the lake.
Blue-lipped and dressed in water's long green silk
she lay for dead.

Then kneeling on the earth,   5
a heroine, her red head bowed,
her wartime cotton frock soaked,
my mother gave a stranger's child her breath.
The crowd stood silent,
drawn by the dread of it.   10

The child breathed, bleating
and rosy in my mother's hands.
My father took her home to a poor house
and watched her thrashed for almost drowning.

Was I there?   15
Or is that troubled surface something else
shadowy under the dipped fingers of willows
where satiny mud blooms in cloudiness
after the treading, heavy webs of swans
as their wings beat and whistle on the air?   20

All lost things lie under closing water
in that lake with the poor man's daughter.

A Difficult Birth, Easter 1998

An old ewe that somehow till this year
had given the ram the slip. We thought her barren.
Good Friday, and the Irish peace deal close,
and tonight she's serious, restless and hoofing the straw.
5   We put off the quiet supper and bottle of wine
we'd planned, to celebrate if the news is good.

Her waters broke an hour ago and she's sipped
her own lost salty ocean from the ground.
While they slog it out in Belfast, eight decades
10   since Easter 1916, exhausted, tamed by pain,
she licks my fingers with a burning tongue,
lies down again. Two hooves and a muzzle.

But the lamb won't come. You can phone for help
and step into the lane to watch for car lights.
15   This is when the whitecoats come to the women,
well-meaning, knowing best, with their needles and forceps.
So I ease my fingers in, take the slippery head
in my right hand, two hooves in my left.

We strain together, harder than we dared.
20   I feel a creak in the limbs and pull till he comes
in a syrupy flood. She drinks him, famished, and you find us
peaceful, at a cradling that might have been a death.
Then the second lamb slips through her opened door,
the stone rolled away.

The Field-Mouse

Summer, and the long grass is a snare drum.
The air hums with jets.
Down at the end of the meadow,
far from the radio's terrible news,
5 we cut the hay. All afternoon
its wave breaks before the tractor blade.
Over the hedge our neighbour travels his field
in a cloud of lime, drifting our land
with a chance gift of sweetness.

10 The child comes running through the killed flowers,
his hands a nest of quivering mouse,
its black eyes two sparks burning.
We know it will die and ought to finish it off.
It curls in agony big as itself
15 and the star goes out in its eye.
Summer in Europe, the field's hurt,
and the children kneel in long grass,
staring at what we have crushed.

Before day's done the field lies bleeding,
20 the dusk garden inhabited by the saved, voles,
frogs, a nest of mice. The wrong that woke
from a rumour of pain won't heal,
and we can't face the newspapers.
All night I dream the children dance in grass
25 their bones brittle as mouse-ribs, the air
stammering with gunfire, my neighbour turned
stranger, wounding my land with stones.

Inversnaid

This darksome burn, horseback brown,
His rollrock highroad roaring down,
In coop and in comb the fleece of his foam
Flutes and low to the lake falls home.

5 A windpuff-bonnet of fawn-froth
Turns and twindles over the broth
Of a pool so pitchblack, fell-frowning,
It rounds and rounds Despair to drowning.

Degged with dew, dappled with dew
10 Are the groins of the braes that the brook treads through,
Wiry heathpacks, flitches of fern,
And the beadbonny ash that sits over the burn.

What would the world be, once bereft
Of wet and of wildness? Let them be left,
15 O let them be left, wildness and wet;
Long live the weeds and the wilderness yet.

GERARD MANLEY HOPKINS
1881

Language in context

The power of language

Key features of the poems are:

1 themes

2 comparisons

3 alliteration

1 THEMES

A **theme** is a major subject or idea which runs through a poem, play or novel. A writer will usually return to a theme several times, dealing with it in different ways and looking at it from a variety of angles.

Common themes include: conflict, parents and children, and the difference between appearance and reality.

A major theme of the poems on pages 150–3 is the relationship between people and nature.

a) In pairs, discuss the following questions about the theme of people and nature:

- What did the child in *Blackberry-Picking* learn each year about nature? How do you feel it affected him?

- In what sense does the nature-lover 'die' in *Death of a Naturalist*? What happens?

- What does the speaker in *Digging* recall about his father's and grandfather's work on the land? What is his own connection with their digging?

- What do people feel about the dead creature in *The Field-Mouse*? What is the connection between the events in the meadow and the people's feelings about news of the wider world?

- What aspect of nature is celebrated in *Inversnaid*? Why should it be so important?

2 COMPARISONS

Poets use comparisons to express their meanings. These comparisons might be:

- literal comparisons
- similes
- metaphors

A **simile** is a means of comparing things in an unusual or unexpected way in which the writer creates an image in the reader's mind. A simile uses the words *like* or *as*. A **metaphor** serves the same purpose, but does not involve the use of *like* or *as*: the person or object is described as though they really were something else.

For example, in Heaney's *Blackberry-Picking* we find:

- a literal comparison:
  its flesh was sweet
  Like thickened wine (lines 5–6)

- a simile:
  big dark blobs burned
  Like a plate of eyes (14–15)

- a metaphor:
  *Then red ones **inked up*** (8)

a) In pairs, find the following lines in the poems on pages 150–3. Then discuss what kind of comparison each one is (not all of them are clear-cut), and make a note of how effective each one is in the context of the poem. For example, you might write down: '*Then red ones **inked up**' METAPHOR. It is as though the red berries were being painted with black ink.*

*Poised **like mud grenades*** (Death of a Naturalist, 30)

*their blunt heads **farting**.* (Death of a Naturalist, 30)

*The squat pen rests; **snug as a gun**.* (Digging, 2)

*A **rat-grey** fungus* (Blackberry-Picking, 19)

*Then the second lamb slips through **her opened door*** (A Difficult Birth..., 23)

*Blue-lipped and **dressed in water's long green silk*** (Cold Knap Lake, 3)

*shadowy under the **dipped fingers** of willows* (Cold Knap Lake, 17)

*the long grass **is a snare drum**.* (The Field-Mouse, 1)

*its black eyes **two sparks burning**.* (The Field-Mouse, 12)

*It curls in agony **big as itself*** *(The Field-Mouse, 14)*

*and **the star goes out** in its eye. (The Field-Mouse, 15)*

*their bones **brittle as mouse-ribs** (The Field-Mouse, 25)*

*the air / **stammering with gunfire** (The Field-Mouse, 25–6)*

*This darksome burn, **borseback brown** (Inversnaid, 1)*

*In coop and in comb **the fleece** of his foam (Inversnaid, 3)*

b) Write some lines of poetry (or a paragraph of descriptive prose) on the theme of people and nature, using all three types of comparison.

> Metaphors and similes are known collectively as **imagery**. If there are several metaphors and similes in a poem all comparing things with animals, for example, we talk about the animal imagery in the poem.

c) In pairs, discuss what kind of imagery can be seen in lines 16, 19 and 27 of Gillian Clarke's poem *The Field-Mouse* (look at the metaphors to do with the field and the land). Write a paragraph to show how that imagery contributes to the meaning of the poem as a whole.

3 ALLITERATION

> **Alliteration** is the repetition of consonant sounds to gain a particular effect.

For example, in the poem *Island Man* on page 142, the repetition of *s* sounds in the following lines possibly echoes the sound of tyres on the road:

Comes back to sands
of a grey metallic soar
>   *to surge of wheels (12–14)*

a) In pairs, discuss what effect the repeated *s* sounds have in lines 15–20 of Gillian Clarke's *Cold Knap Lake*.

b) The nineteenth-century poet Gerard Manley Hopkins was a great admirer of Old English poetry, written in the eighth to eleventh centuries. Poems from that period did not rhyme, but were full of alliteration. Usually, each line was divided into two halves, and words in the first half-line would alliterate with words in the second half-line. For example:

Grendles grape | under geapne hrof
(Grendel's claw, under wide roof – from the Old English epic poem Beowulf)

Or there might be alliteration on one sound in the first half-line and a different sound in the second.

Write a paragraph explaining how Hopkins imitates Old English poetry in *Inversnaid*. Quote three or four examples to show how the alliteration works in half-lines, and comment on its effectiveness.

c) Seamus Heaney is an admirer of Hopkins. Look at lines 12–14 of his *Digging*. Write a paragraph commenting on the way he uses alliteration in a similar style to Hopkins and Old English poetry.

d) In pairs, compare the use of alliteration in Heaney's *Digging*, Clarke's *Cold Knap Lake* and Hopkins's *Inversnaid*. Which poem uses it most effectively, in your opinion? Where does it most successfully help to get the meaning across? (Look back at questions 3b and 3c for ideas on Hopkins and Heaney. For *Cold Knap Lake*, look especially at lines 15–20: how does the alliteration help to convey the meaning?)

Comparing the poetry of Heaney, Clarke and Hopkins

FOUNDATION TIER TASKS

 1 DESCRIBING THE EVENTS

Some of the poems on pages 150–3 tell a story or recount an episode. Pick one of the following and retell what happens as though you were one of the people involved:

Death of a Naturalist
Blackberry-Picking
A Difficult Birth, Easter 1998
Cold Knap Lake
The Field-Mouse

Planning and drafting

Reread the poem you have chosen to write about. Then make notes on:

- the main things that happened
- your feelings as the incident took place, and afterwards

Remember to write as though you were actually there: *Then one of our neighbour's children ran up to us...*

If you were writing about *The Field-Mouse*, you could start:

I remember something that happened last summer, one day when we were cutting hay, down the end of the meadow...

2 CREATING A STORYBOARD

Imagine you were making a short film to illustrate one of the poems on pages 150–3. Draw a storyboard to show five or six key frames and write a commentary to explain what you have done.

Planning and drafting

There are examples of storyboards on pages 10–13 and 30–3. Remember that each frame should have:

- a drawing of what the viewer will see
- an explanation of the kind of shot or angle
- a note on timing
- a statement about any sound effects, music, dialogue or voice-over

Use the storyboards below and opposite, based on Seamus Heaney's *Digging*, as a guide. Frames have been drawn to represent lines 1–5 and 15–19.

SHOT NO.	TIME IN SECONDS	SOUND EFFECTS	DESCRIPTION OF SHOT	SHOT	DIALOGUE
1	00–02	Someone digging in the garden outside.	**Interior shot:** A writer's hand, holding a pen poised over a blank sheet of paper.		**Voice-over:** *Between my finger and my thumb The squat pen rests; snug as a gun.* (lines 1–2)
2	03–04	The digging sound, much louder.	**Exterior:** A spade being thrust into soil by a big hob-nailed boot.		**VO:** *Under my window, a clean rasping sound When the spade sinks into gravelly ground:* (3–4)
3	05–06	The digger's heavy breathing, over the sound of the spade.	**Ext:** looking up at the window. The writer's face appears, looking down to his father, digging.		**VO:** *My father, digging. I look down...* (5)

SHOT NO.	TIME IN SECONDS	SOUND EFFECTS	DESCRIPTION OF SHOT	SHOT	DIALOGUE
9	18–20	Digging from outside.	**Int:** The writer looks up at the wall.		**Voice-over:** *By God, the old man could handle a spade. Just like his old man. (15–16)*
10	21–3	Faint gentle fiddle music, over the digging.	**Int: Close-up** of an old, faded photograph: a farm labourer with a long spade, standing in front of a pile of cut turf.		**VO:** *My grand-father cut more turf in a day Than any other man on Toner's bog. (17–18)*
11	24–6	Fiddle louder as the digging sound fades.	**Ext: Mid-shot** of a little boy, in 1940s clothes – baggy flannel shorts to knees, braces… He carries an earthenware bottle of milk, very carefully.		**VO:** *Once I carried him milk in a bottle… (19)*

FOUNDATION & HIGHER TIER TASK

 WRITING ABOUT THEMES

Compare the ways in which Seamus Heaney, Gillian Clarke and Gerard Manley Hopkins treat the theme of nature and people.

(See pages 158–9 for 'the examiner's view' on how to tackle this question.)

HIGHER TIER TASK

ANALYSING THE LANGUAGE OF POETRY

Select three poems – one by Seamus Heaney, one by Gillian Clarke, and one other – which show how poets use effects such as imagery and alliteration to convey their ideas and develop themes.

Planning and drafting

You could choose to write about Heaney's *Blackberry-Picking*, Clarke's *The Field-Mouse* and Hopkins's *Inversnaid*.

1 Look back at your responses to the different parts of questions 2 and 3.

2 Write about the imagery in:
   - *Blackberry-Picking*: look at lines 4, 8, 14–15, 16, 19
   - *The Field-Mouse*: look at lines 1, 2, 6, 12, 14, 15, 25, 26; and the linked imagery of lines 10, 16, 19 and 27
   - *Inversnaid*: look at lines 3, 7, 8

3 Write about the alliteration in:
   - *Blackberry-Picking*: look at lines 17–19, 21–22
   - *Inversnaid*: throughout the poem
   How do Heaney and Hopkins imitate Old English poetry?

4 Show how imagery and alliteration help the poets to express themselves and develop their themes. For example, how do the alliteration and imagery in *Blackberry-Picking* help Heaney to convey the idea that people have to learn about nature and death?

You could start:

In poetry, the language is part of the meaning…

Compare the ways in which Seamus Heaney, Gillian Clarke and Gerard Manley Hopkins treat the theme of nature and people.

STEP 1: READ THE TEXTS

Poems from the *Anthology* are assessed in Section B of the English Literature paper. This one question, for which you will have 60 minutes, counts for 40% of your total mark for English Literature. You will be assessed on your ability to:

- explore the meaning and context of poems, and give your opinions, supported by references
- analyse the writers' use of language
- show insight into the structures and patterns within the poem
- compare and contrast poems
- evaluate poems (say which you think are particularly effective, and why)

STEP 2: COMPARING POEMS

When comparing several poems it is important to use a reading process. Remember to **reread** your chosen poems, **brainstorm** ideas and **sequence** them using language to show similarities and differences.

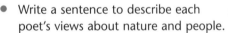 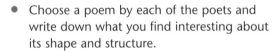

- Write a sentence to describe each poet's views about nature and people.
- Find and write down a quotation to support each of your points.

- Choose a poem by each of the poets and write down what you find interesting about its shape and structure.
- Compare the shape and structure of the poems.
- Explain how each poet uses the shape/structure to support the meaning of the poem.

STEP 3: THE USE OF LANGUAGE

You gain few or no marks for simply identifying a language feature (such as alliteration or metaphor). You gain marks for explaining how a language feature works within the context of a poem.

 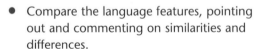

- Find and write down one effective language feature from each of the poems you are comparing.
- Explain why you think that each language feature is effective.

- Compare the language features, pointing out and commenting on similarities and differences.
- Evaluate which of the language features you think is the *most* effective and explain why.

STEP 4: PLANNING AND DRAFTING

Before you start to plan, review what you discussed in response to question 1a on page 154 and make notes. For example, if you chose to write about Seamus Heaney's *Blackberry-Picking*, *Death of a Naturalist* and *Digging*, Gillian Clarke's *The Field-Mouse* and Gerard Manley Hopkins's *Inversnaid*, you could write about:

- the child in *Blackberry-Picking*, who has to learn that death is part of nature
- the effect of the swarming frogs on the nature-lover in *Death of a Naturalist*
- the connection felt by the speaker in *Digging* with his father's and grandfather's work on the land
- the connection between people's feelings about the dead creature in *The Field-Mouse* and the events in the wider world
- the aspect of nature celebrated in *Inversnaid* and its importance to human beings

STEP 5: READING THE POETRY OF HEANEY, CLARKE AND HOPKINS

You are now going to write to compare the work of these three poets. To get a good grade you should:

- compare and evaluate the poems
- fully develop and explain your ideas
- back up your comments with quotations

In the exam, you will have to refer to **two** pre-1914 poems.

STEP 6: SAMPLE ANSWER

Read this introduction from a sample answer.

Beginning your piece of work with a clear plan will help you to cover all parts of the question.

The three poems I have chosen to discuss are: 'Death of a Naturalist' by Seamus Heaney, 'Cold Knap Lake' by Gillian Clarke and 'Inversnaid' by Gerard Manley Hopkins. All three poems deal with the theme of nature and how people interact with it but each poet tackles the theme in their own way. First, I will explain how each poet treats the theme of nature and people in their particular poem. I will then compare the poets' use of language. Finally, I will evaluate how successful each poet has been in his or her purpose.

The theme of nature and people is a recurrent one in the poetry of Seamus Heaney. Being from the country, he is interested in how one affects the other and this is certainly the case in 'Death of a Naturalist'. Heaney writes about his childhood memory of the flax-dam, which 'festered in the heart/Of the townland'. This place is made to seem quite threatening by the words and phrases that Heaney uses to describe it, such as: 'rotted', 'sweltered', 'gargled' and 'bluebottles / wove a strong gauze of sound around the smell.' His description is particularly vivid as it appeals to many of our senses...

Quick tip

Writing about poetry is no different from writing about non-fiction: you still have to make a point, give examples and explain your opinions.

The poetry of Carol Ann Duffy and Simon Armitage

In this unit you will:

- read poems by Carol Ann Duffy, Simon Armitage, Thomas Hardy and Walt Whitman
- compare the poets' use of different poetic forms
- examine the ways in which they achieve their effects

These three poems are by Carol Ann Duffy.

Salome

I'd done it before
(and doubtless I'll do it again,
sooner or later)
woke up with a head on the pillow beside me – whose? –
5 what did it matter?
Good-looking, of course, dark hair, rather matted;
the reddish beard several shades lighter;
with very deep lines around the eyes,
from pain, I'd guess, maybe laughter;
10 and a beautiful crimson mouth that obviously knew
how to flatter …
which I kissed …
Colder than pewter.
Strange. What was his name? Peter?

15 Simon? Andrew? John? I knew I'd feel better
for tea, dry toast, no butter,
so rang for the maid.
And, indeed, her innocent clatter
of cups and plates,
20 her clearing of clutter,
her regional patter,
were just what I needed –
hungover and wrecked as I was from a night on the batter.

Never again!
25 I needed to clean up my act,
get fitter,
cut out the booze and the fags and the sex.
Yes. And as for the latter,
it was time to turf out the blighter,
30 the beater or biter,
who'd come like a lamb to the slaughter
to Salome's bed.

In the mirror, I saw my eyes glitter.
I flung back the sticky red sheets,
35 and there, like I said – and ain't life a bitch –
was his head on a platter.

Stealing

The most unusual thing I ever stole? A snowman.
Midnight. He looked magnificent; a tall, white mute
beneath the winter moon. I wanted him, a mate
with a mind as cold as the slice of ice
5 within my own brain. I started with the head.

Better off dead than giving in, not taking
what you want. He weighed a ton; his torso,
frozen stiff, hugged to my chest, a fierce chill
piercing my gut. Part of the thrill was knowing
10 that children would cry in the morning. Life's tough.

Sometimes I steal things I don't need. I joy-ride cars
to nowhere, break into houses just to have a look.
I'm a mucky ghost, leave a mess, maybe pinch a camera.
I watch my gloved hand twisting the doorknob.
15 A stranger's bedroom. Mirrors. I sigh like this – *Aah.*

It took some time. Reassembled in the yard,
he didn't look the same. I took a run
and booted him. Again. Again. My breath ripped out
in rags. It seems daft now. Then I was standing
20 alone amongst lumps of snow, sick of the world.

Boredom. Mostly I'm so bored I could eat myself.
One time, I stole a guitar and thought I might
learn to play. I nicked a bust of Shakespeare once,
flogged it, but the snowman was strangest.
25 You don't understand a word I'm saying, do you?

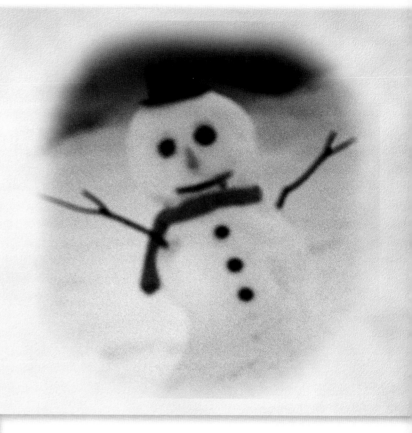

Education *for* Leisure

Today I am going to kill something. Anything.
I have had enough of being ignored and today
I am going to play God. It is an ordinary day,
a sort of grey with boredom stirring in the streets.

5 I squash a fly against the window with my thumb.
We did that at school. Shakespeare. It was in
another language and now the fly is in another language.
I breathe out talent on the glass to write my name.

I am a genius. I could be anything at all, with half
10 the chance. But today I am going to change the world.
Something's world. The cat avoids me. The cat
knows I am a genius, and has hidden itself.

I pour the goldfish down the bog. I pull the chain.
I see that it is good. The budgie is panicking.
15 Once a fortnight, I walk the two miles into town
for signing on. They don't appreciate my autograph.

There is nothing left to kill. I dial the radio
and tell the man he's talking to a superstar.
He cuts me off. I get our bread-knife and go out.
20 The pavements glitter suddenly. I touch your arm.

161

These three poems are by Simon Armitage.

HITCHER

I'd been tired, under
the weather, but the ansaphone kept screaming:
One more sick-note, mister, and you're finished. Fired.
I thumbed a lift to where the car was parked.
5   A Vauxhall Astra. It was hired.

I picked him up in Leeds.
He was following the sun to west from east
with just a toothbrush and the good earth for a bed. The truth,
he said, was blowin' in the wind,
10   or round the next bend.

I let him have it
on the top road out of Harrogate – once
with the head, then six times with the krooklok
in the face – and didn't even swerve.
15   I dropped it into third

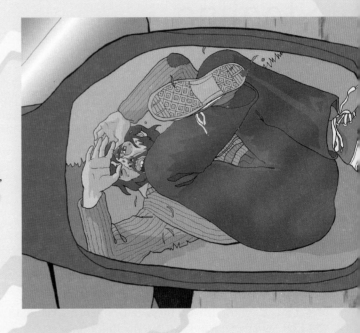

and leant across
to let him out, and saw him in the mirror
bouncing off the kerb, then disappearing down the verge.
We were the same age, give or take a week.
20   He'd said he liked the breeze

to run its fingers
through his hair. It was twelve noon.
The outlook for the day was moderate to fair.
Stitch that, I remember thinking,
25   you can walk from there.

★

Those bastards in their mansions:
to hear them shriek, you'd think
I'd poisoned the dogs and vaulted the ditches,
crossed the lawns in stocking feet and threadbare britches,
5   forced the door of one of the porches, and lifted
the gift of fire from the burning torches,

then given heat and light to streets and houses,
told the people how to ditch their cuffs and shackles,
armed them with the iron from their wrists and ankles.

10   Those lords and ladies in their palaces and castles,
they'd have me sniffed out by their beagles,
picked at by their eagles, pinned down, grilled
beneath the sun.

Me, I stick to the shadows, carry a gun.

★

I've made out a will; I'm leaving myself
to the National Health. I'm sure they can use
the jellies and tubes and syrups and glues,
the web of nerves and veins, the loaf of brains,
5   and assortment of fillings and stitches and wounds,
blood – a gallon exactly of bilberry soup –
the chassis or cage or cathedral of bone;
but not the heart, they can leave that alone.

They can have the lot, the whole stock:
10   the loops and coils and sprockets and springs and rods,
the twines and cords and strands,
the face, the case, the cogs and the hands,

but not the pendulum, the ticker;
leave that where it stops or hangs.

The Man He Killed

'Had he and I but met
    By some old ancient inn,
We should have sat us down to wet
    Right many a nipperkin!

5   'But ranged as infantry,
    And staring face to face,
I shot at him as he at me,
    And killed him in his place.

    'I shot him dead because –
10   Because he was my foe,
Just so: my foe of course he was;
    That's clear enough; although

    'He thought he'd 'list, perhaps,
    Off-hand like – just as I –
15 Was out of work – had sold his traps –
    No other reason why.

    'Yes; quaint and curious war is!
    You shoot a fellow down
You'd treat if met where any bar is,
20   Or help to half-a-crown.'

THOMAS HARDY
1902

Patrolling Barnegat

Wild, wild the storm, and the sea high running,
Steady the roar of the gale, with incessant undertone muttering,
Shouts of demoniac laughter fitfully piercing and pealing,
Waves, air, midnight, their savagest trinity lashing,
5   Out in the shadows there milk-white combs careering,
On beachy slush and sand spirts of snow fierce slanting,
Where through the murk the easterly death-wind breasting,
Through cutting swirl and spray watchful and firm advancing,
(That in the distance! is that a wreck? is the red signal flaring?)
10 Slush and sand of the beach tireless till daylight wending,
Steadily, slowly, through hoarse roar never remitting,
Along the midnight edge by those milk-white combs careering,
A group of dim, weird forms, struggling, the night confronting,
That savage trinity warily watching.

WALT WHITMAN
1856

The power of language

Key features of the poems are:

 rhyme

2 rhythm

3 voice

---

1 RHYME

Rhyme is the effect of bringing together words which end in the same – or similar – sounds:

> I'm sure they can **use**
> the jellies and tubes and syrups and **glues,**

- **Half-rhymes** occur when words sound very similar but are not an exact rhyme:

  > her clearing of **clutter,**
  > her regional **patter,**

- Two successive lines which rhyme are called a **rhyming couplet:**

  > the twines and cords and **strands,**
  > the face, the case, the cogs and the **hands,**

- **Internal rhyme** happens when one word rhymes with another from the middle of a line, rather than at the end:

  > with a mind as cold as the **slice** of **ice**

- A pattern of rhymes in a poem is known as a **rhyme-scheme.**

---

a) In pairs, look through the poems on pages 160–3 and divide them into four groups according to whether they:

- do not rhyme at all
- have a regular rhyme-scheme
- rhyme, or half-rhyme, in some parts but not in others
- are based on half-rhymes

b) Write down examples of:

- rhyme, internal rhyme, half-rhyme and rhyming couplets in the three poems by Simon Armitage. For example, look at:
  - the rhyme in: *Those bastards...* (lines 3–4) and *Hitcher* (3 and 5)
  - half-rhyme in *Hitcher* (9–10, 14–15) and *I've made out a will...* (12 and 14)
  - internal rhyme in *Those bastards...* (5–6), *I've made out a will...* (12) and *Hitcher* (22, 23 and 25)
  - the rhyming couplet in *Those bastards...* (13–14)
- half-rhyme in Duffy's *Salome* (look at the set of half-rhymes all ending with *–ter*) and Whitman's *Patrolling Barnegat* (the *–ing* words)
- rhyme in Hardy's *The Man He Killed*

c) Use the examples from question 1b to write a paragraph comparing the ways in which poets use different kinds of rhyme in order to give their poems a structure and help convey the meaning. For example, compare the uses of:

- rhyme in Hardy's *The Man He Killed* and Armitage's three poems
- half-rhyme in Duffy's *Salome*, Armitage's three poems and Whitman's *Patrolling Barnegat*
- internal rhyme in Duffy's *Stealing*, Armitage's three poems and Hardy's *The Man He Killed*

2) RHYTHM

> The **rhythm** of a poem is its beat, based on its pattern of stressed and unstressed syllables.

a) Reread Hardy's *The Man He Killed*. Copy out the first stanza and mark the heavy stresses. The first line has been done to start you off:

*Had **he** and **I** but **met***

b) Each stanza in Hardy's poem has the same metre (see page 194) – a regular pattern of stressed and unstressed syllables – and this metre creates a definite rhythm. Read the poem out loud, emphasising the regular metre. Then write down some words which describe the rhythm. For example, a poem's rhythm might be described as: *regular* or *irregular*, *insistent* or *subtle*, *slow* or *fast*, *stately and measured* or *jaunty*, *leisurely* or *hasty*...

c) Copy out the first three lines of Armitage's *I've made out a will...* and mark the heavy stresses. Again, describe the overall rhythm of the poem.

d) Write a paragraph comparing the rhythm of *The Man He Killed* with that of *I've made out a will...*
* In what ways are their rhythms similar?
* Hardy writes about killing a man in combat; Armitage asks us to think about our internal organs. Compare the subject matter of the two poems. In what ways are they similar, and why might the two poets have chosen a similar kind of rhythm?

3) VOICE

> **Voice** is the term given to the person who seems to be speaking in a story or poem.

When we read Seamus Heaney's *Digging* (page 151), we assume that the voice of the poem is Heaney himself – because we know that Heaney is a poet who uses his pen just as his father and grandfather used a spade. But in many poems the voice is plainly not the voice of the poet.

a) In pairs, discuss who the voice is of each of the following poems on pages 160–3. How do you know in each case? (For example, the voice of *The Man He Killed* seems to be an infantry soldier, who had enlisted in the army because he was out of work, and had killed a man in combat. The evidence is in lines 5–8 and 13–15.):
* *Salome*
* *Education for Leisure*
* *Those bastards in their mansions*
* *Hitcher*

b) In some poems the voice is a mysterious figure whose background and personality we are left to work out for ourselves. Who is the voice in Carol Ann Duffy's *Stealing* in your opinion? What kind of person are they? How do we know? Although we are not told, where do you think they might be speaking from? Who are they speaking to?

> A **dramatic monologue** is like a soliloquy in a play. The voice of the poem is a character who tells us a story or expresses their thoughts. Dramatic monologues are always in the **first person** (see page 135).

c) Reread Carol Ann Duffy's *Salome* and Simon Armitage's *Hitcher*. These are both examples of short dramatic monologues. Write a paragraph to compare the poems, answering the following questions:
* Who is the voice of the poem in each case?
* What impression do you get of their personality, character or attitude to life?
* What links their two stories?

FOUNDATION TIER TASKS

 1 **DESCRIBING THE EVENTS**

Imagine you were a police officer listening to the person retelling the story in *Stealing*. Write a report, outlining what the person claimed to have done and why they had done it.

Planning and drafting

Reread the poem. Then make notes on the main things that the speaker says about:

- stealing the snowman (lines 1–9):
  - What did they feel about the children's reaction in the morning when they found the snowman gone? (9–10)
  - What did they do with the snowman when they got it home? (16–19)
  - How did they feel in the end? (19–20)
- their reason for breaking into houses (12):
  - What do they do when they have broken in? (13–15)
- stealing because of boredom (21–4):
  - What do you make of their final statement? (25)

Remember to write as though you were a police officer writing a report. You will have to decide whether the person speaking in the poem is male or female.

You could start:

He seemed very prepared to talk about himself and what he had done. I asked him what the most unusual thing was that he had stolen and...

 2 **COMPARING PEOPLE IN TWO POEMS**

Select one poem by Carol Ann Duffy and one by Simon Armitage and compare the ways in which they write about people who have committed a crime, or are about to. What do we know about the people concerned and their crimes? How do we feel about these people, having read what they say about themselves?

Planning and drafting

You could choose to write about Carol Ann Duffy's *Education for Leisure* and Simon Armitage's *Hitcher*.

Use the writing frame opposite as a guide.

FOUNDATION & HIGHER TIER TASK

 COMPARING THE VOICES OF FOUR POEMS

Write about the different voices to be heard in poems by Carol Ann Duffy, Simon Armitage and pre-1914 poets, and the effects they can have upon the reader. In your answer, refer to *Salome* by Duffy, one poem by Armitage and two poems from the pre-1914 selection.

(See pages 168–9 for 'the examiner's view' on how to tackle this question.)

Para	What the people say about themselves	Look at	You could start...
1	Who is speaking in *Education for Leisure* (EL)? Who is speaking in *Hitcher* (H)?	question 3a	*The speaker of this poem seems to be...* *In this poem the speaker is...*
	What they are planning to do (EL) Why they are going to do it (EL) Why they have committed the crime (H)	lines 1, 10–11 2–3	*The speaker lets us know that...* *In* Hitcher *the speaker has already committed the crime...*
2	Their view of themself (EL) Their view of themself (H)	9–10, 15–16 24–5	*He/she sees himself/herself as...* *The speaker in* Hitcher *describes the attack very coldly and in a matter-of-fact tone...*
	Their preparations (EL)	5, 13–14, 17–19	
3	The crime (EL) The crime (H)	20 11–14	*The crime itself is not described; instead...* *This crime has already taken place...*
4	How we feel about it (EL) How we feel about it (H)	11–18, 20 20–5	*Although we do not know exactly what the person is about to do, it seems that we ourselves are the victim...* *From the speaker's description, the crime is extremely violent and probably ends in the victim's death. The speaker's attitude is...*

HIGHER TIER TASK

COMPARING POETS' USE OF RHYME AND RHYTHM

Use one poem by Carol Ann Duffy, one by Simon Armitage and any two pre-1914 poems to write about the ways in which poets use rhyme and rhythm.

You could start:

Poets choose to structure their poems in ways which will bring out the meaning and help them to say what they want to say...

Planning and drafting

You could write about Carol Ann Duffy's *Salome* or *Stealing*, Simon Armitage's *I've made out a will...* or *Hitcher*, Thomas Hardy's *The Man He Killed* and Walt Whitman's *Patrolling Barnegat*.

Look back at your responses to questions 1 and 2 (pages 164–5). If you choose to write about *Salome*, *Hitcher*, *The Man He Killed* and *Patrolling Barnegat*, you could compare:

a) rhyme in:
- *The Man He Killed*
- *Hitcher* (3 and 5)

b) half-rhyme in:
- *Hitcher* (9–10 and 14–15)
- *Salome* (Comment on the slightly comic effect in the way all the half-rhymes mount up, one after the other. Which word do all the half-rhymes lead up to and why is it important to the Salome story?)
- *Patrolling Barnegat* (How does the half-rhyme help to create a structure for a poem which is about the wildness of the elements?)

c) internal rhyme in:
- *Hitcher* (22, 23 and 25)
- *The Man He Killed* (7 and 11)

d) the rhythm of:
- *The Man He Killed*
- *Patrolling Barnegat*

(Compare the rhythms of these two poems. How does the rhythm fit the subject of the poem in each case?)

The examiner's view

Write about the different voices to be heard in poems by Carol Ann Duffy, Simon Armitage and pre-1914 poets, and the effects they can have upon the reader. In your answer, refer to *Salome* by Duffy, one poem by Armitage and two poems from the pre-1914 selection.

STEP 1: READ THE TEXTS

This one question on pre- and post-1914 poetry (Section B of the English Literature paper) counts for 40% of your total mark for English Literature. You will have 60 minutes and a choice of questions; all questions will expect you to write about:

● one poem by Seamus Heaney and one by Gillian Clarke **or** one poem by Carol Ann Duffy and one by Simon Armitage

● two poems from the pre-1914 poetry bank in the *Anthology*

Reread poems which you think may be suitable for this question and choose three that you would like to write about in addition to *Salome*. (For example, you could choose to write about Armitage's *Those bastards in their mansions...* **or** *Hitcher*, Thomas Hardy's *The Man He Killed* and Walt Whitman's *Patrolling Barnegat*.)

STEP 2: COMPARING VOICES

Compare the voices in the poems you have chosen to write about.

● Reread the poems and write down who you think is speaking in each one.

● Why? Explain your decisions and support them with quotes from the poems.

● For each poem, explain why you feel the poet has chosen to write in that voice.

● Which voice is used most effectively in your opinion? Why do you think this?

STEP 3: THE USE OF LANGUAGE

Most of the poems that you will write about will include rhymes and have a particular rhythm. Remember, you must focus on how poets *use* rhyme and rhythm, rather than simply identifying it.

● There is a general point to be made about the difference between most pre- and post-1914 poems' use of rhyme and rhythm. What is this?

● Why, then, does Duffy use rhyme and rhythm so obviously in *Salome*?

● What can you write about the purpose of each of these poems and the methods that the poets have used to fulfil their purpose (e.g. *Duffy has used half rhyme throughout the poem to help build up a sense of anticipation...*)?

● Evaluate which of the poets has succeeded the most in fulfilling their purpose.

STEP 4: PLANNING AND DRAFTING

1 For each of the four poems, make notes in answer to the following questions (look back at question 3 on page 165):

- Who is the voice of the poem in each case?
- What impression do you get of their personality, character or attitude to life?

2 What links the four voices of these poems?

- Can you identify a linking theme? (If you are planning to write on the poems suggested in Step 1, see Foundation Tier task 2 on page 166.)

3 What responses do you have to these voices? Do you generally sympathise with them, for example, or condemn them? Do they fascinate you or repel you?

- Quote from the poems to explain your reactions.

STEP 5: READING PRE- AND POST-1914 POETRY

This is one of the most difficult questions that you will have to tackle under examination conditions. Using the following reading process will help you:

- **Choose** poems that are appropriate for the question being asked.
- **Reread** the question, then **brainstorm** ideas for each poem.
- **Sequence** your ideas using *compare* words and phrases.
- **Write** your response.

STEP 6: SAMPLE ANSWER

Read this introduction from a sample answer.

> In addition to 'Salome' by Carol Ann Duffy, I have chosen to write about
> .... I have chosen these poems as each one has a very distinct voice
> – the reader can clearly identify someone speaking or 'telling the story' of the poem.
>
>   Firstly, I will look at who is speaking in each poem and discuss how their personalities
> and views affect our response. I will then analyse how the poets have created these voices, looking
> at, for example, rhyme and rhythm. Finally, I will assess which of these poems has used voice
> most effectively.
>
>   The voice in 'Salome' is, despite the historical allusion in the title, unmistakeably modern –
> contemporary slang such as 'booze', 'fags' and 'ain't life a bitch' help to create this impression...

> Notice how this student has already shown that they will be evaluating the relative success of the poets. Evaluation is necessary in order to gain an A grade.

! Quick tip Never simply identify a poet's effective use of poetic devices: explain how they are used.

A Kestrel for a Knave

In this unit you will:

● read an extract from a twentieth-century novel

● study how the author creates a character

● analyse comic and serious writing

In the following extract from Barry Hines's *A Kestrel for a Knave*, the main character, Billy Casper, is about to join his class for a games lesson. The extract opens with a description of the games teacher, Mr Sugden.

He walked into the changing room as clean and shining as a boy down for breakfast on his seaside holidays. The other boys were packed into the aisles between the rows of pegs, their hanging clothes partitioning the room
5   into corridors. Mr Sugden was passing slowly across one end of the room, looking down the corridors and counting the boys as they changed. He was wearing a violet tracksuit. The top was embellished with cloth badges depicting numerous crests and qualifications, and on the breast a white athlete carried
10   the Olympic torch. The legs were tucked into new white football socks, neatly folded at his ankles, and his football boots were polished as black and shiny as the bombs used by assassins in comic strips. The laces binding them had been scrubbed white, and both boots had been fastened identically:
15   two loops of the foot and one of the ankle, and tied in a neat bow under the tab at the back.

    He finished counting and rolled a football off the window sill into his hand. The leather was rich with dubbin, and the new orange lace nipped the slit as firmly as a row of surgical stitches. He tossed it up and caught it on the ends of his fingers, then turned round to Billy.

    'Skyving again, Casper?'
20   'No, Sir, Mr Farthing wanted me; he's been talking to me.'

    'I bet that was stimulating for him, wasn't it?'

    'What does that mean, Sir?'

    'The conversation, lad, what do you think it means?'

    'No, Sir, that word, stimult ... stimult-ting.'
25   'Stimulating you fool, S-T-I-M-U-L-A-T-I-N-G, stimulating!'

    'Yes, Sir.'

    'Well get changed lad, you're two weeks late already!'

    He lifted the elastic webbing of one cuff and rotated his fist to look at his watch on the underside of his wrist.
30   'Some of us want a game even if you don't.'

    'I've no kit, Sir.'

    Mr Sugden stepped back and slowly looked Billy up and down, his top lip curling.

    'Casper, you make me SICK.'

'SICK' penetrated the hubbub, which immediately decreased as the boys stopped their own conversations and turned their attention to Mr Sugden and Billy.   35

'Every lesson it's the same old story, "Please, Sir, I've no kit."'

The boys tittered at his whipped-dog whining impersonation.

'Every lesson for four years! And in all that time you've made no attempt whatsoever to get any kit, you've skyved and scrounged and borrowed and …'

He tried this lot on one breath, and his ruddy complexion heightened and glowed like a red   40
balloon as he held his breath and fought for another verb.

'… and … BEG …' The balloon burst and the pronunciation of the verb disintegrated.

'Why is it that everyone else can get some but you can't?'

'I don't know, Sir. My mother won't buy me any. She says it's a waste of money, especially now that I'm leaving.'   45

'You haven't been leaving for four years, have you?'

'No, Sir.'

'You could have bought some out of your spending money, couldn't you?'

'I don't like football, Sir.'   50

'What's that got to do with it?'

'I don't know, Sir. Anyway I don't get enough.'

'Get a job then. I don't…'

'I've got one, Sir.'

'Well then! You get paid, don't you?'   55

'Yes, Sir. But I have to gi' it to my mam. I'm still payin' her for my fines, like instalments every week.'

Mr Sugden bounced the ball on Billy's head, compressing his neck into his shoulders.

'Well you should keep out of trouble then, lad, and then…'

'I haven't been in trouble, Sir, not…'   60

'Shut up, lad! Shut up, before you drive me crackers!'

He hit Billy twice with the ball, holding it between both hands as though he was murdering him with a boulder. The rest of the class grinned behind each other's backs, or placed their fingers over their mouths to suppress the laughter gathering there. They watched Mr Sugden rush into his changing room, and began to giggle, stopping immediately he reappeared waving a pair of giant blue   65
drawers.

'Here Casper, get them on!'

He wanged them across the room, and Billy caught them flying over his head, then held them up for inspection as though he was contemplating buying. The class roared. They would have made Billy two suits and an overcoat.   70

'They'll not fit me, Sir.'

The class roared again and even Billy had to smile. There was only Mr Sugden not amused.

'What are you talking about, lad? You can get them on, can't you?'

'Yes, Sir.'

'Well they fit you then! Now get changed, QUICK.'   75

Billy found an empty peg and hung his jacket on it. He was immediately enclosed in a tight square as two lines of boys formed up, one on each side of him between the parallel curtains of clothing. He sat down on the long bench covering the shoe racks, and worked his jeans over his pumps. Mr Sugden broke one side of the square and stood over him.

'And you want your underpants and vest off.'   80

'I don't wear 'em, Sir.'

As he reached up to hang his trousers on the peg, his shirt lap lifted, revealing his bare cheeks, which looked as smooth and boney as two white billiard balls. He stepped into the shorts and pulled

them up to his waist. The legs reached halfway down his shins. He pulled the waist up to his neck
85 and his knees just slid into view. Boys pointed at them, shouting and laughing into each other's
faces, and other boys who were still changing rushed to the scene, jumping up on the benches or
parting the curtains to see through. And at the centre of it all, Billy, like a brave little clown, was
busy trying to make them fit, and Sugden was looking at him as though it was his fault for being
too small for them.

90 'Roll them down and don't be so foolish. You're too daft to laugh at, Casper.'

No one else thought so. Billy started to roll them down from his chest, each tuck shortening the
legs and gathering the material round his waist in a floppy blue tyre.

'That'll do. Let's have you all out now.'

He opened the door and led them down the corridor and out into the yard. Some boys waited
95 until he had gone, then they took a run and had a good slide up to the door, rotating slowly as they
slid, and finishing up facing the way they had come. Those with rubber studs left long black streaks
on the tiles. The plastic and nailed leather studs cut through the veneer and scored deep scratches in
the vinyl. When they reached the yard, the pad of the rubber studs on the concrete hardly differed
from that in the changing room or the corridor, but the clatter produced by the nailed and plastic
100 studs had a hollow, more metallic ring.

The cold caught Billy's breath as he stepped outside. He stopped dead, glanced round as though
looking to escape, then set off full belt, shouting, across the concrete on to the field. Mr Sugden set
off after him.

'Casper! Shut up, lad! What are you trying to do, disrupt the whole school?'

105 He gained on Billy, and as he drew near swiped at him with his flat hand. Billy, watching the
blows, zig-zagged out of reach, just ahead of them.

'I'm frozen, Sir! I'm shoutin' to keep warm!'

'Well don't shout at me then! I'm not a mile away!'

They were shouting at each other as though they were aboard ship in a gale. Mr Sugden tried to
110 swat him again. Billy sidestepped, and threw him off balance. So he slowed to a walk and turned
round, blowing his whistle and beckoning the others to hurry up.

'Come on, you lot! Hurry up!'

They started to run at speeds ranging from jogging to sprinting, and arrived within a few seconds
of each other on the senior football pitch.

115 'Line up on the halfway line and let's get two sides picked!'

They lined up, jumping and running on the spot, those with long sleeves clutching the cuffs in
their hands, those without massaging their goosey arms.

'Tibbut, come out here and be the other captain.'

Tibbut walked out and stood facing the line, away from Mr Sugden.

120 'I'll have first pick, Tibbut.'

'That's not right, Sir.'

'Why isn't it?'

''Cos you'll get all the best players.'

'Rubbish, lad.'

125 'Course you will, Sir. It's not fair.'

'Tibbut. Do you want to play football? Or
do you want to get dressed and and go and
do some maths?'

'Play football, Sir.'

130 'Right then, stop moaning and start
picking. I'll have Anderson.'

He turned away from Tibbut and pointed
to a boy who was standing on one of the

intersections of the centre circle and the halfway line. Anderson walked off this cross and stood behind him. Tibbut scanned the line, considering his choice.   135

'I'll have Purdey.'

'Come on then, Ellis.'

Each selection altered the structure of the line. When Tibbut had been removed from the centre, all the boys sidestepped to fill the gap. The same happened when Anderson went from near one end. But when Purdey and Ellis, who had been standing side by side, were removed, the boys at their   140 shoulders stood still, therefore dividing the original line into two. These new lines were swiftly segmented as more boys were chosen, leaving no trace of the first major division, just half a dozen boys looking across spaces at each other; reading from left to right: a fat boy; an arm's length away, two friends, one tall with glasses, the other short with a hare-lip; then a space of two yards and Billy; a boy space away from him, a thin boy with a crew-cut and a spotty face; and right away from these,   145 at the far end of the line, another fat boy. Spotty Crew-Cut was halfway between the two fat boys, therefore half of the length of the line was occupied by five of the boys. The far fat boy was the next to go, which halved the length of the line and left Spotty Crew-Cut as one of the end markers.

Tibbut then selected the tall friend with glasses. Mr Sugden immediately selected his partner. They separated gradually as they walked away from the line, parting finally to enter their respective   150 teams. And then there were three: Fatty, Billy, and Spotty Crew-Cut, blushing across at each other while the captains considered. Tibbut picked Crew-Cut. He dashed forward into the anonymity of his team. Fatty stood grinning. Billy stared down at the earth. After long deliberation Mr Sugden chose Billy, leaving Tibbut with Hobson's choice; but before either Billy or Fatty could move towards their teams, Mr Sugden was already turning away and shouting instructions.   155

'Right! We'll play down hill!'

The team broke for their appropriate halves, and while they were arguing their claims for positions, Mr Sugden jogged to the sideline, dropped the ball, and took off his tracksuit. Underneath he was wearing a crisp red football shirt with white cuffs and a white band round the neck. A big white 9 filled most of the back, whiter than his white nylon shorts, which showed a slight fleshy tint through   160 the material. He pulled his socks up, straightened the ribs, then took a fresh roll of half inch bandage from his tracksuit and ripped off two lengths. The torn bandage packet, the cup of its structure still intact, blew away over the turf like the damaged shell of a dark blue egg. Mr Sugden used the lengths of bandage to secure his stockings just below the knees, then he folded his tracksuit neatly on the ground, looked down at himself, and walked on to the pitch carrying the ball like a plum pudding on   165 the tray of his hand. Tibbut, standing on the centre circle, with his hands down his shorts, winked at his Left Winger and waited for Mr Sugden to approach.

'Who are you today, Sir, Liverpool?'

'Rubbish, lad! Don't you know your club colours yet?'

'Liverpool are red, aren't they, Sir?'   170

'Yes, but they're all red, shirts, shorts and stockings. These are Manchester United's colours.'

'Course they are, Sir, I forgot. What position are you playing?'

Mr Sugden turned his back on him to show him the number 9.

'Bobby Charlton. I thought you were usually Denis Law when you were Manchester United.'

'It's too cold to play as a striker today. I'm scheming this morning, all over the field like Charlton.'   175

'Law plays all over, Sir. He's not only a striker.'

'He doesn't link like Charlton.'

'Better player though, Sir.'

Sugden shook his head. 'No, he's been badly off form recently.'

'Makes no odds, he's still a better player. He can settle a game in two minutes.'   180

'Are you trying to tell me about football, Tibbut?'

'No, Sir.'

'Well shut up then. Anyway Law's in the wash this week.'

Language in context

The power of language

Key features of the text are:

1 character description

2 dialogue

3 comic and serious writing

1 CHARACTER DESCRIPTION

A writer does not always have to let us know what a character is thinking or feeling. We can learn a great deal about them from a description of their **appearance** and an account of their **actions**.

For example, Barry Hines's picture of Mr Sugden opens with:

He was wearing a violet tracksuit ... embellished with cloth badges depicting numerous crests and qualifications (appearance)

and

He finished counting and rolled a football off the window sill into his hand. (actions)

a) Write down three further quotations from the extract to illustrate the two types of description listed above: description of appearance and description of actions.

b) Reread:

- the description of the way Sugden is dressed at the beginning of the extract (lines 7–15: *He was wearing ... at the back.*)

- the account of his preparations once he has reached the football pitch (157–66: *The team broke ... of his hand.*)

Write a short paragraph explaining in what ways these descriptions help to create a picture of the character and an impression of the kind of person he is. Look at the ways in which his appearance and his actions are described.

2 DIALOGUE

A novelist also reveals a great deal about a character through **dialogue**.

An examination of Sugden's dialogue shows that his speeches contain a large number of exclamation marks and question marks.

An **exclamation** can express a sudden reaction (*Oh, no!*), a strong assertion (*I will not!*), an emotion such as surprise (*I don't believe it!*) or a powerful personal feeling (*I can't stand that music!*). It ends in an **exclamation mark**.

a) Why do you think there are so many exclamations in Sugden's speech? In pairs, discuss what this tells you about him, and his attitude to the boys, especially Billy.

A **rhetorical question** is one that does not expect an answer.

For example, we might say to somebody *Are you crazy?* or *What kind of answer is that?*

b) Sugden's speech contains several rhetorical questions. For example:

What are you trying to do, disrupt the whole school?

Find two rhetorical questions that he asks Tibbut. (Remember that a rhetorical question can have an answer: it's just that no answer is expected.)

A statement with a brief question added on to the end is called a **tag question**. (The additional question element is called the **question tag**.)

We use tag questions all the time in speech:

It's OK, isn't it?

Got a new car, have they?

I'd have told you, wouldn't I?

c) Sugden's speeches contain a large number of tag questions. For example:

I bet that was stimulating for him, wasn't it?

Find examples of others.

d) Write a paragraph to explain what Sugden's dialogue reveals about the kind of person he is. For example, what can we tell from the fact that his speeches are full of exclamations, rhetorical questions and tag questions?

3 COMIC AND SERIOUS WRITING

A Kestrel for a Knave is an example of a novel which mixes the comic and the serious.

This is a novel which has very serious things to say about the life that Billy Casper leads; but some episodes, such as the one featuring Sugden, are mainly comic.

Comic dialogue

a) Reread the section of dialogue in which Tibbut questions Sugden about the position he has decided to play (lines 168–83: from *'Who are you today, Sir, Liverpool?'*). Write a short paragraph commenting on the comic effect of this dialogue and what it adds to our impression of Sugden. Think about:

- the fact that Tibbut winks at his Left Winger (166–7)
- what lies behind Tibbut's reply *'Course they are, Sir, I forgot.'* (172)
- Sugden's opinion of his abilities as a footballer (175: *I'm scheming...*)
- the serious arguments that Sugden comes up with for being Bobby Charlton rather than Denis Law (175–9)

- the way Sugden 'wins' the argument (181)
- the comic anti-climax which concludes the dialogue (183)

Serious narrative

b) Reread the description of the boys as they leave the building and enter the yard (94–111: *He opened the door ... to hurry up.*). Write a paragraph to explain how the writing enables us to see, hear and feel what is happening. Look, for example at:

Some boys waited...

Those with rubber studs...

but the clatter...

The cold caught...

They were shouting...

blowing his whistle...

Comedy and seriousness mixed

Barry Hines uses a comic episode to make some serious points.

c) Reread the account of Billy putting on the shorts (lines 76–92: *Billy found an empty peg ... floppy blue tyre.*). Write about the mixture of comic and serious elements at this point in the novel. For example:

- Make a note of the comic descriptions. Look at what happens when Billy pulls the shorts up to his neck (84–5) or rolls them down from his chest (91–2).
- Which serious points are being made in this account? Look, for example, at lines 80–3, where Sugden tells Billy to remove his pants and vest:
  - Reread the sentence *As he reached up ... billiard balls.* Do you find this description funny, sad, or both?
  - What does this moment suggest about Billy's home life and how well he is looked after?
  - How far would you say that Billy was being bullied by Sugden here?

FOUNDATION TIER TASKS

 WRITING A SCENE

Write a page of another scene which involves Mr Sugden, Billy Casper and some of the boys. You could choose to continue the existing episode or create a completely new one.

Planning and drafting

Reread the extract so that you have a clear idea of the ways in which the characters speak and behave.

Pay attention to:

- creating character through descriptions of appearance and actions (look back at question 1)
- revealing character through dialogue (look back at question 2)
- making serious points through comic narrative (look back at question 3)

If you continue the existing scene, you could start:

Sugden placed the ball on the centre spot and looked around at his team…

If you decide to write a completely new scene, you could start:

That afternoon, Billy was late getting to Geography. It didn't usually matter, as Braithwaite, the teacher, was invariably late as well. But today Braithwaite was ill. And taking the class in his place was Sugden…

or

Nobody had seen Billy taking the apples. But, as he scrambled over the brick wall and dropped on to the pavement, who should he run straight into but Sugden…

or

Billy, Tibbut and the others had no idea why they had been summoned to see the Head. All they knew, as they waited outside his study, was that there was another teacher in there with him… and his voice was familiar…

 WRITING ABOUT THE CREATION OF A CHARACTER

Write about the methods Barry Hines employs to create the character of Mr Sugden.

Planning and drafting

Write about:

- the description of his appearance and actions
- what we learn by studying what he says
- the serious points which are made through the character and the scenes in which he appears

Use this writing frame as a guide.

Para	Writing features	Look back at	You could start…
Sugden's appearance and actions			
1	his appearance	Q1b	*Barry Hines introduces Sugden with a description of…*
	his actions	Q1b	
What Sugden says			
2	exclamations	Q2a, Q2d	*Sugden's dialogue reveals a great deal about him. For example…*
3	rhetorical questions	Q2b, Q2d	*The fact that his speech contains a lot of rhetorical questions shows that…*
	tag questions	Q2c, Q2d	
4	comic dialogue	Q3a	*One of the most revealing sections of dialogue comes at the point where…*
Sugden as a comic character who allows the writer to make serious points			
5	more serious points	Q3c	*Although Sugden can be viewed as a comic character…*

FOUNDATION & HIGHER TIER TASK

 WRITING ABOUT BILLY'S WORLD

A Kestrel for a Knave opens with the following description. When you have read it, write about the impression you have formed of the kind of life Billy Casper leads. In your answer, refer to this extract and the one on pages 170–3.

(See pages 178–9 for 'the examiner's view' on how to tackle this question.)

HIGHER TIER TASK

ANALYSING THE MIXTURE OF COMEDY AND SERIOUSNESS

Analyse the ways in which Barry Hines mixes comic and serious writing in *A Kestrel for a Knave*.

Planning and drafting

1 Give examples of comic writing. (See questions 1b and 3a.)

2 Give examples of serious writing. (See question 3b, and the extract below.)

3 Show how Barry Hines succeeds in getting serious points across in scenes which are mainly comic. (See questions 1b and 3c.)

There were no curtains up. The window was a hard edged block the colour of the night sky. Inside the bedroom the darkness was of a gritty texture. The wardrobe and bed were blurred shapes in the darkness. Silence.

5 Billy moved over, towards the outside of the bed. Jud moved with him, leaving one half of the bed empty. He snorted and rubbed his nose. Billy whimpered. They settled. Wind whipped the window and swept along the wall outside.

10 Billy turned over. Jud followed him and cough-coughed into his neck. Billy pulled the blankets up round his ears and wiped his neck with them. Most of the bed was now empty, and the unoccupied space quickly cooled. Silence. Then the alarm rang. The noise brought Billy upright, feeling for it in

15 the darkness, eyes shut tight. Jud groaned and hutched back across the cold sheet. He reached down the side of the bed and knocked the clock over, grabbed for it, and knocked it farther away.

'Come here, you bloody thing.'

20 He stretched down and grabbed it with both hands. The glass lay curved in one palm, while the fingers of his other hand fumbled amongst the knobs and levers at the back. He found the lever and noise stopped. Then he coiled back into bed and left the clock lying on its back.

25 'The bloody thing.'

He stayed in his own half of the bed, groaning and turning over every few minutes, Billy lay with his back to him, listening. Then he turned his cheek slightly from the pillow.

30 'Jud?'

'What?'

'Tha'd better get up.'

No answer.

'Alarm's gone off tha knows.'

35 'Think I don't know?'

He pulled the blankets tighter and drilled his head into the pillow. They both lay still.

'Jud?'

'What?'

'Tha'll be late.' 40

'O, shut it.'

'Clock's not fast tha knows.'

'I said SHUT IT.'

He swung his fist under the blankets and thumped Billy in the kidneys. 45

'Gi'o'er! That hurts!'

'Well shut it then.'

'I'll tell my mam on thi.'

Jud swung again. Billy scuffled away into the cold at the edge of the bed, sobbing. Jud got out, sat on the edge 50 of the bed for a moment, then stood up and felt his way across the room to the light switch. Billy worked his way back to the centre and disappeared under the blankets.

'Set t'alarm for me, Jud. For seven'

'Set it thi sen.' 55

'Go on, thar up.'

Jud parted Billy's sweater and shirt, and used the sweater for a vest. Billy snuggled down in Jud's place, making the springs creak. Jud looked at the humped blankets, then walked across and pulled them back, 60 stripping the bed completely.

'Hands off cocks; on socks.'

For an instant Billy lay curled up, his hands wafered between his thighs. Then he sat up and crawled to the bottom of the bed to retrieve the blankets. 65

'You rotten sod, just because tha's to get up.'

'Another few weeks lad, an' tha'll be getting up wi'me.'

He walked out on to the landing. Billy propped himself up on one elbow.

'Switch t'light out, then!' 70

Jud went downstairs. Billy sat on the edge of the bed and re-set the alarm, then ran across the lino and switched the light off. When he got back into bed most of the warmth had gone. He shivered and scuffled around the sheet, seeking a warm place. 75

A Kestrel for a Knave opens with the following description. When you have read it, write about the impression you have formed of the kind of life Billy Casper leads. In your answer, refer to the extracts on pages 170–3 and page 177.

STEP 1: READ THE TEXT

You will have to answer one question on a post-1914 prose text in Section A of the English Literature paper. There will be a choice of two questions on each text. All questions will be assessed using the same criteria; each question will assess your ability to:

- focus on the question
- explain the writer's methods
- refer to details from the novel and use quotes appropriately

STEP 2: FOCUS ON THE QUESTION

The particular question that we are focusing on concerns your opinion about the kind of life Billy leads, with special reference to two particular episodes. Focus on the question in front of you, not one that you have answered recently or one that you would rather tackle!

- What details do we learn about the sort of life Billy leads from these two episodes?
- Find and write down quotations to support your views.

- In your opinion, what is the author's purpose in these two scenes?
- What methods does the writer use to help to fulfil his purpose?
- How successfully do you think the author fulfils his purpose?

STEP 3: THE USE OF LANGUAGE

You have already looked at the way Barry Hines uses dialogue in the episode with Sugden (see questions 2a–d on pages 174–5). How does he use dialogue in the opening section of the novel?

- Identify three pieces of dialogue in this opening section and write them down.
- Explain what each one tells us about the sort of life Billy leads. For example: *Jud's first words show that he is short-tempered, aggressive and foul-mouthed. Sleeping in the same bed as such a brother must...*

- Explain what effect the use of dialect spellings has on our view of Billy.
- How does this help to fulfil the author's purpose?

STEP 4: PLANNING AND DRAFTING

When answering this question, aim to write about the following points:

Billy's home life

From the extract on page 177, write about:

- the bedroom
- sharing a bed with his brother
- the way his brother treats him

From the extract on pages 170–3, write about:

- the way he is looked after by his mother (lines 31–57 and 82–4)

Billy's life at school

From the extract on pages 170–3, write about:

- games lessons
- the way he is treated by Sugden (see question 3c on page 175)
- his relationship with the other boys (look at 63–91)

STEP 5: READING AND WRITING ABOUT POST-1914 PROSE

Writing about your reading of a post-1914 prose text will be marked in the same way as all of your other reading assessments. The examiner will look for evidence of analysis; do not just retell the story, or write all you know about a character, but:

- make a **point** related to the question
- find an **example** to back up your point
- **explain** your point

You should also:

- explain the writer's **methods**
- show evidence of a **personal interpretation** (give your own opinions about the text)

STEP 6: SAMPLE ANSWER

Read this introduction from a sample answer.

We learn a lot about the kind of life Billy Casper leads from these two episodes. The novel opens with a vivid picture of Billy's home life and this first scene is the more serious of the two because we see glimpses of the sort of relationship that Billy has with his step-brother, Jud. Jud bullies Billy on several occasions in this first scene, most notably when Hines writes, 'He [Jud] swung his fist under the blankets and thumped Billy in the kidneys.' Bullying, or the threat of violence, is present throughout the novel and it re-occurs in the games lesson when Sugden bullies Billy before, during and after the football match.

   We also discover from the opening scene that Billy lives a deprived life, having to share not only his room, but also his bed with his brother. This puts Billy in a position where he can be readily bullied, but it also helps the writer to draw a picture of the sort of material background that Billy comes from...

> Note how this student has linked the two episodes, rather than writing about each one separately. This way of answering a question is usually only attempted by students who gain a B grade or above.

! Quick tip Use a reading process of read, brainstorm, sequence and write for all of your reading assessments.

An Inspector Calls

In this unit you will:

- read an extract from the opening of a post-1914 play
- examine some dramatic conventions
- study the historical and social context and a major theme of the play

The year is 1912 and a prosperous Midlands family have just finished their evening meal. The father, Arthur Birling, takes the opportunity to have a talk with his son Eric (in his early twenties) and a young man called Gerald Croft, who has just become engaged to Birling's daughter, Sheila.

BIRLING	I'm delighted about this engagement and I hope it won't be too long before you're married. And I want to say this. There's a good deal of silly talk about these days – but – and I speak as a hard-headed business man, who has to take risks and know what he's about – I say, you can ignore all this silly pessimistic talk. When you marry, you'll be marrying at a very good time. Yes, a very good time – and soon it'll be an even better time. Last month, just because the miners came out on strike, there's a lot of wild talk about possible labour trouble in the near future. Don't worry. We've passed the worst of it. We employers at last are coming together to see that our interests – and the interests of Capital – are properly protected. And we're in for a time of steadily increasing prosperity.
GERALD	I believe you're right, sir.
ERIC	What about war?
BIRLING	Glad you mentioned it, Eric. I'm coming to that. Just because the Kaiser makes a speech or two, or a few German officers have too much to drink and begin talking nonsense, you'll hear some people say that war's inevitable. And to that I say – fiddlesticks! The Germans don't want war. Nobody wants war, except some half-civilized folks in the Balkans. And why? There's too much at stake these days. Everything to lose and nothing to gain by war.
ERIC	Yes, I know – but still—
BIRLING	Just let me finish, Eric. You've a lot to learn yet. And I'm talking as a hard-headed, practical man of business. And I say there isn't a chance of war. The world's developing so fast that it'll make war impossible. Look at the progress we're making. In a year or two we'll have aeroplanes that will be able to go anywhere. And look at the way the auto-mobile's making headway – bigger and faster all the time. And then ships. Why, a friend of mine went over this new liner last week – the *Titanic* – she sails next week – forty six thousand eight hundred tons – forty six thousand eight hundred tons – New York in five days – and every luxury – and unsinkable, absolutely unsinkable. That's what you've got to keep your eye on, facts like that, progress like that – and not a few German officers talking nonsense and a few scaremongers here making a fuss about nothing. Now you three young people, just listen to this – and remember what I'm telling you now. In twenty or thirty years' time – let's say, in 1940 – you may be giving a little party like this – your son or daughter might be getting engaged – and I tell you, by that time you'll be living in a world that'll have forgotten all these Capital versus Labour agitations and all these silly little war scares. There'll be peace and prosperity and rapid progess everywhere – except of course in Russia, which will always be behindhand naturally.
MRS B.	Arthur!
	As MRS BIRLING *shows signs of interrupting.*

| BIRLING | Yes, my dear, I know – I'm talking too much. But you youngsters just remember what I said. We can't let these Bernard Shaws and H. G. Wellses do all the talking. We hardheaded practical business men must say something sometime. And we don't guess – we've had experience – and we know. | 35 |

| MRS B. | (*rising. The others rise*) Yes, of course, dear. Well – don't keep Gerald in here too long. Eric – I want you a minute. | 40 |

She and SHEILA *and* ERIC *go out.* BIRLING *and* GERALD *sit down again.*

BIRLING	Cigar?
GERALD	No, thanks. Can't really enjoy them.
BIRLING	(*taking one himself*) Ah, you don't know what you're missing. I like a good cigar. (*Indicating decanter.*) Help yourself.
GERALD	Thank you.	45

BIRLING *lights his cigar and* GERALD, *who has lit a cigarette, helps himself to port, then pushes the decanter to* BIRLING.

| BIRLING | Thanks. (*confidentially*) By the way, there's something I'd like to mention – in strict confidence – while we're by ourselves. I have an idea that your mother – Lady Croft – while she doesn't object to my girl – feels you might have done better for yourself socially — |

GERALD, *rather embarrassed, begins to murmur some dissent, but* BIRLING *checks him.*

| | No, Gerald, that's all right. Don't blame her. She comes from an old country family – landed people and so forth – and so it's only natural. But what I wanted to say is – there's a fair chance that I might find my way into the next Honours List. Just a knighthood, of course. | 50 |

| GERALD | Oh – I say – congratulations! |
| BIRLING | Thanks. But it's a bit too early for that. So don't say anything. But I've had a hint or two. You see, I was Lord Mayor here two years ago when Royalty visited us. And I've always been regarded as a sound useful party man. So – well – I gather there's a very good chance of a knighthood – so long as we behave ourselves, don't get into the police court or start a scandal – eh? (*laughs complacently*) | 55 |

GERALD	(*laughs*) You seem to be a nice well-behaved family—
BIRLING	We think we are—
GERALD	So if that's the only obstacle, sir, I think you might as well accept my congratulations now.	60
BIRLING	No, no, I couldn't do that. And don't say anything yet.
GERALD	Not even to my mother? I know she'd be delighted.
BIRLING	Well, when she comes back, you might drop a hint to her. And you can promise her that we'll try to keep out of trouble during the next few months.

They both laugh.

ERIC *enters*

ERIC	What's the joke? Started telling stories?	65
BIRLING	No. Want another glass of port?
ERIC	(*sitting down*) Yes, please. (*takes decanter and helps himself*) Mother says we mustn't stay too long. But I don't think it matters. I left 'em talking about clothes again. You'd think a girl had never had any clothes before she gets married. Women are potty about 'em.
BIRLING	Yes, but you've got to remember, my boy, that clothes mean something quite different to a woman. Not just something to wear – and not only something to make 'em look prettier – but – well, a sort of sign or token of their self-respect.	70
GERALD	That's true.
ERIC	(*eagerly*) Yes, I remember – (*but he checks himself*)
BIRLING	Well, what do you remember?	75
ERIC	(*confused*) Nothing.
BIRLING	Nothing?

GERALD	(*amused*) Sounds a bit fishy to me.	
BIRLING	(*taking it in same manner*) Yes, you don't know what some of these boys get up to nowadays. More money to spend and time to spare than I had when I was Eric's age. They worked us hard in those days and kept us short of cash. Though even then – we broke out and had a bit of fun sometimes.	80
GERALD	I'll bet you did.	
BIRLING	(*solemnly*) But this is the point. I don't want to lecture you two young fellows again. But what so many of you don't seem to understand now, when things are so much easier, is that a man has to make his own way – has to look after himself – and his family too, of course, when he has one – and so long as he does that he won't come to much harm. But the way some of these cranks talk and write now, you'd think everybody has to look after everybody else, as if we were all mixed up together like bees in a hive – community and all that nonsense. But take my word for it, you youngsters – and I've learnt in the good hard school of experience – that a man has to mind his own business and look after himself and his own – and—	85 90
	We hear the sharp ring of a front door bell. BIRLING *stops to listen.*	
ERIC	Somebody at the front door.	
BIRLING	Edna'll answer it. Well, have another glass of port, Gerald – and then we'll join the ladies. That'll stop me giving you good advice.	95
ERIC	Yes, you've piled it on a bit tonight, Father.	
BIRLING	Special occasion. And feeling contented, for once, I wanted you to have the benefit of my experience.	
	EDNA *enters.*	
EDNA	Please, sir, an inspector's called.	
BIRLING	An inspector? What kind of inspector?	100
EDNA	A police inspector. He says his name's Inspector Goole.	
BIRLING	Don't know him. Does he want to see me?	
EDNA	Yes, sir. He says it's important.	
BIRLING	All right, Edna. Show him in here. Give us some more light.	
	EDNA *does, then goes out.*	
	I'm still on the Bench. It may be something about a warrant.	105
GERALD	(*lightly*) Sure to be. Unless Eric's been up to something. (*nodding confidentially to* BIRLING) And that would be awkward, wouldn't it?	
BIRLING	(*humourously*) Very.	
ERIC	(*who is uneasy, sharply*) Here, what do you mean?	110
GERALD	(*lightly*) Only something we were talking about when you were out. A joke really.	
ERIC	(*still uneasy*) Well, I don't think it's very funny.	
BIRLING	(*sharply, staring at him*) What's the matter with you?	
ERIC	(*defiantly*) Nothing.	115
EDNA	(*opening door, and announcing*) Inspector Goole.	
	The INSPECTOR *enters, and* EDNA *goes, closing the door after her. The* INSPECTOR *need not be a big man but he creates at once an impression of massiveness, solidity and purposefulness. He is a man in his fifties, dressed in a plain darkish suit of the period. He speaks carefully, weightily, and has a disconcerting habit of looking hard at the person he addresses before actually speaking.*	
INSPECTOR	Mr Birling?	
BIRLING	Yes. Sit down, Inspector.	
INSPECTOR	(*sitting*) Thank you, sir.	

BIRLING	Have a glass of port – or a little whisky?	120
INSPECTOR	No, thank you, Mr Birling. I'm on duty.	
BIRLING	You're new, aren't you?	
INSPECTOR	Yes, sir. Only recently transferred.	
BIRLING	I thought you must be. I was an alderman for years – and Lord Mayor two years ago – and I'm still on the Bench – so I know the Brumley police officers pretty well – and I thought I'd never seen you before.	125
INSPECTOR	Quite so.	
BIRLING	Well, what can I do for you? Some trouble about a warrant?	
INSPECTOR	No, Mr Birling.	
BIRLING	(*after a pause, with a touch of impatience*) Well, what is it then?	130
INSPECTOR	I'd like some information, if you don't mind, Mr Birling. Two hours ago a young woman died in the Infirmary. She'd been taken there this afternoon because she'd swallowed a lot of strong disinfectant. Burnt her inside out, of course.	
ERIC	(*involuntarily*) My God!	
INSPECTOR	Yes, she was in great agony. They did everything they could for her at the Infirmary, but she died. Suicide, of course.	135
BIRLING	(*rather impatiently*) Yes, yes. Horrid business. But I don't understand why you should come here, Inspector—	
INSPECTOR	(*cutting through, massively*) I've been round to the room she had, and she'd left a letter there and a sort of diary. Like a lot of these young women who get into various kinds of trouble, she'd used more than one name. But her original name – her real name – was Eva Smith.	140
BIRLING	(*thoughtfully*) Eva Smith?	
INSPECTOR	Do you remember her, Mr Birling?	
BIRLING	(*slowly*) No – I seem to remember hearing that name – Eva Smith – somewhere. But it doesn't convey anything to me. And I don't see where I come into this.	145
INSPECTOR	She was employed in your works at one time.	
BIRLING	Oh – that's it, is it? Well, we've several hundred young women there, y'know, and they keep changing.	
INSPECTOR	This young woman, Eva Smith, was a bit out of the ordinary. I found a photograph of her in her lodgings. Perhaps you'd remember her from that.	150
	INSPECTOR *takes a photograph, about postcard size, out of his pocket and goes to* BIRLING. *Both* GERALD *and* ERIC *rise to have a look at the photograph, but the* INSPECTOR *interposes himself between them and the photograph. They are surprised and rather annoyed.* BIRLING *stares hard, and with recognition, at the photograph, which the* INSPECTOR *then replaces in his pocket.*	
GERALD	(*showing annoyance*) Any particular reason why I shouldn't see this girl's photograph, Inspector?	
INSPECTOR	(*coolly, looking hard at him*) There might be.	
ERIC	And the same applies to me, I suppose?	155
INSPECTOR	Yes.	
GERALD	I can't imagine what it could be.	
ERIC	Neither can I.	
BIRLING	And I must say, I agree with them, Inspector.	
INSPECTOR	It's the way I like to go to work. One person and one line of inquiry at a time. Otherwise, there's a muddle.	160
BIRLING	I see. Sensible really. (*moves restlessly, then turns*) You've had enough of that port, Eric.	
	The INSPECTOR *is watching* BIRLING *and now* BIRLING *notices him.*	
INSPECTOR	I think you remember Eva Smith now, don't you, Mr Birling?	

The power of language

Key features of the text are:

1 dialogue and stage directions

2 genre

3 historical and social context

---

1 DIALOGUE AND STAGE DIRECTIONS

> **Dialogue** is the term given to the conversation between characters in plays and fiction.

This scene from *An Inspector Calls* is a good example of the ways in which characters reveal something about themselves through the dialogue.

a) Write down what we learn from Mr Birling's speeches about his attitudes to:

- women (from lines 70–2: *Yes, but ... self-respect.*)
- his youth (79–81: *Yes, you don't ... cash.*)
- the view that people ought to look after each other (85–6: *But what ... his own way –*)
- his own experience of the world (97–8: *And feeling ... experience.*)
- the reported suicide (137–8: *Yes, yes ... Inspector—*)
- Eric's drinking (162: *You've had ... Eric.*)

> **Stage directions** are notes in the script which provide information about the play's performance not already made clear in the dialogue.

Stage directions are usually written in italics and can give information about:

- **the set:**
  The dining room of a fairly large suburban house belonging to a prosperous manufacturer...
- **a new character:**
  ARTHUR BIRLING is a heavy-looking, rather portentous man in his middle fifties...
- **what is happening on stage at that moment:**
  EDNA goes out. They now have all the glasses filled.

- **how a character says something:**
  GERALD (politely)
- **what a character does:**
  BIRLING Yes, of course. (Clears his throat)

b) Find examples of different types of stage direction in the extract from *An Inspector Calls*.

c) Write a paragraph commenting on the usefulness and significance of the stage direction in each of the following quotations. What does it tell us about the character or the situation in each case, and why is it important?

- BIRLING   so long as we behave ourselves, don't get into the police court or start a scandal – eh? (*laughs complacently*) (lines 56–7)
- ERIC   (*eagerly*) Yes, I remember – (*but he checks himself*) (74)
- BIRLING   (*solemnly*) But this is the point... (84)
- BIRLING   that a man has to mind his own business and look after himself and his own – and—

  We hear the sharp ring of a front door bell. BIRLING stops to listen. (91–2)
- INSPECTOR   (*coolly, looking hard at him*) There might be. (154)

---

2 GENRE

> **Genre** is the name given to a particular kind of writing with its own typical features.

To remind yourself about genre, look back at page 124.

An Inspector Calls has been described as a **psychological mystery drama**.

a) Mystery writers create **suspense** by deliberately withholding information from us. List some of the questions which remain to be answered by the end of this section of the play. Look, for example, at:

- Eric's behaviour and Birling's and Gerald's reactions to it (74–80)
- Birling's reactions to the name Eva Smith (143, and145–6)

- the Inspector's behaviour (especially 152–4 and preceding stage direction)
- the Inspector's strange name and his identity (101 and 122–6)

 3 HISTORICAL AND SOCIAL CONTEXT

> When we study a piece of writing it is important to bear in mind its **context**: the historical period and the society in which it was written.

Context

An Inspector Calls was completed in 1945; but Priestley set the play in the spring of 1912 because he wanted audiences to view their own society with the perspective of the previous half century.

a) In groups, discuss what you know about the period 1912–45. In particular, think about:

- the *Titanic*
- the two world wars
- the Russian Revolution
- the General Strike

b) Then reread the extract up to the point where Mrs Birling and Sheila leave (line 40). List the opinions that Birling expresses which we know to be completely misguided, bearing in mind what actually happened in the first four decades of the twentieth century.

For example, look at his comments about:

- *silly talk* (2–4)
- *labour trouble in the near future* (5–7)
- *a time of steadily increasing prosperity* (7–9)
- the prospect of war (12–20)
- developing technology and progress (20–7)
- 1940 (28–32)
- Russia (32–3)

Dramatic irony

> Sometimes a character says something which has a different and more serious meaning to the audience, because they know something that the character does not. When this happens, we say that the playwright has used **dramatic irony**.

This happens, for example, when Birling confidently expresses opinions about the absolutely unsinkable *Titanic* (25) or any of the other things referred to in question b above: in each case, we know something that he doesn't.

c) Write a paragraph commenting on Birling's misguided optimism and the way it is presented to us by Priestley's use of dramatic irony. Given how wrong-headed Birling's opinions and predictions are, how should we view his later advice to Gerald and Eric (84–92)?

The theme

> A **theme** is a major subject or idea which runs through a poem, play or novel. A writer will usually return to a theme several times, dealing with it in different ways and looking at it from a variety of angles.

To remind yourself about themes, look back at page 154.

d) It is often said that a major theme of *An Inspector Calls* is **responsibility**. One of the Inspector's most important statements, just before he leaves the Birling household at the end of the play, is *We don't live alone. We are members of one body. We are responsible for each other.*

Write a paragraph to explain how this theme is introduced in the opening section of the play on pages 180–3. Look, for example, at:

- lines 7–9: *We employers at last are ... prosperity.*
- 85–92: *But what so many ... and his own – and —*
- 137–8: *Yes, yes ... here, Inspector—*
- 148–9: *Oh – that's it, is it? ... changing.*

Writing about the language and techniques of 20th-century drama

FOUNDATION TIER TASKS

 1 WRITING DIALOGUE

Write a scene in a play between three or four people that reveals something of the character and personality of each one, but leaves some unanswered questions.

Planning and drafting

Think carefully about who the people are and what you want to reveal about their characters and personalities. Try to create people who are very different. For example, you might have:

- a confident businessman or woman in their mid-fifties, rather like Mr Birling
- a cheerful typist in their twenties
- a teenager
- someone in their eighties who is a little infirm
- a professional person, such as a doctor or teacher

Make sure that there is a mixture of ages, genders and backgrounds.

- Place them in a particular **setting** and create a **situation** that they are faced with. Think up a setting and situation which are challenging or awkward. For example, a lift that has broken down between floors, a windswept station platform late at night, a surprise birthday party that is going horribly wrong, an embarrassing interview, an arrest...
- Make the characters say and do things which leave some intriguing unanswered questions for the audience to ponder.

For example, you could start with the following stage directions:

The cramped interior of an office lift. The floor indicator next to the door shows clearly that the lift has become stuck between floors. Standing impatiently in one corner of the lift is Sir Toby Beamish, managing director of Beamish Enterprises...

2 WRITING ABOUT CHARACTERS

What do we learn about Mr Birling at the beginning of the play? In what ways is the Inspector contrasted with Birling, when we first meet him?

Planning and drafting

First make notes on the two characters, finding evidence in the extract. Look back at your responses to the questions on pages 184–5. Then think about the differences between them. Use the writing frame below as a guide.

Para	Evidence in the extract	Look back at
Evidence from stage directions about Birling		
1	The opening stage directions	the introduction to Q1b
	Stage directions in the script	Q1c
Evidence from the dialogue about Birling		
2	His attitudes	Q1a
	His misguided opinions	Q3b
	His views on our responsibilities to one another	Qs 3c, 3d
Unanswered questions about Birling		
3	His reactions to the mention of Eva Smith	Q2a
Evidence from stage directions about the Inspector		
4	When he enters	lines 116–17
	When he speaks	line 139
	The way he behaves	Q1c
Evidence from the dialogue about the Inspector		
5	His replies	line 154
	His way of working	lines 160–1
	His calm control	line 163
Unanswered questions about the Inspector		
6	Who is he?	lines 122–6

FOUNDATION & HIGHER TIER TASK

 WRITING ABOUT DRAMATIC CONVENTIONS

Write about Priestley's use of the stage directions in this extract from *An Inspector Calls*, describing the different ways in which they are employed and the various functions they perform.

(See pages 188–9 for 'the moderator's view' on how to tackle this question.)

Para	You could start...
1	The stage directions at the beginning of the play describe Birling as 'a heavy-looking, rather portentous man in his middle fifties'...
	They also reveal other things about him...
2	Birling is a man who believes that...
	He also expresses confident opinions about...
	The speech which sums up Birling's philosophy is...
3	By the end of this opening section, the audience has been left with some important questions about him...
4	In contrast to Birling, the Inspector 'need not be a big man'...
	At one point, he interrupts Birling...
	When Gerald asks why he isn't allowed to see the photograph...
5	While Birling is always declaring his opinions, the Inspector gives nothing away...
	He likes to work methodically...
	He seems to know exactly what the others are thinking...
6	The most important question...

HIGHER TIER TASK

 ANALYSING THE SCENE

Write a study of the extract from *An Inspector Calls* explaining how an understanding of the historical and social context of the play, and the use of dramatic irony, help shape audience responses, especially to the theme of responsibility.

Planning and drafting

BACKGROUND

The following additional information might help you to understand more about the historical context:

- *Priestley first had his idea, about a mysterious Inspector visiting a family, before the Second World War.*
- *He returned to the idea in 1944 and wrote the play very quickly in the winter of 1944–5.*
- *As there was no London theatre available, the play was first staged in two theatres in Moscow, in 1945. It opened in London in 1946.*

1 WRITING ABOUT THE HISTORICAL CONTEXT

Look at your responses to questions 3a and 3b.

2 ANALYSING PRIESTLEY'S USE OF DRAMATIC IRONY

Look back at 3c.

3 SHOWING HOW DRAMATIC IRONY IS USED IN INTRODUCING THE THEME OF RESPONSIBILITY

Look at your answer to 3d.

- Remember that, just before he leaves the Birling household at the end of the play, the Inspector says: *We don't live alone. We are members of one body. We are responsible for each other.*

You could start:

Although Priestley wrote this play in 1944–5, he decided to set it in the spring of 1912...

The moderator's view

Write about Priestley's use of the stage directions in this extract from *An Inspector Calls*, describing the different ways in which they are employed and the various functions they perform.

STEP 1: READ THE TEXT

The post-1914 drama assignment is part of your English Literature coursework and is worth 10% of your final mark. Remember to respond to plays as drama as well as texts. In this assignment you should make sure that you:

- respond critically, sensitively and in detail using evidence from the text to support your ideas
- explore the interaction of language, structure and form
- consider alternative approaches and interpretations
- relate the play to its social, cultural and historical context and literary tradition

STEP 2: STAGE DIRECTIONS

A playwright can use stage directions for various reasons (see questions 1a–c on page 184).

- Find and write down all the examples of stage directions in the extract on pages 180–3.
- Put them into groups according to whether they tell us about (a) the way a character says something, or (b) an action being performed on stage.

- Explain how these directions back up what we know about characters from their speeches.

STEP 3: DIALOGUE

One purpose of stage directions is to indicate to the director and actors the way in which the playwright wants certain lines to be spoken.

- Write down three stage directions of your own which explain how a particular speech from the play should be spoken.
- How would each of these three directions affect the audience's response to the speech?

STEP 4: PLANNING AND DRAFTING

Look at your responses to questions 1a–c on page 184.

Give examples of different kinds of stage direction and comment on the dramatic effects they achieve. For example, look at stage directions which give information about:

- the set (Do these help us determine the social and historical context of the play?)
- a new character (How do these help form our first impression of a character?)
- what is happening on stage
- what a character does

STEP 5: READING AND RESPONDING TO POST-1914 DRAMA

Now use everything you have learned in this unit to answer the task on *An Inspector Calls*. Remember that you are awarded marks for the 'quality of written communication' for all your coursework assignments. You should:

- make sure that your work is legible, accurate and that the meaning is clear
- use an appropriate structure and style of writing

STEP 6: SAMPLE ANSWER

Read this introduction from a sample answer.

In comparison with the plays of Shakespeare, there are many stage directions in An Inspector Calls. In the following piece of coursework, I am going to identify the different kinds of stage directions in the opening section of the play and explain how these are used by the playwright. However, the underlying reason for all of these stage directions is to clarify the playwright's intentions to the director and the audience.

The play is meant to be seen as drama and not simply as a text. Similarly, the stage directions should inform the production process, not be read like part of a novel. Whereas Shakespeare's absence of stage directions allows directors to set his plays within almost any time or place, Priestley uses stage directions to place this play very firmly within a particular historical and social context...

> This student has written a very clear opening. They clearly state what they will cover and, in the second paragraph, are starting to analyse the effect of Priestley's stage directions.

Quick tip   Get to know the 'assessment objectives' for the different tasks: find out what the examiner wants, to make sure that you cover everything.

Shylock and the pound of flesh

In this unit you will:

- study one of Shakespeare's characters with an understanding of the social and historical influences and the cultural context in which he was created
- examine Shakespeare's language
- compare different interpretations of the character

In the opening of Shakespeare's *The Merchant of Venice*, the young Bassanio asks his friend, the merchant Antonio, if he will lend him some money so that he can present himself to the rich heiress Portia as a would-be husband. Antonio readily agrees, but explains that, not having enough in the bank, he will have to borrow the three thousand ducats that Bassanio needs. In the scene which follows (Act 1 Scene 3), Bassanio is discussing the possibility of a loan with the money-lender Shylock. Thinking it over, Shylock asks...

SHYLOCK	– may I speak with Antonio?
BASSANIO	If it please you to dine with us –
SHYLOCK	Yes, to smell pork, to eat of the habitation which your prophet
	the Nazarite conjured the devil into. I will buy with you, sell with you,
	talk with you, walk with you, and so following; but I will not eat with you, 5
	drink with you, nor pray with you. What news on the Rialto?
	Who is he comes here?

Enter ANTONIO

BASSANIO	This is Signor Antonio.	
SHYLOCK	[*Aside*] How like a fawning publican he looks!	
	I hate him for he is a Christian;	10
	But more, for that in low simplicity	
	He lends out money gratis, and brings down	
	The rate of usance here with us in Venice.	
	If I can catch him once upon the hip,	
	I will feed fat the ancient grudge I bear him.	15
	He hates our sacred nation, and he rails	
	Even there where merchants most do congregate	
	On me, my bargains, and my well-won thrift	
	Which he calls interest. Cursed be my tribe	
	If I forgive him!	20
BASSANIO	Shylock, do you hear?	
SHYLOCK	I am debating of my present store,	
	And by the near guess of my memory	

	I cannot instantly raise up the gross	
	Of full three thousand ducats. What of that?	25
	Tubal, a wealthy Hebrew of my tribe,	
	Will furnish me. But soft, how many months	
	Do you desire? [*To Antonio*] Rest you fair, good signor!	
	Your worship was the last man in our mouths.	
ANTONIO	Shylock, albeit I neither lend nor borrow	30
	By taking nor giving of excess,	
	Yet to supply the ripe wants of my friend	
	I'll break a custom. [*To Bassanio*] Is he yet possessed	
	How much ye would?	
SHYLOCK	Ay, ay, three thousand ducats.	35
ANTONIO	And for three months.	
SHYLOCK	I had forgot, three months; [*To Bassanio*] you told me so.	
	Well then, your bond; and let me see – but hear you,	
	Methoughts you said you neither lend nor borrow	
	Upon advantage.	40
ANTONIO	I do never use it.	

To prove that there is nothing wrong with lending money for interest, Shylock then tells them the Bible story of Jacob, who profited when looking after his uncle Laban's sheep. But Antonio is not impressed…

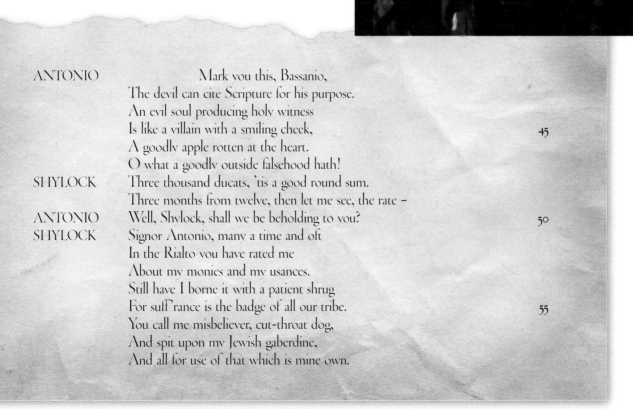

ANTONIO	Mark you this, Bassanio,	
	The devil can cite Scripture for his purpose.	
	An evil soul producing holy witness	
	Is like a villain with a smiling cheek,	45
	A goodly apple rotten at the heart.	
	O what a goodly outside falsehood hath!	
SHYLOCK	Three thousand ducats, 'tis a good round sum.	
	Three months from twelve, then let me see, the rate –	
ANTONIO	Well, Shylock, shall we be beholding to you?	50
SHYLOCK	Signor Antonio, many a time and oft	
	In the Rialto you have rated me	
	About my monies and my usances.	
	Still have I borne it with a patient shrug	
	For suff'rance is the badge of all our tribe.	55
	You call me misbeliever, cut-throat dog,	
	And spit upon my Jewish gaberdine,	
	And all for use of that which is mine own.	

191

	Well then, it now appears you need my help.	
	Go to, then, you come to me, and you say,	60
	'Shylock, we would have monies' – you say so,	
	You that did void your rheum upon my beard,	
	And foot me as you spurn a stranger cur	
	Over your threshold: monies is your suit.	
	What should I say to you? Should I not say	65
	'Hath a dog money? Is it possible	
	A cur can lend three thousand ducats?' Or	
	Shall I bend low, and in a bondman's key,	
	With bated breath and whisp'ring humbleness,	
	Say this:	70
	'Fair sir, you spat on me on Wednesday last,	
	You spurned me such a day, another time	
	You called me dog: and for these courtesies	
	I'll lend you thus much monies.'	
ANTONIO	I am as like to call thee so again,	75
	To spit on thee again, to spurn thee too.	
	If thou wilt lend this money, lend it not	
	As to thy friends, for when did friendship take	
	A breed for barren metal of his friend?	
	But lend it rather to thine enemy,	80
	Who if he break, thou mayst with better face	
	Exact the penalty.	
SHYLOCK	Why look you how you storm!	
	I would be friends with you and have your love,	
	Forget the shames that you have stained me with,	85
	Supply your present wants, and take no doit	
	Of usance for my monies, and you'll not hear me.	
	This is kind I offer.	
BASSANIO	This were kindness.	
SHYLOCK	This kindness will I show.	90
	Go with me to a notary, seal me there	
	Your single bond, and, in a merry sport,	
	If you repay me not on such a day,	
	In such a place, such sum or sums as are	
	Expressed in the condition, let the forfeit	95
	Be nominated for an equal pound	
	Of your fair flesh, to be cut off and taken	
	In what part of your body pleaseth me.	
ANTONIO	Content, in faith! I'll seal to such a bond,	
	And say there is much kindness in the Jew.	100
BASSANIO	You shall not seal to such a bond for me;	
	I'll rather dwell in my necessity.	

ANTONIO	Why, fear not, man, I will not forfeit it.
	Within these two months, that's a month before
	This bond expires, I do expect return 105
	Of thrice three times the value of this bond.
SHYLOCK	O father Abram, what these Christians are,
	Whose own hard dealings teaches them suspect
	The thoughts of others! Pray you tell me this:
	If he should break his day what should I gain 110
	By the exaction of the forfeiture?
	A pound of man's flesh, taken from a man,
	Is not so estimable, profitable neither,
	As flesh of muttons, beefs, or goats. I say
	To buy his favour, I extend this friendship. 115
	If he will take it, so; if not, adieu,
	And for my love, I pray you wrong me not.
ANTONIO	Yes, Shylock, I will seal unto this bond.
SHYLOCK	Then meet me forthwith at the notary's.
	Give him direction for this merry bond, 120
	And I will go and purse the ducats straight,
	See to my house left in the fearful guard
	Of an unthrifty knave, and presently
	I'll be with you. *Exit*
ANTONIO	Hie thee, gentle Jew. 125
	The Hebrew will turn Christian, he grows kind.
BASSANIO	I like not fair terms and a villain's mind.
ANTONIO	Come on, in this there can be no dismay,
	My ships come home a month before the day.

Exeunt

Here are some images of Shylock as he has been played by different actors.
From left: David Calder, Warren Mitchell and Laurence Olivier.

The power of language

Key features of the performances are:

1. Shakespeare's language
2. setting
3. interpretation

1 LANGUAGE

Most of this scene (from line 8 onwards) is in **verse**. The pattern of light and heavy stresses in a line of verse is known as the **metre**.

Regular metre

a) The metre of the following three lines is totally regular. To hear this regular metre in Shakespeare's verse, read the lines out loud, emphasising the heavily stressed syllables:

- If **I** can **catch** him **once** u**pon** the **hip** (14)
- Your **worship was** the **last** man **in** our **mouths** (29)
- You **shall** not **seal** to **such** a **bond** for **me** (101)

b) To become more familiar with Shakespeare's metre, copy out the following lines and underline the stressed syllables:

- *A goodly apple rotten at the heart.* (46)
- *And all for use of that which is mine own.* (58)
- *My ships come home a month before the day.* (129)

c) The six lines above are all totally regular in their metre. Write down what you notice in each line about:

- the pattern of light and heavy stresses
- the number of syllables

d) Most lines are not regular. Find the opening two lines of Shylock's aside (*How like ... a Christian*, lines 9–10). Read the lines aloud several times. Although different actors will perform them in different ways, many will place the stresses something like this:

How like a **fawn**ing **pub**lican he **looks**

I hate him for he is a **Christ**ian

Write a brief comment on the lines, explaining how the stress pattern helps to convey the meaning and the speaker's mood. For example, where do the heavy stresses fall? Where do you find two heavy stresses next to each other?

Iambic pentameter

Just as music has bars, so verse has **feet**. Shakespeare's verse has five feet in a complete line.

A five-feet line is called **pentameter** (*pent* = five; *meter* = measure).

A foot which contains an unstressed syllable followed by a stressed one (the standard beat – *dee*-**dum**) is called an **iamb**.

Verse which has five iambs per line as its standard rhythm is therefore called **iambic pentameter**. Iambic pentameter which does not rhyme is also known as **blank verse**.

e) Make up some regular iambic pentameter lines which could serve as newspaper headlines. For example:

Milan to sell their Irish striker, Byrne

United Nations aids Afghanistan

Election set for June the twenty-first

Henry Goodman (left) and Patrick Stewart as Shylock.

2 SETTING

> The **setting** of a film is the particular time and place in which the events of the story happen. If a Shakespeare film or stage play is set in a period which is neither Shakespeare's own time nor the period when the story took place, we call it a **period analogue** production.

An *analogue* is simply a parallel. For example, Shakespeare's *King Richard III*, which shows the rise to power of a bloody tyrant, has been set in the 1930s to draw parallels with Hitler.

a) Look carefully at the photographs of the different Shylocks on pages 193–4. Henry Goodman was in a period analogue production, set in central Europe in the 1930s. The other four are examples of period analogue (one set in the 1890s and one set in the early 20th century), **Shakespearean** and **modern** settings. (Look at the section on Shakespeare's *Romeo and Juliet*, page 14.) Study the characters' costumes and work out which Shylock was in which setting.

b) Trevor Nunn chose a period analogue interpretation of the play to remind audiences of events which took place in central Europe in the 1930s. In groups:
- discuss what you know about (a) anti-Semitism, and (b) the Holocaust
- find moments in the scene – particular lines or characters' reactions – which might remind an audience of the persecution of the Jews under Hitler. For example, look at lines 16–20 (*He hates ... forgive him!*), 51–76 (*Signior Antonio ... spurn thee too.*) and 125–7 (*Hie thee ... villain's mind.*)
- consider how this 1930s setting affects the way you view Shylock and Antonio. Do you have more, or less, sympathy for Shylock? Do you think of Antonio as a Nazi? What might Shylock's fate be in a society like this?

3 INTERPRETATION

> An **interpretation** of a play is someone's idea about what it means. We say that a director or an actor is interpreting a script by performing it in certain ways and making the audience notice particular things in order to bring out chosen meanings.

One of the main decisions any actor or director has to make about Shylock is: does he offer the flesh bond in this scene as a genuine attempt to win Antonio's friendship; or as an attempt to trick him into putting his life in danger? Henry Goodman's Shylock did the first; Patrick Stewart's the second.

a) In groups of three, act out the scene from line 83 (*Why look you how you storm!*) to the end:
- as though Shylock were perfectly genuine and honest, regarding the offer as a kind of joke
- as though Shylock were perfectly genuine and honest, and wanted Antonio to understand that the offer is part of a serious attempt at reconciliation
- as though Shylock were a villain attempting to trap Antonio (but not so obviously as to let Antonio see that he is plotting)
- in any other way that you think might work

Then reread the earlier part of the scene and discuss which of the versions you find most convincing and believable. Take into account what Shylock says at lines 14–15 (*If I can ... bear him*), 19–20 (*Cursed ... forgive him!*), 84–8 (*I would be ... kind I offer.*) and 115 (*To buy...*).

b) Write up your discussion in a paragraph headed *How genuine is Shylock's offer?*

FOUNDATION TIER TASKS

 SUMMARISING THE STORY

Reread Act 1 Scene 3 of Shakespeare's *The Merchant of Venice* and summarise the main events in your own words.

Use the starters in this writing frame to remind you what happens.

 CREATING A STORYBOARD

In the 1994 television version of *The Merchant of Venice*, the director Alan Horrox decided to show us the moment when the bond is signed and sealed, and then show us Shylock's reaction after Antonio and Bassanio have left, even though the scene does not exist in Shakespeare's text.

Draw up a storyboard of your own version of this moment.

Lines	Starters
1–6	*Shylock asks if he may speak with Antonio, but he refuses to…*
8–20	*When Antonio arrives, Shylock expresses his feelings to us in an aside. He says…*
22–8	*Shylock hasn't got the money to lend to Antonio, but says that he can…*
42–7	*Antonio is not impressed by Shylock's Bible story and says…*
51–74	*Shylock reminds Antonio about the way he has treated him in the past…*
75–82	*Antonio responds angrily…*
83–98	*Shylock calms him down and makes an unexpected offer. He will lend Antonio the money and, if…*
101–24	*Bassanio doesn't like the sound of it, but Antonio accepts and arranges to meet Shylock…*
125–9	*Antonio is not worried by the terms of the bond because…*

Planning and drafting

CREATING A STORYBOARD

First look at the storyboards for *Romeo and Juliet* on pages 10–13. Notice that, for each shot, there is:

- a comment about any sound effects or music
- a description of what the viewer will see
- a drawing
- dialogue (which you do not need to include)

INTERPRETING SHYLOCK'S ACTIONS

Look back at question 3 on interpretation (page 195) and decide whether your Shylock is genuine in his offer or a villainous plotter.

Make sure that your storyboard brings out the chosen interpretation clearly.

CHOOSING A SETTING

Is yours a historical, Shakespearean, modern or period analogue production? If it's period analogue, when is it set?

Where should the signing of the bond take place? What difference can it make if Shylock is 'on home territory' or not? Or if the scene takes place in public or in private? Possible locations include:

- Shylock's house or workplace
- Bassanio's or Antonio's house
- a busy street or square
- a deserted place in the city
- a public place such as a café or an inn

or any other location of your choice.

DECIDING WHAT TO SHOW

You could include the following shots:

- Antonio and Shylock signing the bond
- wax dripping on to the bond and receiving the imprint of Antonio's seal ring
- Antonio shaking hands with Shylock and then leaving
- Shylock's reaction after Antonio departs

FOUNDATION & HIGHER TIER TASK

COMPARING INTERPRETATIONS OF SHYLOCK

In the 1994 television version of *The Merchant of Venice*, Shylock (played by Bob Peck) was plainly a villain who made his offer of the bond as a deliberate attempt to trap Antonio. In the 1999 production at the Royal National Theatre, Henry Goodman's Shylock was a decent man who offered the bond genuinely as a way of becoming friends with Antonio after years of mutual dislike and suspicion.

Compare these two approaches and say which you prefer as an interpretation of Shylock in Act 1 Scene 3 of the play.

(See pages 198–9 for 'the moderator's view' on how to tackle this question.)

HIGHER TIER TASK

COMPARING CUT AND UNCUT VERSIONS

Directors usually cut lines or whole scenes from Shakespeare's text when they are preparing a performance.

This can happen because the full text is very long (*Hamlet* can run to over four hours if it isn't cut), or perhaps because there are lines or scenes which might not work for a modern audience (some of Shakespeare's clowns can be very unfunny these days). Film versions often use only a fraction of the full text.

Cuts can also be made, however, which affect the interpretation. When David Calder played Shylock in 1993, the following lines were cut:

If I can catch him once upon the hip,
I will feed fat the ancient grudge I bear him.   (lines 14–15)

and

*   Cursed be my tribe*
If I forgive him!   (lines 19–20)

Discuss what effect these cuts might have on our interpretation of Shylock's motives and give your opinion on whether it was right to cut lines which can affect the interpretation in this way.

Planning and drafting

WHERE DO THE CUTS OCCUR?

First reread the scene, paying particular attention to the speech from which the lines were cut. What else is Shylock saying during the speech? What is the context of the cut lines?

HOW IMPORTANT ARE THEY?

Decide how significant these cuts are. What information is the audience deprived of if the lines are not spoken?

COMPARE A CUT AND AN UNCUT VERSION

What differences are there in the way we might view a Shylock whose speeches included these lines and one from whose speeches these lines were cut?

IS IT RIGHT TO CUT THEM?

Consider the views that cutting lines 14–15 and 19–20:

- is right, because otherwise people only see Shylock after that as a scheming villain, not as a complex human being
- is wrong, because they are a clear statement that Shylock means Antonio harm, and this is something we need to know from the outset

---

You could start:

Directors nearly always make some cuts to a Shakespeare script when they are preparing a performance. In the 1993 production of The Merchant of Venice...

In the 1994 television version of *The Merchant of Venice*, Shylock (played by Bob Peck) was plainly a villain who made his offer of the bond as a deliberate attempt to trap Antonio. In the 1999 production at the Royal National Theatre, Henry Goodman's Shylock was a decent man who offered the bond genuinely as a way of becoming friends with Antonio after years of mutual dislike and suspicion.

Compare these two approaches and say which you prefer as an interpretation of Shylock in Act 1 Scene 3 of the play.

STEP 1: READ THE TEXT

Your Shakespeare coursework is particularly important because it can make up 5% of your final mark for English and 10% of your final mark for English Literature (as the pre-1914 drama assignment).

There are three main assessment objectives for coursework on Shakespeare. You will be assessed on your ability to:

- read with insight, make textual references and develop your own personal response
- explore how language contributes to meaning
- consider alternative approaches to, and interpretations of, texts
- relate the play to its social, cultural and historical context and literary tradition

STEP 2: FOCUS ON THE QUESTION

Look back at the script on pages 190–3 and ask yourself the following questions:

- Does Shylock appear to be a good man or a bad man from what he says to Antonio and the way he behaves?
- How did you respond to Shylock's account of being spat upon and insulted?
- Thinking about these two men, would you say that Shylock is from the outset a bad man plotting against Antonio's life, or an essentially good man who has been badly treated in the past but wants to make friends with Antonio?

STEP 3: THE USE OF LANGUAGE

Select three statements from (a) Shylock and (b) Antonio that help to support your view of each character.

STEP 4: PLANNING AND DRAFTING

Look back at the script on pages 190–3 and think about the way Shylock is presented to us through his speeches and actions. Then decide what you feel about his offer of the bond. Make notes under four headings:

1 **Describe what Shylock says and does**

Look at:

- Shylock's conversation with Bassanio and his reaction to being invited to eat with Antonio (1–6)
- his aside to the audience as Antonio enters (9–20):
  - Why does he hate Antonio?
  - What does he say he will do if he gets the chance?
- his reaction when Antonio accuses him of hypocrisy and deceit (51–74). What does he feel about:
  - Antonio's past treatment of him?
  - the fact that Antonio now needs his help?
  - how he should react to Antonio's request for help?

2 **Interpret his statements and actions**

Look at the bond (83–117):

- Is it a genuine offer of friendship, in your opinion, or part of a plot to trap Antonio? You could include the paragraph you wrote in answer to question 3b on page 195.

3 **Study the language**

Then look back at the section on Shakespeare's language (page 194) and add comments to your notes to show how the metre helps to express the meaning.

4 **Evaluate the two interpretations**

Finally, explain why you prefer Patrick Stewart's or Henry Goodman's interpretation of Shylock.

STEP 5: READING AND RESPONDING TO SHAKESPEARE

Now write your answer. Remember to back up your opinions by referring to the text and using quotes.

STEP 6: SAMPLE ANSWER

Read this introduction from a sample answer.

> I think that Shakespeare wrote this scene in such a way that the reader can decide upon their own meaning. Shylock is a complex character and his actions are open to interpretation. Directors and actors have chosen to portray Shylock in many different ways, all of which can be supported by reference to the text.
>
> When we first encounter Shylock in Act 1 Scene 3...

This student has indicated that they will compare different interpretations of this scene, evaluate which they think to be the most effective and support their answer with reference to the text – all crucial to success in this question.

Quick tip Remember to use the point–example–explanation structure to make sure that you back up everything you say by referring to the text.

Glossary

of English and English Literature terms

Abstract noun The label we give to something we cannot touch, such as an emotion, feeling or idea, e.g. *a thriving* **family** *and* **community** *that has* **skills** *and* **resources**. (p. 55, p. 74)

Accent The term used to describe the way people pronounce words according to their regional or social background. (pp. 144–5)

Acrostic A form in which the first – or sometimes the last – letter of each line goes to form a key word or phrase. (p. 84)

Active and passive In an active sentence, the subject performs the action; in a passive sentence, the subject is on the receiving end of the action, e.g. *Ostman* **had** *no choice...* (active), *the story* **was picked up** *by other papers...* (passive). (p. 95)

Adjective A word which gives information about a noun or pronoun. A group of words which does this is called an **adjective phrase**, e.g. *gruesome deaths,* **savage** *butchery, a* **horrific** *scene*. (p. 45, pp. 54–5, p. 74, p. 115)

Adverbials Words or phrases which add important information to a sentence, answering questions such as When? How? and Where? e.g. *Meanwhile, a witness, Ellen Stanton, told police she had seen Alfred Stratton ... tearing* **at high speed away from the shop**. (pp. 84–5, pp. 114–15)

Alliteration The repetition of consonant sounds to gain a particular effect, e.g. *But when the bath was filled we found a fur* (p. 155)

Angles Camera shots from different directions and heights. (p. 15, pp. 34–5)

Audience The people who are expected to read or see a text – the group to whom that text is addressed. The term can refer to readers, listeners, film/television audiences, or users of information technology. (p. 44)

Autobiography A written account of the writer's own life. (p. 135)

Biography A written account of someone else's life. (p. 135)

Blank verse *See* **Metre**

Chronological writing Writing in which events are described in the order in which they happened. *See also* **Non-chronological writing** (p. 94)

Conditional sentence A sentence in which one thing depends upon another. The **conditional clause** in the sentence will usually begin with the words *if* or *unless*, e.g. *If you do not have a smoke alarm, fit one. Do not open the front door unless...* (p. 85)

Context The society, the historical period and the culture in which something was written. (p. 144, p. 185)

Creole *See* **Pidgin**

Cutting The action of changing from one film shot to another. (p. 15, p. 35)

Dialect A variety of language used by a particular group of people, which has distinctive features of vocabulary and grammar. (pp. 144–5)

Dialogue The spoken exchanges between characters in plays and fiction. (pp. 174–5, p. 184)

Directive *See* **Imperative**

Direct speech A speaker's exact words reproduced in writing. In **indirect** (or **reported**) **speech**, we report what was said but do not use the speaker's exact words, e.g. *'...and don't break anything!'* (direct speech), *Ostman said the Sasquatches chatted among themselves* (reported speech). (p. 134)

Discourse markers Adverbials and other phrases which help to structure a text are sometimes known as discourse markers, e.g. *Firstly, On the other hand.* (p. 115)

Dramatic irony In plays, an effect in which a character says something which has a special significance for the audience, because they know something that the character does not. (p. 185)

Dramatic monologue A poem in which the voice is a character who tells us a story or expresses their thoughts, as in a soliloquy in a play. *See also* **Voice** (p. 165)

Duration The set amount of time for an audience to experience all or part of a moving-image text. (p. 35)

Exclamation An exclamation can express a sudden reaction, a strong assertion, an emotion such as surprise or a powerful personal feeling. It ends in an **exclamation mark**. (p. 174)

Frame A single image on a strip of film, or a 'frozen' television image. A photograph taken from a film or television frame is known as a **still**. (p. 15, p. 34)

Framing The skill of placing people or objects in different positions within the edges of the film frame to get particular effects. (p. 15, p. 34)

Genre A particular kind of book or film with its own special and recognisable features – such as horror, Western or science fiction. (p. 124, pp. 184–5)

Graphic novel A story which is told through a combination of words and images. It closely resembles a cartoon-strip in its style and narrative. (p. 25)

Graphics The art of putting images and lettering together for a special effect. (p. 24)

Iambic pentameter *See Metre*

Image An illustration, such as a photograph or a drawing, used by an advertiser to achieve a particular effect. *See also Imagery* (p. 55)

Imagery The collective term for metaphors and similes. An image in poetic language is a picture in words which helps to get across an idea. (p. 125, pp. 154–5)

Imperative The form of the verb used to give a command, issue a warning or make a request. The imperative form is used in **directives** – sentences which ask/tell someone to do something, e.g. *Be prepared, Don't engage in conversation, Share a taxi with a friend...* (p. 54, p. 84)

Intro The opening paragraph or sentence of a newspaper article. (p. 104)

Juxtaposition Placing one item next to another for particular effect. Writers often juxtapose incidents or facts in order to make a particular point. (p. 135)

Metaphor A way of comparing things without using the words *like* or *as*, where the writer writes about something as if it really were something else, e.g. *...the long grass is a snare drum.* *See also Simile* (p. 125, pp. 154–5)

Metre The pattern of light and heavy stresses in a line of poetry. A verse line can be divided into **feet** (the equivalent of bars in music). A five-feet line is known as **pentameter**. A foot which contains an unstressed syllable followed by a stressed one is called an **iamb**. Verse which has five iambs per line as its standard rhythm is therefore called **iambic pentameter**. Iambic pentameter which does not rhyme is also known as **blank verse**. (p. 194)

Montage The skill of joining shots together in a sequence to convey a particular meaning (a French word, pronounced *mont-arje*). (p. 15)

Narrative Another term for a story or account. Biographies, autobiographies, novels and short stories are all examples of **narrative texts**. (p. 24)

Non-chronological writing Writing which organises events in a different order from the one in which they happened. *See also Chronological writing* (p. 114)

Panning Moving the camera across a scene in a single shot. (p. 15)

Paragraph A block of sentences linked together by one main idea or subject. (p. 64, p. 105)

Parenthesis A word or phrase inserted into a sentence to provide additional information, placed between commas, brackets or dashes, e.g. *Then, in 1910, the murder of two miners...* (pp. 94–5)

Passive *See Active*

Period analogue The setting of a Shakespeare film or stage play in a period which is neither Shakespeare's own time nor the period when the story took place. (p. 195)

Person *See Verb*

Pidgin A language which grew up when European traders made contact with African or Asian language communities and they needed to exchange simple information. A **creole** is a pidgin which has become the mother-tongue of a community. (p. 145)

Presentational devices Examples of the use of text and image to gain particular effects. (p. 55, p. 73)

Question tag *See Tag question*

Quote Someone's word-for-word comment reported in a news article, e.g. *Dr David Vaughan said, 'We have increased carbon dioxide...* (p. 45)

Rhetorical language Language used for particular effects, especially in important speeches. It includes structures such as lists (e.g. *government of the people, by the people, for the people*) and repetition (e.g. *afraid of today, afraid of tomorrow and ... afraid of each other*). (p. 65)

Rhetorical question A question that does not expect an answer. (p. 174)

Rhyme The effect of bringing together words which end in the same – or similar – sounds. **Half-rhymes** occur when words sound very similar but are not an exact rhyme. Two successive lines which rhyme are called a **rhyming couplet**. **Internal rhyme** happens when one word rhymes with another from the middle of a line, rather than at the end. A pattern of rhymes in a poem is known as a **rhyme-scheme**. (p. 164)

Rhythm The beat of a poem, based on its pattern of stressed and unstressed syllables. (p. 165)

Setting The particular time and place in which a film or stage director sets the story. (p. 14, p. 195)

Shot A single uninterrupted run of the camera. Shots include **close-ups**, for example, where the camera is very near to the subject, or **long-shots**, taken from further away. (p. 14, p. 34)

Simile A way of comparing things in an unusual or unexpected way, in which the writer creates an image in the reader's mind. A simile uses the words *like* or *as*, e.g. *her hair stood out from her head like a crest of serpents.*
See also **Metaphor** (p. 125, pp. 154–5)

Slogan A short, catchy phrase designed to stick in the memory, most often used in advertising, e.g. *All bubble, no squeak!* (p. 35)

Stage directions Notes in a play script which provide information about the play's performance not already made clear in the dialogue. (p. 184)

Standard English The dialect of English which is normally used for writing and public communication, and is most widely understood. (p. 144)

Structure The structure of a text is the way it is organised, laid out or shaped. (p. 64)

Syntax Another name for sentence grammar. (p. 144)

Tabloid A popular, small-format newspaper such as the *Daily Mail*, the *Mirror* or the *Sun*. (p. 105)

Tag question A statement with a brief question added on to the end. The additional question element is called the **question tag**, e.g. *'You get paid, **don't you**?'* (p. 175)

Target group The particular audience at which an advertisement is aimed. (p. 35)

Tense The form of the **verb** which shows when something happens – either the past, the present or the future, e.g. *Our fathers **brought forth** (past), Now we **are engaged** (present), **shall** not **perish** from the earth (future)*. (p. 64)

Theme A major subject or idea which runs through a poem, play or novel. A theme is usually returned to several times, dealt with in different ways and looked at from a variety of angles. (p. 15, p. 154, p. 185)

Topic heading A brief title which summarises the content of a paragraph. (p. 105)

Typography A term used in graphics for the way words are written, drawn or printed. (p. 24)

Verb A word that expresses an action, a happening, a process or a state. Verbs can be in the **first person** (*I hope to, We soon learned*), the **second person** (*You'll see*) or the **third person** (*It's a great way, She enjoyed herself, Conservation can be hard work*). (p. 84, p. 135, p. 145)

Vocabulary The term given to a writer's choice of words. (pp. 54–5)

Voice The term given to the person who seems to be speaking in a story or poem. (p. 165)

Voice-over In moving-image media, a voice heard without the speaker being seen. (p. 35)

Glossary

of 'examiner's terms'

The following terms are specifically aimed at helping students understand the language of the examination papers, as well as some of the terms within this book.

Article A piece of non-fiction writing in a newspaper, magazine or reference book.

Assessment objectives The skills in English which are tested in exams and coursework.

Brainstorm An intensive planning stage to help to generate ideas or solve problems.

Compare Highlight the similarities and differences between two items.

Convey 'Communicate' or 'get across' a message.

Criticise If you criticise a text, you analyse it and judge how effective it is.

Cultures and traditions A particular set of customs, attitudes or beliefs that characterise a group of people, which may have been handed down from generation to generation.

Device A literary tool which is used to try to create a particular effect in a piece of writing, or to draw a particular response from a reader or listener.

Draft One version of a piece of writing.

Effective An effective piece of writing is one that has fulfilled its purpose.

Essay A short piece of non-fiction writing dealing with a particular topic.

Evaluate To judge what something is worth or to place a value on something relative to something else.

Focus A point on which you should fix your attention.

Follow an argument Make sure that you understand what the writer is trying to say on a particular subject.

Form The kind of writing you are reading or producing, e.g. a letter, a newspaper article, a leaflet...

Foundation tier A level of entry at GCSE at which grades C–G can be gained.

Higher tier A level of entry at GCSE at which grades A*–D can be gained.

Interaction The way something acts or works in relation to something else. For example, in many media texts, text and illustrations interact to get across a particular message.

Layout The design of text and illustrations on the page.

Media A means for communicating information – newspapers, cinema, radio, television...

Plan An outline for a piece of writing, in note form.

Pre-1914 poetry bank The selection of sixteen poems in the AQA *Anthology* by poets who wrote before 1914.

Presentation The ways in which the material is presented, or laid out, on the page in order to gain the reader's interest, or to enhance the meaning of the item.

Purpose The reason why a text is written.

Sequence To place things in a successive order.

Sustained writing Continuous writing of a reasonable length (not simply notes).

Text Any piece of printed or written language.

The specifications at a glance

Below are the summaries of what has to be studied for English Specification A and English Literature Specification A. The annotations show which parts of the exam papers and coursework assignments are covered by the units in this book.

- Star-cross'd lovers
- People are...
- No-one wants jigging mouses!
- Ice titan
- Two thousand years of history

- A message from the president
- Save the rainforest!
- Crimestoppers

- Poetry from different cultures

- Snow monster
- Mysteries of the dead
- The finger of fate

- Shylock and the pound of flesh

- Star-cross'd lovers
- People are...
- No-one wants jigging mouses!
- Ice titan
- Two thousand years of history

- The vulture woman
- Outsiders

GCSE English Specification A

Paper 1   30% of total marks
Foundation and Higher tier – 1 hour 45 minutes

Section A
Reading response to non-fiction/media texts.   15%

Section B
Choice of one from three or more questions testing
writing which seeks to argue, persuade or advise.   15%

Paper 2   30% of total marks
Foundation and Higher tier – 1 hour 30 minutes

Section A
Reading response to poetry from different cultures
and traditions in the AQA *Anthology*.   15%

Section B
Choice of one from three or more questions testing
writing which seeks to inform, explain or describe.   15%

Coursework   40% of total marks
Speaking and Listening

- Three assessed activities   20%
- Two responses to Reading and two responses to Writing, comprising:
  - Shakespeare*   5%
  - Prose Study*   5%
  - Media   5%
  - Original Writing   5%

GCSE English Literature Specification A

Written paper	**70% of total marks**

Foundation and Higher tier – 1 hour 45 minutes

Section A
One question based on post-1914 prose. There will be a choice of questions.　　30%

Section B
One question based on pre- and post-1914 poetry from the AQA *Anthology*. There will be a choice of questions.　　40%

Coursework	**30% of total marks**

Task 1: Pre-1914 drama (Shakespeare)*　　10%
Task 2: Pre-1914 prose*　　10%
Task 3: Post-1914 drama　　10%

- A Kestrel for a Knave

- The poetry of Seamus Heaney and Gillian Clarke
- The poetry of Carol Ann Duffy and Simon Armitage

- Shylock and the pound of flesh

- An Inspector Calls

* indicates a 'cross-over' piece (i.e. it can be used to meet the coursework requirements of both GCSE English Specification A and GCSE English Literature Specification A).